SERIOUS MATTERS

Psychological Question-Answer Stories

Volume 1

Brigitte Halenta

About This Book

This volume isn't just another psychological guide—it's a repository of real-life psychological dilemmas and expert solutions. For over three decades, Licensed Clinical Psychologist and Psychotherapist Brigitte Halenta has been a trusted voice in Germany for individuals seeking advice on matters of the heart, the mind, and the soul. While her advice has been shaped by her experiences in Germany, the universal themes and actionable guidance found within these pages transcend borders and are relevant for anyone, anywhere. Published in various newspapers, her responses to readers' letters have touched countless lives. And now, for the first time, these valuable exchanges have been translated into English and curated into a book series, available in both eBook and paperback formats.

"Serious Matters – Psychological Question-Answer Stories" is the inaugural book in this series, containing more than 150 selected question-and-answer pairs spread across nearly 460 pages. Each correspondence provides not only a glimpse into the unique circumstances of real individuals but also offers actionable, expert advice for those who find themselves in similar predicaments.

This is no AI-generated content or abstract theorization. These are genuine letters from real people—people like you. People who have faced challenges, asked questions, and found answers that have led to meaningful changes in their lives.

And this is just the beginning. This book is the first in a series that will feature over 1000 more question-and-answer pairs in future volumes, offering a robust and evolving guide to navigating the human experience.

Psychological and Medical Disclaimer

The letters and responses presented in "Serious Matters – Psychological Question-Answer Stories Vol.1" are based on real-life queries from readers and the responses provided by a psychologist in a newspaper format. These are intended for educational and illustrative purposes only and do not serve as psychological or medical advice. They are neither comprehensive nor a substitute for personalized consultation with qualified healthcare or mental health professionals.

By engaging with this material, readers acknowledge that the content herein is specific to individual cases and circumstances and should not be generalized. No doctor-patient or therapist-client relationship is established by reading or relying upon this content. Readers are strongly advised to seek professional medical or psychological advice, diagnosis, or treatment for any specific medical or psychological conditions or concerns they may have.

While efforts have been made to maintain accuracy and relevance of the content at the time of publication, psychological and medical information is subject to change, and errors may occur. The author and publisher disclaim all liability for any inaccuracies, errors, or omissions in this work, and shall not be held responsible for any damages or consequences that may arise from the use, interpretation, or misuse of the information contained within.

If you have underlying medical conditions or serious psychological issues, consult with a qualified physician or psychotherapist in your area.

If you are curious:

You can sign up for the newsletter at brigittehalenta.de. This way, you will not only receive information about new releases and special promotions, but also get exclusive insights into all other book projects by Brigitte Halenta.

Imprint

Serious Matters
Psychological Question-Answer Stories
Volume 1

© 2013-2022 Brigitte Halenta
First Edition published in September 2023
Second Edition published in October 2024
Published and Copyright managed by David Halenta
Translation by David Halenta, Benjamin Halenta

Design, Layout, and Typesetting by Moojox Media.
Cover image by David Halenta

For more information about Brigitte Halenta and her other works, please visit the author's website: www.brigittehalenta.de.

ICS:121024132502

<h1 align="center">Foreword by the Publisher</h1>

Dear Readers,

Before you delve into the fascinating world of psychological question-answer stories penned by my mother, I'd like to offer a few personal words to you.

My mother, Brigitte Halenta, sadly passed away at the age of 85, surrounded by her closest family in Thailand. She was not only an extraordinarily gifted author but also a profound psychologist with a remarkable understanding of human emotions. From a young age, she discovered her passion for writing, and it was only a matter of time before she incorporated her professional expertise as a psychologist into her literary works.

But my mother wasn't just exceptional in her professional field; she was also a wonderful mother who tirelessly devoted herself to her children. She was always there for us when we needed her, supporting us with her love and rich life experience until her last breath. Her absence leaves a void that can never be completely filled.

v

We deeply miss her, and it is an honor for me to finally make her work accessible to a broader audience through this series, available in both e-book and paperback formats and in both German and English.

I wish you an enriching read and hope that you can benefit as much from my mother's insights as I, and many others who had the fortune to know her, have.

With warm regards,

David Halenta

Note to the Reader:
Please understand that we have had to omit a few question-and-answer pairs from the German edition for this translated version. This decision was made to avoid misunderstandings and potential legal complications, particularly in the U.S., especially concerning sensitive topics such as sexual identity.

Foreword

For over thirty years, alongside my work in my private practice as a licensed psychotherapist for depth-psychologically founded psychotherapy, I have managed an advice column for various newspapers. The concerns were always serious matters, motivating people to pick up the pen and unburden their souls by writing about their troubles.

Sometimes, confiding in an unknown person and seeking advice is easier than approaching acquaintances, friends, or relatives. On the other hand, most of the letter-writers (the majority of whom were women) were naturally afraid that they might be identified by their families or others based on their specific problems if they were published. Therefore, all letters were heavily altered in terms of real facts.

Places or names that could have provided clues were never mentioned, and familial and occupational circumstances were swapped out, as were the ages and the number of children mentioned. Most letters also had to be shortened or smoothed out, as people in distress often write in a disjointed and difficult-to-understand manner.

This was sometimes not easy, as the specific problem should be retained, as should the diversity of life circumstances and personal writing style. My revision of the letters led to curious results several times, in that completely unknown people to me felt concerned and complained.

However, these reactions have also shown me that the described problems are widespread. Thus, you will find here more than 150 advice letters from the last years, distilled and sorted into five major problem areas:

- Problems with oneself
- Problems in relationships
- Problems with family
- Problems with children
- Problems with others

Advice can often feel like a burden, or even an intrusion. In my answers, I always wanted to provide more than just instructions for action, which usually cannot be followed anyway because powerful other motives oppose them; thus, I have tried to offer the letter-writers a look "behind the scenes"—into the unconscious psychodynamics that produced and maintain the current conflict. When I have succeeded in this, I have received wonderful feedback.

I wish you, dear reader, a beneficial experience in reading these stories, especially where you can identify with the problems described.

Yours
Brigitte Halenta

Table Of Contents

Problems With Oneself 21

Problems in Relationships 119

Problems With Family 231

Problems With Others 395

Problems With Oneself

*The hardest battle
is not the one with the world,
but the one with oneself.*

—Brigitte Halenta

Has Her Obsession with Cleaning Rubbed Off On Me?

After a long and draining emotional battle, I have managed to separate from my wife, or rather, convinced her to move out. The house we've lived in for twenty-one years was inherited from my parents; so, it was clear from the start that she would be the one to leave. Our only son is studying in another city and only comes to visit me since the separation. My ex-wife's place is too small to accommodate him. I have been living alone in the house for four months now, and our son recently came for the first time to stay for two weeks during his semester break. His mocking comments left me feeling somewhat disoriented and insecure, which is why I'm writing to you.

My son laughed himself silly over what he calls my "rituals" and all the rules I have set up. It was only through his reactions that I became aware of what has happened to me. I separated from my wife, in part, because I could no longer tolerate her obsession with order and cleanliness. Now, my son shows me that I am doing the very same things I fought against in her for years. I may do things differently than she did, but at the core, I have also developed a system similar to hers and expect others to follow it. While I can do whatever I want in my own house and expect guests to behave according to my wishes, the mere fact that I'm no better than my ex-wife frightens me.

How can this be? Before my marriage, I lived in a shared apartment and was anything but tidy. When we got married, I mocked my wife's cleaning obsession in the same way my son mocks me today. I have always preached freedom from such compulsive systems and had countless arguments with my wife about it. And now, I am doing the same thing. As if her obsession with cleanliness has rubbed off on me. I don't want to be like this! How can I break free?

Answer

Cleanliness obsession isn't contagious in the conventional sense like a cold, as you're already aware, but it can be psychologically infectious in various complex ways. You've lived for twenty-one years with a woman who was compulsively neat and organized, and it's left its mark. In at least the early years of the marriage, amid all your protests, you also likely tried to understand her and please her. You began to see things through her eyes, and that subtly changed your own attitudes without you realizing it. This identification with your wife's views can only become evident when she's no longer present, and that's exactly what's happening now. Your son has merely held up a mirror for you.

It makes a difference whether you are, so to speak, the perpetrator or the victim. In relation to your ex-wife, you were in the victim role, and your protest possibly applied more to that role than to the issues themselves. Now you're the "perpetrator," in the sense that you're setting the rules, and your son is protesting against them, even if the contents are different from those of his mother.

Whether you have to remove your shoes at the door or take them straight to the basement is irrelevant; what's troubling is the obligation, the "having to." You've spent twenty-one years always paying attention to what your wife wanted; you'll probably need more than four months to purge such a compulsive system from your mind and emotions.

However, it could also be that you eventually discover that you are actually just as compulsively inclined as your ex-wife. Relationships generally don't happen unless there's a certain soul affinity. Understanding another person also always means that you have elements within yourself that resonate.

I Work Too Much

I am a young, probationary teacher and a single mother of two daughters aged eight and eleven. I always thought that my life would get easier after passing my exams. But the exam pressure has been off for six months now, and I am still as stressed as before. I simply work too much, and too little time remains for me and the children. I have chronic sleep deprivation and often feel correspondingly miserable. I find no time for things that would be good for me, like my beloved choir and also sports. I want to be there for the children on the precious weekend, but that doesn't always work out because I still have corrections and lesson preparations to do.

Of course, I am ambitious and have set goals. I would like to work in teacher training someday. That's why I am also happy to take on special tasks and projects. But all of this also takes time beyond the normal working hours. I passed all my exams with top grades, meaning my school also expects good performance from me. Older colleagues can't be a role model for me. Only a few give full commitment; most make life rather easy for themselves, in my eyes. But I think we owe it to the students to give them our best.

A friend told me about a time management seminar. Could something like this be useful to me? I think it's all just a matter of time, and if one could learn to organize oneself better, I would gladly learn that. But unfortunately, with the children, so much unforeseen stuff happens that good planning is very difficult. Do you think this could solve my problems?

Answer

For a short time—mind you, for a short time—your problems would be very solvable with two extra days in the week. It wouldn't take long before you had filled those too, but at least for a short time... You unfortunately define yourself only through performance. If you don't perform enough, you quickly feel worthless and unloved. Meanwhile, the demands placed on you from the outside are nowhere near as bad as the ones you impose on yourself. It is you who demands 120% performance from yourself and is relentless.

The instance within ourselves that sets commands and restrictions is called the Superego. Your Superego is huge and dominates your entire emotional life. Usually, the authorities of childhood are immortalized in this instance. So you might ask yourself who was so strict and pleasure-hostile with you in your childhood as you are with yourself today.

Above all, you are afraid to fail in front of this strict Superego. Because if you can't satisfy it, your self-esteem plummets. All the people around you who supposedly expect top performance will not devalue you as you do when you're not good. Perhaps you fend off an impending depression with this perfectionism; in any case, fear sits at the back of your neck and drives you to constant peak performances. In that regard, a better time management seminar will help you little. I find psychotherapy more useful, where you can learn to be kinder to yourself and accept time as a real constant.

Your own children also have a claim to your best. The best for children is always love and time. If you drive yourself like this, you will also drive your children. They should function and nothing else, so that they fit into your schedules. It is high time for the whole family to change course so that everyone doesn't get sick.

You need to find a livable balance between career and family. That will probably mean that you will have to wait to realize your ambitious plans until the children are older.

The Decision Is Difficult for Me

I urgently need help making a decision regarding a family matter. My only daughter from my first marriage is celebrating the baptism of her son this coming Sunday. The little one is the first grandchild, and I would very much like to be there. The problem is that my current husband refuses to come because he would encounter my first husband, my daughter's father, at the celebration. He holds a grudge against this man that he can't let go of.

He actually took his wife away from him after just one year of marriage. My daughter was one year old at the time. We, the two who were cheated on, became friends, later got married, and have had a good marriage for almost twenty years. I think that after twenty years, one could finally forget the old stories, especially since my first husband has been married to a completely different woman for many years. So my husband wouldn't even encounter his ex-wife.

However, he is determined not to attend this baptism, even though he has otherwise been a good father to my daughter. He says he has no problem if I go to the baptism alone. Nevertheless, I find myself in great uncertainty. Should I stand by my husband and follow his decision, or should I comply with my daughter's wish, who really wants me to be there? I feel that whatever I do, someone will be hurt.

Answer

The old stories are indeed very complicated and have undoubtedly left some scars. Nevertheless, I think, like you, that it's time to bury them. If your husband still avoids encountering the old rival, it can only mean that part of the old issues are still alive for him. Perhaps your husband still imagines the other as being more powerful, seductive, etc., and he doesn't want to expose himself to such uncomfortable feelings of inferiority.

If your behavior doesn't give him any reason to feel this way, it could reassure and secure him if you tell him clearly in a quiet moment that he is the only and most important man for you. Don't say, "He knows that!" Hearing it clearly from your mouth is something completely different than silent certainty.

As for your decision to attend or not attend the baptism, you give your own wishes too little importance. You want to please both your husband and your daughter, and that's not possible. The conflict can only be somewhat resolved if you follow your own heart, and that is pulling you towards the baptism. The problem isn't yours, but your husband's. In understanding conversations afterward, you can help him resolve it.

I Feel Guilty About My Dog's Death

I'm currently living in England, but at the moment I'm on vacation and staying with my mother, who always reads your newspaper. I thought I would like to know what you think of my story. My mother always tries to comfort me, but that just makes me sadder. I always have to think about my dog Lena, who died because of my fault. She was a mixed breed, not unlike a Golden Retriever. I got her as a birthday present from my father when I was fourteen; he only had one more year to live at that time. From then on, we were inseparable. She would be twelve years old today, which is not old for a dog.

Four months ago, my employer offered me a great opportunity that represented a big career step for me—I was to go to England for two years for the company. I couldn't refuse the offer, but I knew immediately that this would cause a big problem with Lena. She couldn't stay alone with my mother, as my mother herself requires care. Taking her to London was also not an option. So with a heavy heart, I looked for a new owner for Lena. But no one wanted her. Everyone expected illnesses from a nearly twelve-year-old dog and declined.

Finally, through an ad, I found a farmer and his wife who wanted to keep her on their farm. They were animal lovers, the woman said on the phone. When I visited, I only dealt with the woman, whom I found nice. The farm was well-kept, so I left Lena there with a heavy heart. After three days, I went back to see how things were going. Lena greeted me joyfully; we went for a walk as if everything were as usual. We agreed that they would notify me immediately if there were any problems with Lena. When I drove away, she followed the car for a bit, but then turned around and ran back, much to my relief. I drove to London thinking she was in good hands. The first few weeks there were so hectic for me that I forgot all about Lena. Today, I deeply regret that.

When I finally called after nearly two months to inquire about Lena, I spoke to the man for the first time. He was very brusque and gave me the feeling that I was bothering him. He tried to brush me off. When I kept asking more urgently about Lena, he said they had had enough trouble with the dog and had her euthanized. I was stunned. When I accused them of not notifying me, he simply hung up. I called several more times, but the phone was always hung up as soon as I mentioned my name. However, I did manage to reach the woman once; she was also very curt but said that Lena didn't have to suffer. I feel so guilty. Lena could still be alive if I hadn't forgotten her.

Answer

You are linking your feelings of guilt about forgetting Lena amid all the new demands in London with the death of the dog. However, this is not logically compelling. She could have theoretically been fine during that time, or the new owners could have had her put down on the first day of your absence. I think your feelings of guilt run deeper. You can't forgive yourself for choosing to prioritize your own interests over the dog. Even if Lena had been well taken care of by the new family, a feeling of guilt would have remained. Lena was the companion of your youth and also a keepsake of your father. Giving her away probably feels like betraying your father.

Perhaps the intensity with which you blame yourself also involves some unconscious anger at your mother. It's easier to be angry with yourself than with a mother who needs care. But to your spontaneous feelings, it would have been your mother who should have continued to provide Lena with a familiar home. Animals that we love deeply can also be experienced as a substitute for a lost person, but perhaps more often they represent a part of ourselves. Thus, we give them the care and love that we ourselves would have liked to receive.

Accept the departure of Lena; it is also a farewell to your youth and maybe once again to your father. You're only hurting yourself by constantly pondering whether and how her death could have been prevented. She had twelve good years with you and has now found her peace. You have set out to take your own life into your own hands, and that is exactly what needs to be done now.

You are linking your feelings of guilt about forgetting Lena amid all the new demands in London with the death of the dog. However, this is not logically compelling. She could have theoretically been fine during that time, or the new owners could have had her put down on the first day of your absence. I think your feelings of guilt run deeper. You can't forgive yourself for choosing to prioritize your own interests over the dog. Even if Lena had been well taken care of by the new family, a feeling of guilt would have remained. Lena was the companion of your youth and also a keepsake of your father. Giving her away probably feels like betraying your father.

Perhaps the intensity with which you blame yourself also involves some unconscious anger at your mother. It's easier to be angry with yourself than with a mother who needs care. But to your spontaneous feelings, it would have been your mother who should have continued to provide Lena with a familiar home. Animals that we love deeply can also be experienced as a substitute for a lost person, but perhaps more often they represent a part of ourselves. Thus, we give them the care and love that we ourselves would have liked to receive.

Accept the departure of Lena; it is also a farewell to your youth and maybe once again to your father. You're only hurting yourself by constantly pondering whether and how her death could have been prevented. She had twelve good years with you and has now found her peace. You have set out to take your own life into your own hands, and that is exactly what needs to be done now.

I'm Not a Fearful Type

First of all, I want to say that I am generally not a fearful person. On the contrary, my courage has proven itself in many situations of daily life, both here and during an extended stay in the Philippines. My wife knows that she can rely on me in all situations, and I don't want to undermine her trust in me at all. Therefore, you will understand that I am somewhat unsettled by two experiences I want to tell you about in recent weeks.

I was doing a heating repair in a friend's basement when, due to a draft, the heavy iron door closed and could not be opened from the inside. My phone was upstairs in the apartment. My friend was out getting replacement parts. I was sure he would be back within an hour at most. He returned after just two minutes and freed me. But in those two minutes, I went through hell. Unfortunately, that wasn't all. For nights afterward, I had nightmares from which I woke up sweating. For days afterward, the situation in the basement kept popping back into my mind, immediately followed by palpitations. As I said, I'm not a fearful type and find my reaction to this small incident exaggerated and incomprehensible.

The other experience concerns a movie I watched in which a hostage is transported in the trunk of a car. The image of the man tied up like a package won't leave my mind, also associated with the palpitations that then immediately set in. I don't want to bother anyone with these trifles. Can you give me some advice? One should be able to get a handle on such moods! But how?

Answer

I understand well why your experiences are unsettling you. Unfortunately, you don't write anything else about your life situation, so I can only answer very generally. Since we are constantly changing, it also happens again and again that we discover new things about ourselves. You have just discovered a readiness for fear in yourself, deviating from your self-image.

What you experienced in the locked basement was a panic reaction. The television image also triggers the same reaction, albeit more mildly. Fear is part of life; it is a signal that we should hear in order to protect ourselves from worse things. Accept this experience! You too have fears, so you don't have to be a fearful type for a long time. The question is only why fear shows up in situations that are actually quite harmless for you in reality.

Perhaps being locked up or tied up has some symbolic meaning for you that you react so strongly to. Consider whether in your current life situation, in family or job, you feel trapped or bound in some way, so that you have lost your freedom of movement. In any case, your two bouts of anxiety are a signal that something is currently wrong in your life.

Maybe tell your wife about what you have experienced, even if your image as the unassailably brave man suffers as a result. Your wife surely has fears too. If you both can talk about this topic, it will do you both good and you will feel close to each other. Feelings can't be so easily controlled. The only appropriate way to deal with them is to perceive them and then let them be as they are.

The Feelings of Anxiety Are Unbearable

I am thirty-eight and had my first heart attack a year and a half ago; before that, I was always healthy. The doctors couldn't find anything, and the pills they gave me were useless. Lately, the attacks are coming more frequently with rapid heartbeats, sweating, and quite strong feelings of anxiety. In my opinion, the feelings of anxiety are unbearable. The attacks come either at night or during the day when I am alone.

I am now trying to make sure that someone is always near me. During the day, colleagues are around, in the morning my thirteen-year-old daughter is in the car, but driving home alone in the car is already a risk, especially over the weekend. My wife refuses to take my illness into account. She does not want to work less, even though she has only been working full-time for two years, and she does not want to give up any of her many hobbies over the weekend, which require her to leave the house.

I am deeply disappointed in my wife and have told her this repeatedly, but she does not change. How can I bring her to understand?

Answer

You expect your wife and daughter to put their own interests aside and be fully there for you whenever you deem it necessary. The reassuring presence of your family members alleviates your fear of fear, so that in their presence the dreaded attacks do not occur at all. But this expectation turns your wife into a nurse, and she is rightfully resisting that.

If anyone needs to come to an understanding, it is you.

Today, it is increasingly believed that there is hardly any disease that is not also causally involved with psychological factors. If the doctors cannot find organic reasons for your heart attacks, then your attacks are caused solely by psychological conflicts. These psychological conflicts are usually unconscious.

So there is something in your unconscious emotional life that scares you a lot. This unknown something will continue to manifest itself, possibly ever more loudly, until you listen to your body's language and address this fear-inducing issue yourself.

In the long run, avoidance will not help, even if you manage to employ your entire family and acquaintances to accompany you permanently. I strongly advise you to undergo therapeutic treatment. If you succeed in slowly bringing the currently unconscious problems into consciousness so that you can talk about them, the heart attacks will also subside.

I Can't Indulge Myself

We went on a company trip to Copenhagen. Everyone came back to the ship laden with shopping, but I didn't buy anything. "You're just stingy," said a colleague who is actually quite close to me. I laughed at the moment, but her words have not left me in peace. Since then, I have been thinking about whether I am stingy or not.

I am thirty-two, single, and an administrative assistant. I have a large two-room apartment and, by my standards, am well-furnished. The furniture I have consists of all antique pieces, which I searched for a long time and which were not cheap. My clothing is similar; it is not necessarily so fashionable, but when I buy something, it must be of good material and well-crafted. I'm happy to spend money on that. In that sense, I don't think I'm stingy.

However, when I compare myself with my colleagues, there might be some truth to the accusation. They all indulge in much more luxury. They spend a lot of money on various trinkets, often go out to eat, go to the movies every week, swimming, or to the sauna. For example, I went to the sauna once, and I liked it. But I didn't go again because fourteen euros for two hours seemed too much to me.

On such occasions, I do have my doubts. I live frugally, as I've learned, and can't indulge myself as much as others do. The aforementioned colleague says: You have to pamper yourself. I can only marvel at that. Is that true?

Answer

Your colleague is right. When we're adults, we have no more entitlement to being pampered by others, and where it still happens, those are gifts that are not to be taken for granted. Our ongoing need for care and pampering, we have to satisfy ourselves, by doing good things for ourselves, just as our parents used to do for us. Your parents seem to have only provided the absolute necessities—though of good quality.

As a result, you as an adult can also only cater to your basic needs. Anything beyond that seems like luxury to you, and luxury was probably considered superfluous or even reprehensible in your parents' house. What your parents didn't allow, you can't allow for yourself today. If you did, you would probably feel guilty. Your parents were obviously people with a serious outlook on life who not only denied themselves any luxury but also little joy in life. Both are closely related.

If you can't spend fourteen euros for two hours in a sauna today, you're only seeing one thing and its price, not that you're affording yourself two hours of fun, well-being, and enjoyment. Whether you're stingy, I can't judge; but what is certain is that you don't value your feelings much. Only when you take your inner world of feelings, moods, desires, and needs more seriously will it also become easier for you to spend money on them.

Roller Coaster of Emotions

The last four months have been an emotional roller coaster for me. I envy other people who have a peaceful life. I'm only twenty-six and feel like I've already experienced much more than my peers. At twenty-one, I got married for the first time to my childhood love, with whom I have a now four-year-old son. The marriage fell apart after two years because we didn't understand each other at all. Today, we can communicate quite well regarding our son. My ex-wife is very ambitious and wants to build a career, which still surprises me because she used to be rather shy and fearful. Then I met a woman who I briefly thought was my absolute dream woman, but she wasn't, and I sank into deep depression.

My second wife saved me from this. We got along right away, got married quickly, and a child was on the way. When my wife was three months pregnant, I was diagnosed with testicular cancer. I fell into a deep hole again. I started to feel better only when our son was born and I had gotten through the surgery and radiation therapy well. The little one is now one and a half and is developing splendidly. When my older son comes for the weekend, the two play together really well.

So far, so good, but then I met a colleague at a training event. It was love at first sight. With her, I've experienced things that I hadn't with any other woman. After three months of a secret affair, I decided, with a heavy heart, to tell my wife everything and demand a separation. I managed the first part, but hadn't yet talked about separation. Then came the holidays.

I spent four weeks in Sweden with my wife and kids and noticed how my feelings for my dream woman weakened. When we met again, the sparkle was gone from both sides. I decided to stay with my wife, if she forgives me. She did, and things are somewhat back on track for us. But recently, I accidentally saw my girlfriend again, and it hit me like a lightning bolt. Suddenly, it no longer seems impossible that my feelings could flip again. That scares me. Can't I do anything against this roller coaster of emotions?

Answer

You'll probably have to accept that you are a person who lives in extremes. Ecstatic one moment and despondent the next—that's your nature. That's why you also experience more than other people whose emotional levels fluctuate more around the central axis. From their perspective, you are probably envied for your exciting life.

I can well understand that you find the extreme ups and downs of your emotions frightening. However, you can learn to handle this predisposition well. In general, you should always give yourself enough time before making life-changing decisions. In the case of your dream woman, three months weren't enough to be really sure of your feelings. Emotional security does exist, the right decision at the right place, but it takes time to mature.

Love at first sight and everything built on this pattern stands on very shaky legs, because it can't really be about reality that quickly, but only about fantasy and mutual attributions. The dream woman remains a dreamed woman, even when you think you're holding her in reality. Only in reality, over longer periods, will it become clear what is real with her and what is dreamed.

This means that you have projected the fulfillment of your wishes, and sooner or later, harsh reality catches up with you. So you have to learn to recognize your projections. Dreaming is allowed, but you should not confuse your dreams with reality. So if you accidentally see the lost dream woman and immediately start dreaming, it's not necessarily bad, but you should wake up from the dream before turning back to your family.

My Wild Years

My wife is urging me to write to you because she's running out of patience with me. We've known each other for fourteen years, she's seen my wilder years, but when our first child came along eight years ago, I became more stable. My dream was always to be an actor, but I realized that you can't build a family on that. I did theater in school, and after graduation, under my parents' pressure, I reluctantly studied pedagogy. During that time, I also performed street theater and initiated theater projects. After finishing my degree in pedagogy, even my parents had nothing against me studying acting. When a prestigious school accepted me, I was ecstatic.

I was only able to act on smaller stages for two years after graduating. Since the income was too low, I decided to become a teacher. We now have three kids; I teach at a comprehensive school, my wife at an elementary school. We can afford a good standard of living, which I highly value and don't want to give up.

Over the years, I thought I'd moved on from acting and was content with my life. But lately, I've had doubts. My wife says she doesn't recognize me anymore, that I've lost my laughter. She has a point. The lightness I once had is long gone. When I look closely, I realize I'm not doing well at all.

I have sleep problems, irregular heartbeats, feel overwhelmed by constant work for school, and find it hard to motivate myself for anything beyond the daily grind. My wild life before settling down feels like a distant dream now. I guess I have to give that up for a family. Where's my problem? I can't see it.

Answer

"Two souls, alas, are dwelling in my breast" - You're familiar with this feeling and can't imagine that these two souls can interact. You deliberately excluded theater to become entirely stable and conventional. This was undoubtedly reasonable for starting a family, and your parents likely approved. But for creatively inclined people, it's insufficient to always be sensible, as this neglects their artistic side. It appears you're suffering from reactive depression due to suppressing your creative abilities and needs. Unlived lives make us depressed.

It seems you've constructed an either-or scenario in your mind, allowing you to live only one side. You lacked financial security as an actor, and now, as a well-placed teacher, you miss the thrill of the stage. This might be influenced by your parents' attitudes, but today it's a conflict within you. Since you can't reconcile these two sides, you also fail to find reasonable compromises in the external world. Maybe you should consider coaching to explore or develop ways to bring some excitement and color into your stable life as a teacher. Even if time is tight, there will always be opportunities to express your acting side.

Your mood can drastically improve when you acknowledge that something important is missing in your life. Only then is it possible to dream again. And from some pipe dreams, solid castles are built one day. Giving up on dreams serves no one well.

I Get Bored So Quickly

Somehow, I seem to be wired differently than other people, and that makes me unhappy. I would like to know if there's anything that can be done about it. I'm experiencing a great disappointment for the third time in my life. It's not other people who are disappointing me; I'm doing it to myself. Let me tell you what's happening to me right now. So, I'm now thirty-seven, and for the past three years, I've been working toward a single goal: I wanted to open a small café and host exhibitions and readings there. I thought this was my life's dream.

The café has been in operation for over six months now. It's situated in an ideal location, and the interior is beautiful. With the help of friends, I've been able to realize all my ideas. We are only open on weekends, selling coffee and homemade cakes in the afternoon and hosting readings, performances, or occasional musical events in the evenings. We also have a permanent exhibition. The program is diverse, and I am overwhelmed with offers. The financials are also working out, albeit a bit tighter than estimated. In short, things are going well; I'm getting a lot of recognition, but—and this is my problem—I find it all dreadfully boring.

I've essentially experienced this multiple times already. I really wanted to study Art History. To achieve this goal, I completed my high school diploma and fought for a place at my preferred university. After two semesters, I lost interest and dropped out. At eighteen, I waged a campaign to win over an-

other woman's man. When I finally had him, I lost interest in him. It's always the same.

This can't go on. I find myself browsing job listings in the newspaper. I should be content with my success, but I'm dissatisfied. Is there a way for me to change this?

Answer

There certainly is a way. You have already proven multiple times that you can achieve what you set out to do; it's just that you can't be satisfied with what you've achieved. Until now, you've always fought for external goals; this time, if contentment is your goal, it's an internal one. Unfortunately, you've written nothing about your biographical background, so I can only rely on speculation.

Your condition is more common than you might think. You're not alone. There are many people who live more in their dreams than in reality. The dream is furnished in all details with a perfection that reality usually cannot deliver. As long as the hope of realizing the dream mobilizes all your energy, you're happy. But once the goal is reached, you have to confront the limitations of reality and lose interest. This is a form of narcissism, usually rooted in childhood.

Important caregivers have always seen the child for what they should be and not what they really are. Love was given only for performance, for fulfilling the expectations of others, and not for developing one's own needs. Such a child had to always be strong; their weak sides were treated as temporary disturbances. Once grown up, such a person treats others—and themselves— just as they've learned. In psychotherapy, you can learn to perceive your true needs. Only satisfying genuine needs will make you happy and content in the long run.

I Can't Find Joy

Ever since my wife told me that I haven't laughed in three weeks, I have to admit to myself that my mood has been low for some time now. I do everything that is expected of me, but I find no joy in it. It particularly strikes me when I come home from work and our eight-month-old daughter crawls toward me beaming with joy. Sure, I pick her up and cuddle her, but I can't bring myself to be silly and frolic around with her on the floor like I did a few weeks ago. Everything just seems overwhelming, and after work, I just want to be left alone.

On all accounts, I have enough reason to be happy. We had severe worries about our daughter for months. She was born with a hole in her heart. Most likely, she would have needed surgery, but during the last check-up, we were told that the hole had closed on its own and surgery is no longer required. Our little one is now as healthy as any other child. While my wife was jubilant, I felt barely relieved and still can't quite grasp it. I'm generally a serious person. I was raised by my father alone after my parents separated, and there wasn't much to laugh about.

Another problem at my workplace that had frustrated me has fortunately been resolved. After much uncertainty and unpleasant surprises, my immediate boss has finally been transferred, and things are going well with the new one. However, my current mood is inexplicably bleak. I can't find joy in anything. Is this depression? Or what else could be wrong with me?

Answer

It does sound like depression, but it's certainly not baseless. All emotional states have causes, even if they're not immediately comprehensible. The fact that you're experiencing this bleak mood just as the stressors weighing on your soul are lifting is not unusual. As long as you're fully invested in coping with day-to-day life, you're fully present, but the moment you could relax, the extent to which you've suffered becomes evident. This is particularly true when today's problems are unconsciously charged with emotional energies from the past.

You only hint at your personal history in a single sentence, but behind those few words, one can sense an entire drama. The hole in your daughter's heart was a devastating blow that also reactivated your emotional "hole," metaphorically torn into your heart by your parents' separation. Your daughter is now healthy, but the revived sadness from your childhood still lingers and weighs you down. Similarly, the issue at your workplace probably involves more than just a disappointing boss; your subconscious likely associates him with parental authority figures.

Your childhood wounds probably still reside within you, and as long as life doesn't burden you too much, you can keep them repressed. The events of the past year have broken through that repression. You now need psychotherapeutic help to emerge from the gloom of your childhood mood so that you can find joy in your healthy daughter and improved work situation in the present.

I Can't Do Anything Right

I'm currently very unhappy in my marriage, perhaps you can tell me what I'm doing wrong. I've been married for five years to a man who is extremely busy with his career. It was my wish to give up my job to fully devote myself to the children. Since my husband has so little time, I handle everything related to the family alone. My husband practically does nothing; I have complete freedom, but afterward, he is satisfied with nothing. I do my best to meet his standards, but according to him, I never do anything right. There's always criticism, and sometimes he's even offended if I haven't considered something that, in his opinion, I should already know. He does appreciate my efforts, at least he always emphasizes this in front of others.

The latest example is our move, which I practically handled alone. When everything was done, he returned from a business trip abroad and had something to complain about in everything. He finds the new couch set unprofessional, the colors of the curtains too loud, and his books in the office are not in the old order. But when I tried to find out beforehand what he would like, my questions were just a nuisance to him. I could have cried. When I tried to explain how disappointed I was, he didn't respond to my feelings but gave detailed reasons why his criticism was justified.

I've reached a point where I can't bear it anymore. I had the same experience at home. My mother was never satisfied with what I did, or how I looked. That's still the case today. When we saw each other after a year-long break, the first thing she said to me was: Why did you choose to wear a red sweater, when red doesn't suit you at all? As a child, I was always blamed for everything, and my brother always got off scot-free. I moved out early because I was fed up; now it feels like I have the same with my husband, and that makes me unhappy. What am I doing wrong?

Answer

You're doing quite a lot wrong, and that's why your unhappiness is largely self-made. You are an adult and are choosing to live with this man. While you can't change your mother, you can certainly change a partner who doesn't love you, because what he is displaying can't really be called love. He'll claim he loves you, but in reality, he just needs you so he can focus on his career while still maintaining his idea of a family. How you feel as a person is largely irrelevant to him, as long as you meet his expectations.

You actually don't stand a chance to meet his standards because his expectations are unpredictable and because, like your mother, he takes his aggression out on you. If you make your self-worth entirely dependent on your husband, as you do, it's a surefire way to make yourself unhappy.

Rather, you should pat yourself on the back more often and refuse to accept retrospective criticism. If he doesn't contribute beforehand, he has no right to criticize afterward. This will be hard for you because you've learned from your family of origin to adapt completely and to forgo independence in the hope of being loved. That didn't work with your mother, and it won't work with your husband, whom you've chosen based on the same relationship pattern.

As a child, you couldn't afford to be angry, but in adult relationships, anger can be important for self-esteem. If you could muster some anger at your husband, who is exploiting you quite selfishly, it would likely be easier for you to set boundaries. What becomes of the relationship after that largely depends on your husband's ability to change.

I Had a Blackout

For the last fourteen days, I've been back at work, and I think my colleagues haven't noticed anything. Officially, I had a severe flu, from which I could only recover slowly, making a four-week sick leave seem plausible to everyone. But in reality, I completely lost it and spent five days in a psychiatric ward. I am still taking a medication to calm me down. When I tried to stop it, I couldn't sleep. I still can't understand how something like this could happen. It frightened me. The doctor in the clinic reassured me, saying that this could happen to anyone under stress, but that provides little comfort. I have always thought that I had good control over myself.

The day started off innocently. It was a Saturday; we were invited out in the evening, and in the afternoon we planned to go for a small bike ride with the kids, weather permitting. I drove to the office in the morning because we were under deadline pressure with a new project, and I wanted to quickly email some data to an employee. However, I ended up staying longer at the office than planned because a graphic crashed, and I didn't get home until after our usual lunchtime. Unfortunately, I forgot to inform my wife about the delay by phone. When I got there, she had already eaten with the kids and locked herself in her room. I was angry that there was no food on the table for me.

There was a huge argument. A bike ride and the invitation were out of the question. The kids retreated, crying, to their rooms. My wife brought up everything that had accumulated over the years. In between, a call came from a colleague who fed me new information, according to which my promotion to department head was in question again. That was too much. When my wife then threatened to leave, I completely lost it. The last thing I thought was that I was about to smash everything.

In fact, I only demolished a small table and a chair. I didn't hit my wife, just shouted horrible things that I can't remember. Then I stormed out, shouting that I was going to kill myself, which I vaguely remember. My wife sent the police and an emergency doctor after me; I only regained clarity once I was in the clinic.

I never want this to happen again under any circumstances. It was a nightmare. I have talked things over with my wife, but the stress at work, of course, continues. How should I behave, or what should I look out for?

Answer

You seem to work in a company where the exploitation of employees' labor is the principle, so that only those who fully dedicate themselves to the company will advance in their career. This always means that family life suffers, along with the time for rest and regeneration. The fact that your wife feels so neglected that she threatens to leave after such a delay indicates that she feels neglected.

Probably this has been the case for a long time. She is now just as shocked about your blackout as you are and therefore ready for reconciliation. But unless you fundamentally change something, the next conflict is predestined. Such a blackout is a symptom, just like anxieties or depression; symptoms arise under the specific conditions of a situation, and you cannot expect them to disappear and never recur if the situation remains the same.

You are very ambitious and have set goals; a professional career is as much a goal as a harmonious family. Your life was falling apart on the day that led to the blackout. Your prospect of becoming a department head seems to have burst, and your wife is threatening to leave you. It must have been boundless rage that you first directed at the furniture and then at yourself. Because such primitive rage doesn't fit with your controlled self-image, consciousness turns off. This can indeed happen easily, but those who are particularly at risk are performance-oriented people like you, who otherwise always suppress their feelings.

If you understand this context, you can also see how you can proceed if you want to avoid further blackouts. You have to take care of your neglected emotional life; this will surely also improve your relationships with your wife and children. This will not be possible without reconsidering your career goals. A coach could help you with that.

I'm Seeking the Truth

I'm totally confused. I lie awake at night, wracking my brain for the truth. It's been like this for weeks. Ever since I met a family from my childhood again. They were our neighbors back then and had children my age. I was four when we moved away. I remember that my parents used to argue a lot even then. Anyway, my parents separated soon after. My father got custody of me and my younger brother, my mother disappeared forever. Only bad things were said about her. In my father's entire extended family and from my stepmother, I never heard a neutral word about my mother. She was the absolute failure, alcoholic, lazy, and stupid.

She's been dead for over ten years. By chance, when I was pregnant with my first child, I found out that she had taken her own life with pills at the age of forty-two. Back then, it didn't affect me much. It fit the bad image I had of her. But now I see it in a completely different light. The former neighbor, who didn't even know that my parents had separated shortly after their move, told me things that left me astonished.

My mother would have been a beautiful, lively woman with whom she had done a lot. She would have been interested in art and literature and studied a few semesters of German literature before getting married. The former neighbor knew nothing of alcohol problems, but my mother would have been very kind and patient with us children and would have always played imaginary stories for us with puppet shows. However, she also often cried because my father was away so much.

The former neighbor also said that the divorce did not surprise her because the parents did not match at all. My father came from a long tradition of farmers, my mother from the city and the daughter of artists. I know nothing about my mother's family and am now researching it. This all upsets me incredibly. My father had a tantrum when I addressed him about it. I'm searching for the truth and am torn back and forth. Who should I believe?

Answer

Fate, which placed your former neighbor in your path, meant well for you. The new information about your mother is a real gift for which you can be grateful. Your shock is understandable. The bad image of your mother, which you have never questioned, has collapsed. Since this concerns such an important person as your mother, your self-image as her daughter is also affected. It's not about objective truth but subjective truth that helps you form a secure, conflict-free identity. Your father and his family have pieced together their subjective truth in such a way that they could live well with it. The bad part about this is that they destroyed your image of your mother.

At four years old, every child has developed an intense bond with their mother. Moreover, the mother is the most important female person for the daughter, against whom the child measures her own femininity. Losing the mother is bad enough; having her spoken ill of is a deep injury to the child. This injury, which has certainly left its mark on your life, can now heal.

There are always multiple truths, and in this case, I would trust the neighbor who has no vested interest in her stories more. Feeling like the daughter of this beautiful and artistically gifted woman will surely give you a better self-image than seeing yourself as the daughter of a stupid alcoholic.

Your mother was obviously very unhappy in this marriage and could not assert herself against your father's clan. Who knows why she left her children behind? If you investigate, you may uncover even more facts that have been concealed or distorted. You will have to rewrite the story of your childhood, but it looks like you can only win from this.

I Don't Feel Equal

I have a problem that has been bothering me since my childhood, and I somehow can't get it under control, or I obviously don't recognize what exactly I am doing wrong. I feel inferior to others and often feel down. Among the people I know, I am not popular and am often treated condescendingly, which hurts me deeply. I am married, and my three children are grown up. After having already undergone therapy, I assert myself quite well in the domestic area and am treated with respect and esteem by my husband and in-laws. However, I don't do as well with my children. I am directly afraid of their sometimes mocking remarks and get stuck in a speech jam because my thinking is blocked.

Basically, I am probably a loner. I enjoy being alone, especially in nature. Here I get to know and identify plants and insects, which is very satisfying for me. But my entire social life is overshadowed by this problem. I constantly find that I am obviously being avoided, which is evident, for example, by people demonstratively turning their backs on me at events or avoiding me while shopping. However, I do strive for casual contacts like the occasional coffee gathering, a chat with the neighbor, or with old acquaintances.

With my friends, of whom I now only have two, I rank pretty low, or I often miss the respect, so I feel hurt in my sense of honor. If someone appears who is more important, I am left standing. This has been the case since I was a child in kindergarten. I then feel very lonely and rejected. I would like to have your advice on how I can manage to feel equal to others. How should I behave so that people find it pleasant to meet me or have me around.

Answer

Your problem has a long history, probably going back to before your time in kindergarten. You had severe experiences of rejection as a child, from which you then drew the obvious conclusion: I am not important, I am not lovable. As a result, you have built up conscious and above all unconscious self-images that are all deficient, so you first want from other people what could heal these fragile self-images: respect. - I would interpret this desire for respect as a deep need to be adequately perceived at all. If that does not happen, what you call your hurt sense of honor today expresses a very old pain about the disregard of your person.

You therefore encounter other people largely unconsciously based on this early relational pattern, which includes from the outset that you are the small, the worthless, the inferior, and the others are the great and valuable ones. But on the real level today, you are also an adult and equal and are seen as such by others. The discrepancy between external appearance and internal condition leads to what is now called a communication disorder, in which all participants feel uncomfortable. That's why people prefer to avoid you.

In mature, adult relationships, it is usually about a balanced ratio of giving and taking. Other people certainly find you nice and appreciate your company if you offer attention, interest, and affection. However, you can hardly do this due to your inner condition. I think you should go back into psychotherapy, this time into a depth-psychologically based one, so that you can get to the root of your problems this time.

I Wanted to Change My Life

As far back as I can remember, I have been overweight. After my second child, at a height of 1.72 meters, I reached my record weight of 104 kg. I hardly dared to leave the house. Due to my husband's job, we often have social obligations. Every celebration was a nightmare for me. For years, I dreamed about how my life would change if I had a normal figure like others. I wanted to go to the swimming pool more often with the kids, do sports in general, dress nicely, do more, and meet more people. I always told myself, if I were slimmer, I would do all of this.

Now I am thinner because I starved off thirty-six kilograms in one and a half years, and my dream could become a reality. But nothing has changed. I am extremely angry with myself. I still sit at home just like before, can't manage to go to the swimming pool or to jazz gymnastics, and still can't open my mouth in front of people. I always thought my problem was my overweight, but that was apparently not it. What's wrong with me? To my horror, I'm starting to binge eat again.

Answer

You are like many people who look for a reason why they aren't doing all the great things they could be doing. Everything is postponed into the future: When I am thinner, when I no longer smoke, when I have a boyfriend or a girlfriend, when I drink less alcohol, when the kids are older — and so on. In most cases, the drive to do something right now is lacking, and it is easy to foresee that reduced weight or grown-up kids will change nothing about that.

That you have no drive, whether thick or thin, that you sit around listlessly and feel inhibited and shy among people, is the actual problem. You eat too much because you are depressed, not the other way around. With excessive eating, all feelings that do not fit into your life and therefore must be suppressed are kept in check. You learned this technique as a child, which is why you have always been overweight.

Eating is a very pleasurable process for all living beings and is therefore always suitable for comforting and calming us. However, food preparation and eating is, even if we do not register it at all, a highly aggressive activity. Each individual action is aggressive: cutting, chopping, hacking, frying, chewing, gulping down, swallowing, and so on. Nothing remains of the objects of our eating pleasure; they are totally destroyed. Thus, anger can be vented with eating when we are actually unconsciously angry and mean, or dissatisfied with our life situation. Excessive hunger is therefore also always excessive anger in the stomach.

With your months of fasting, you have already shown a great deal of self-discipline. But the suppressed aggression continues to be directed either against you, making you depressed, or is unleashed in excessive eating. If you don't want to fall into a debilitating cycle of fasting and eating, you should seek psychotherapeutic help to work on the underlying aggression problem.

I'll Never Make It

I insisted on training in a technical profession against my parents' views, where so far only a few girls work. The first year of training didn't cause me any problems at all, I was actually very confirmed in my decision because I enjoyed the work. I had a great young training supervisor. Another girl had started the training with me, but I didn't have much contact with her. The second year of training has been running for three months now, and I am close to giving up.

I already get stomachaches on Sunday afternoon when I think about having to go back the next morning. I moved to a different department. Now I am the only girl, and my training supervisor is an older man. As far as I can tell, he is quite nice. He takes special care of me, asks if I understood everything, and provides extra explanations. This embarrasses me. I already get palpitations when I see him coming, and I can hardly understand anything because I get so nervous.

I don't think the demands have increased much, but all the self-confidence I had from the first year is gone. I feel dumber than everyone else and now have the feeling: I'll never make it. It makes me very angry that my parents are now triumphing. I would really like to complete the training, but I am completely discouraged.

Answer

The fact that you have asserted yourself in your unusual career choice against your parents shows that you have your own ideas for shaping your life and also the strength to realize them against resistance. Don't give up just yet! At the moment, you feel very unhappy in your situation. You will probably feel a little better when you better understand the situation.

You are currently gaining important experiences about yourself! If you want to learn and achieve something, you have more trust and accordingly more security towards people like your young training supervisor, perhaps towards women in general. In the older training supervisor, you unconsciously may encounter your father, who doesn't believe you can do anything. The feeling: I can't make it, is probably a very old feeling, and it was first the important adults in your life like your parents who repeatedly said to you: You won't make it. Now you want to prove to yourself and others with your career choice that you can make it.

You will make it if you consciously acknowledge the old feelings of failure and fear alongside the new reality: The older training supervisor is also helpful and friendly and believes in me, and the others (are they perhaps always the young ones?) can't do everything better than me either. This doesn't completely eliminate your fears, but they will slowly weaken. Be patient with yourself.

Learning processes take time. You are currently learning against your fears and discouragement that you can achieve something if you want to, even though you are "just" a girl. In addition, you learn that parents are not always right. This makes the parents smaller and you a bit bigger. This is part of growing up. You also have to take time for that.

I Am Afraid of Menopause

I am very depressed after a visit to my sister and can't get out of this mood. I hadn't seen her in six years. She is eight years older than me. I have just turned forty-nine. We both have a similar family situation, except that her children are older than mine. But my sister is suffering terribly from menopausal symptoms.

I have only known her as a very active woman who is never overwhelmed. During this reunion, I was truly shocked by her condition. She has become a burden to herself and her family. She is a walking complaint and can no longer find joy in anything. The hormone replacement therapy she is taking has no effect. I could visibly see her suffer through one hot flash after another.

On this occasion, it also became clear to me that our mother had to suffer from menopause in the same way. I took home a truly frightening image. A conversation with my doctor couldn't really calm me down either. He said that I should just let everything come naturally; for now, I have no complaints. My menstruation is still regular. But that can change quickly, as I've seen among my acquaintances. Most people my age that I know are already having issues with it, although not as severe as my sister. So, my concern remains!

I want to know how I can prevent the fate of my mother and sister. In my bookstore, I saw that there are many books on the subject, but where should I start?

Answer

Your concern likely serves a purpose. Take it as an invitation to think about your current life situation. We are always afraid of tomorrow when we owe something to today. You live your own life, and just because your mother and sister have problems with menopause doesn't mean you have to as well. Physical processes like puberty, pregnancy, illness, or menopause also have a psychological aspect; and how we experience something is strongly influenced by our inner attitude towards it.

If you are already afraid of your menopause, which hasn't even started yet, you will most likely experience it badly, fulfilling your own prophecy. The best prevention you are looking for lies in living your life satisfactorily now and having plans, perspectives, and new goals for the future.

Menopause usually coincides with changes in the family. The children become independent, and thus fulfilling life tasks diminish. This situation requires a double reorientation: firstly, you have to find a new attitude towards your body, which is clearly no longer young, and secondly, determine your new role in life. Where both are only experienced as a lack or overwhelm, the way to complaints and illness is near.

If you can accept the physical change as a natural developmental process, if you understand the liberation from family obligations as a new form of freedom, then a positive new phase of life begins in this period, and the complaints that menopause brings will be relatively small. Books on the subject can certainly help. Focus first on the books that bring the new freedom and the given new perspectives to the foreground.

I Don't Know What Suits Me

My husband is taking up a new position at the turn of the year. He is very proud to have reached this position so quickly, and I want to support him in every way. We will be moving and meeting many new people. I'm a little scared of that because I feel quite insecure when it comes to clothing.

When I observe other women my age, almost thirty, I get the impression they know much better what suits them than I do. Of course, I can get advice, but that's not what I mean. Rather, it's that special self-assuredness that I lack, which other women have when they wear beautiful clothes.

My husband wants me to look elegant and accordingly buys me expensive clothes, so that I make an appearance as a refined lady by his side. But without him, I would not dare to go out in public dressed like that. In my parents' home, the motto was simple and genuine. Don't stand out and nothing fake. For example, we had hardly any jewelry. My husband constantly brings me striking costume jewelry from his travels and expects me to wear it.

We were invited to a get-to-know-you party with my husband's new colleagues. I wore a long green silk dress with what I considered to be overly ostentatious Italian jewelry. My husband was pleased with me, and supposedly I made a strong impression on his boss, but I felt completely out of place the whole time. The other women, some of whom were older than me, were much less dressed up than I was and wore more casual, trendy clothes. But that's how it always is for me. Why can't I find a style that really suits me and makes me feel comfortable?

Answer

You are mixing two different aspects of your problem: the external view of your so-called style of dressing and your inner perception of how you feel with it. You have already found a style, or perhaps just a style that impresses, that pleases your husband and his boss, and perhaps the wives of his colleagues were jealous, who knows.

But behind the ladylike façade still sits the little girl who is ashamed when she stands out. I think that little girl needs to grow up so she can choose for herself what she likes. You will only find a match between your outward appearance and your inner perception if you dress in a way that pleases you.

The self-assuredness to wear striking clothes that you admire in other women comes, if it is genuine, from the fact that these women express their own image of themselves through their clothing.

You, on the other hand, conform to the desired images of others. You were the well-behaved, inconspicuous daughter of your parents; now you are the ladylike wife of a successful man. But who are you just for yourself? That's what you have to find out.

Escape into Illness

I was on a retreat for six weeks and had a little affair with a man who is a year older than me. I am twenty-four. Now this man wants to visit me at home. He is very decisive in everything he does, and I actually admire that, but I would much prefer it if he didn't come. I also have an almost-fiancé here, and I have enough problems with him as it is.

He and both families are pressuring us to get married, and I have half-agreed to do it in the fall. I have also been offered further training at my workplace. For this, I would have to go to Munich for half a year. I'm actually very tempted; I've almost given my boss a yes, but I don't want to confront my boyfriend with it. I already know he'll be against it because we would have to postpone the wedding.

If my affair from the retreat also shows up now, the stress will simply be too much for me; I'll definitely collapse again. I had to go on the retreat because I was very sick before. I had terrible circulation problems and back pain. How should I be-have now? All of this weighs on me like millstones. My entire re-covery is already gone.

Answer

I am not at all surprised that you are already at the end of your tether. You're probably constantly pondering what the right thing to do is, and the 'right' thing for you is always the solution that hurts no one and satisfies everyone. However, this ideal solution does not exist! Your own desires and needs often have to be asserted against the expectations of those around you.

You don't dare to say a clear no when you feel no. So you always say both no and yes at the same time. This is very clear even in your short letter: You've gone so far in accommodating your vacation acquaintance that he feels entitled to visit you, yet at the same time, you reject him. You give your boss a commitment even though you haven't talked to your boyfriend yet. You want to get married, and you don't want to.

Your ambivalence puts you in such difficult situations that only illness remains as an escape route. With the illness, you escape the necessity of having to solve your problems.

Perhaps you don't have to get sick again if you make it clear to your fling from the retreat that you consider the relationship to be over. The clearest thing to me is your desire for professional development. Make it clear to your boyfriend that this training is important to you. He probably takes his job seriously too.

If he can't understand your desires at all, you should reconsider whether he is really the right partner for you. The separation from your family and boyfriend, associated with the training, could perhaps also contribute to you becoming more independent.

The Joy of Life Is Gone

I'm turning to you because I hope for some advice: I don't recognize myself anymore. I have always been a strong woman, have mastered my life, raised children without a man, and have gained a position of trust in the company where I have worked for twenty-one years now. In theory, I could enjoy my life now, where I have no immediate worries. But for some time, I've been increasingly aware that all my former zest for life has disappeared.

I took my last trip two years ago, since then I've spent all my vacations at home, always with good reasons, but the truth is that I just can't get myself going. Even the simplest things, like buying new shoes or the like, have become a huge task that I can't tackle. So everything remains undone; I only do the bare minimum. Even most of my hobbies—I was an active member of a gymnastics club for half my life—I have let slide. I no longer understand myself and am annoyed with myself for becoming such an old aunt. But life is not over at fifty-four!

So far, I have blamed everything on my various illnesses. An old gallbladder problem has resurfaced, and I also have gout and circulatory problems. But even now, after a cure has made me feel much better, I am absolutely listless and have no desire for anything. Dark thoughts about illness and death keep coming to me. I have always tried to make something out of life, but now everything seems useless and meaningless to me.

I wonder what I am here for. My work is also not going as well as it used to. I can't concentrate well and always feel like everyone is deliberately making things difficult for me. My only purpose in life is watching TV, sleeping, and eating well. This can't go on like this!

Answer

No, your life really shouldn't continue like this. Perhaps the fact that you've managed to write this letter is already the first step toward change. The most important thing is always to take a close look at how we are really doing. You describe a condition that can be termed as depression. Typical for depressive states are your lack of drive, the feeling of being overwhelmed, the gloomy mood, withdrawal from contacts, your difficulty in concentrating, and your preoccupation with death and illness.

In most cases, the reasons for depression are not physical. Depressions are triggered by certain emotional experiences, often related to loss. When loved ones die, leave, turn away, or are no longer reachable, we suffer a loss. But there are also invisible losses: farewell to youth, beauty, or health, to unbroken working capacity, farewell to a hope that has accompanied us for a long time.

What triggered your depression, I can't say. But aging alone already brings with it many unavoidable losses. We need to mourn what we lose. Only when a loss has been mourned can we turn to new people and things. The depression that paralyzes us from participating in life is like emotionally playing dead for fear of mourning. Take your depression as a chance to come to terms with yourself and your life. Perhaps a book can help you in this regard. Take a look at your bookstore; there are many helpful books on this topic.

My Ambition Is Getting in the Way

I have problems that I probably create myself, but I don't know how to change that. I am twenty-four and, after completing a carpentry apprenticeship, I am now going back to school to get my high school diploma. I am actually happy that I finally made this decision, but I have a major problem that is getting worse every day.

I always want to be the best, i.e., give the best answers, write the best papers, etc. If I am not absolutely sure that my answer is correct, I prefer to say nothing at all. Afterwards, I get annoyed when I would have known something but remained silent.

The worst part is with the written assignments, because no sentence seems good enough to me when I think about what the teacher will say about it. I just can't get anything down on paper. This characteristic of mine is slowly driving me crazy. My girlfriend says my ambition is getting in the way. Do you think so too?

Answer

For you, achievement seems to be the only way to feel loved and valuable, which is why you try so hard. You have to be the best to ward off your fears of not being loved and recognized. In that regard, your girlfriend is correct. Your exaggerated ambition is more likely to hinder you from achieving your possible performance than to support you.

Look around and see if there are people in your life who like you just as you are, simply because you are you, and not because you accomplish something special. In school, you should try to focus entirely on the task at hand; that means staying completely in the present and not worrying about how your actions will be evaluated in the future. When you are fully engaged, performance tends to happen naturally.

From this perspective, it is not your ambition that is in the way, but your fear of not receiving recognition. You are probably also more compliant in your relationships with people than is good for you. You need to learn to take your own needs as seriously as others' expectations of you.

Translated to your current problem, this means: Your desires to qualify are important; the subject matter you are currently dealing with is important; the teacher is merely someone to help you achieve your goals. If you can't become more relaxed, school will only become a source of stress, but learning should also be fun. It should not be just about a grade, but also about a development process; engaging with the content of our culture can enrich you and expand your horizons.

If you cannot find a different attitude towards performance on your own, you should seek professional help. Counseling centers and psychological practices are the right places to go. You are well on your way to developing a learning and working disorder.

I Doubt My Feelings

I'm currently very insecure and no longer trust my feelings. I moved here six months ago because my boyfriend lives here. We have an apartment together and plan to get married soon. I've also found a new job here that I'm very hopeful about. I've looked forward to this move for months and to finally be with my boyfriend, as I was really suffering from longing before.

Until now, I've lived in a different state where my parents also live, and where I went to school and completed my apprenticeship. But ever since I've been here, I've had a complete turnaround in my feelings! I can't really be happy about everything I've longed for. Inside, I feel completely stiff. Work is going well, but I've become really nasty to my boyfriend.

I'm also disturbed by a recurring dream I've had four times. I wake up at night crying. Each time, in the dream, my bicycle has been stolen. In reality, the bicycle is a gift from my boyfriend that I'm very attached to. I don't understand at all why I'm in such a bad mood, when everything is, or could be, as I've dreamed it would be. Can you explain this to me?

Answer

You are experiencing something that many people go through: even a turn for the better is often hard to handle. Any major change in life is a stressful situation in which we need all our strength to adapt to the new circumstances. Therefore, not only death, divorce, or illness can shake our emotional balance but also joyful events like weddings, births, or even just passing exams.

So take your time to settle into your new life situation. Allow yourself to try many things; to make mistakes; to find that some things in reality look quite different than in your dreams. Six months is a very short time to handle all the adjustment and change issues.

There may be another reason for your inner stiffness and sadness, expressed in dreams about the lost bicycle. Perhaps, in anticipation of your new life with your boyfriend, you've forgotten to say goodbye to your old life. I think that you have left behind many things that you are attached to, like your bicycle, in the city of your childhood.

We cannot avoid saying goodbye, that is, mourning everything we have to let go of in order for something new to be possible at all. A chapter in your life has ended, a new one is beginning. Only once you've adequately mourned the departure from your parents, friends, and the places of your childhood can you truly feel happy in your new life.

Why Always Me?

I am forty-four years old, currently not working because I have four school-aged children to take care of. My husband is self-employed and very busy, so I'm responsible for everything. I'm the proverbial family manager. I enjoy it and find it fulfilling. That's not my problem, but I've noticed that in our large circle of friends and acquaintances, I'm always the one who does everything. Many a party or outing with the kids would not have happened if I hadn't stepped in.

I make the calls, I bake most of the cakes for events, I shop for a bedridden neighbor even though others live closer, I step in when someone needs a babysitter. But when I'm in need, no one is there.

So, I had a falling out with a close friend. I just lost it. I have her eldest son, who's in the same class as one of our daughters, over for lunch twice a week, but she can't even give me a firm commitment that she'll drive my younger two to music lessons in three weeks. I don't think it's just this one friend; I feel like everyone else just looks out for themselves, and I'm the only fool who's always there for others.

Of course, this makes me very popular and I often hear: if it weren't for you, but I don't really need that. I actually have enough on my plate with my own family. But that's just how I am. Perhaps you become this way when you grow up in a large family. We were five siblings, and we all pitched in and stood up for each other. Nowadays, people are all selfish, it seems to me, waiting to be served rather than taking initiative themselves. I wonder why I always have to make the effort; I would also like to receive something for once.

Answer

The answer is pretty simple: In the social structure, roles are assigned not by supernatural powers but by the behavior that people exhibit. Who will play what role is often incredibly quickly determined in the first few minutes of an encounter. This applies equally to couples and to mothers in a playgroup. In your circle of friends, you have taken on the role of the one who is always available because you have offered it through your behavior. Everyone now assumes that you will never say "no," that you're always strong, helpful, and uncomplaining. This is very convenient for others. They can treat you like an institution and don't have to think about how you might feel—and that's exactly how you feel: exploited.

A circle of friends doesn't function like a family, where mutual solidarity is required. Here, the strong prevail, and you could call that selfish. But everyone has to learn to set boundaries to find a balanced ratio of give and take for themselves. For you, this means that you must demand more for yourself from others. You are too much on the giving side. Of course, this will not make you popular with those who have known you differently. This might be harder for you to bear than you thought. In this respect, the argument with your friend is something new for both of you. If there's to be a reconciliation, the relationship will be stronger than before. Otherwise, perhaps it's not a big loss.

But also consider: Every society needs committed, proactive people like you. If you accept your role and don't necessarily expect something in return or gratitude, then you can also be happy with it.

What to Do About Nightmares?

I am not writing to you because I occasionally have bad dreams, but because I have been having terrible nightmares three to four times a week for about a year now. Most of the time, I can't fall back asleep afterward, and the next day I not only lack sleep but can't shake off the terrible mood from the dream, which spoils my entire day. I have come to fear going to sleep. All the advice I've received so far has not helped. I've tried drinking calming tea in the evenings, moving my bed, leaving the light on at night, writing down the dreams, and much more. But nothing changes, whether I am at home or on vacation in Mallorca.

I am forty-eight years old and married without children. My marriage is average. If that were the reason, many more people would have nightmares. I am very satisfied and successful in my profession. We can afford everything we desire. We travel a lot with our caravan. The nightmares are ruining my joy for life. At first, I always told my husband about them. He can't stand to hear about them anymore, but I still have to dream them.

I always find myself somehow in confined spaces that I can't escape from. Sometimes it's in a skyscraper on the thirtieth floor or in an airplane, other times it's in some sort of tube deep underground. I am not alone, but I don't see the others; I only know that they mean me harm and I am very afraid. It always takes an agonizingly long time until it happens, but it happens: Someone passes judgment on me.

Exactly what it is, I never know. I start to cry and beg for mercy. Then usually different things happen, like there being a terrible noise and someone says it's a plane taking off, or rats whose tails someone has cut off run over my feet. This continues until I feel sick and have to gag. The dream always ends with someone pulling slimy worms from my mouth. Endlessly. It doesn't stop until I wake up in horror.

Can you interpret these dreams for me? And is it true that you stop dreaming them if you know the interpretation?

Answer

The idea that the correct interpretation could stop the nightmares is not entirely wrong, but it would have to be the right interpretation, and that's not easy to find. Dream books are no help at all; you need patient work with a psychotherapist for that. Your subconscious produces these dreams, so only you can know what they mean.

It is generally assumed that particularly impactful or unprocessed experiences are what come forth in nightmares. Even if individual aspects of your dreams vary, it seems to be a recurring dream dealing with the same theme.

I know too little about you to say much about these nightmares. It would be important to get medical clearance to confirm you are organically healthy. Then it would be interesting to find out what happened a year ago when these dreams started. In content, I think that, besides fear, disgust is the strongest emotion in these dreams. The worms coming out of your mouth is a powerful image.

As a psychotherapist, one might think that these nightmares are expressing deeply repressed experiences of abuse. But without having spoken to you, that is pure speculation. However, it likely involves traumatic experiences trying to come into the light of consciousness.

You should take the fact that these nightmares have been troubling you so frequently and for a year now seriously. This is not harmless, but rather a warning sign you should heed. Seek psychotherapeutic treatment.

Spring Makes Me Sad

The warm breezes are blowing again, and everyone is delighted as if something special is happening. I feel completely different and just have to let it out. Giving me the courage to do so is the acquaintance of another woman who feels the same as I do.

Apparently, we are both alone in the world with our feelings. Everyone else around me goes crazy at this time of the year. They buy flowers, plants, and seed bags like mad, and constantly burst into exclamations of joy because some little tree is green again. To me, all of this seems ridiculous and exaggerated.

I actually dislike this season and it puts me in a bad mood. I can't keep up with the pace that others suddenly adopt. Everyone seems excited, just because the sun is shining and it's getting warmer.

I get hay fever from the birch trees and prefer to barricade myself in my room on weekends. Then my friends and colleagues criticize me for not participating in outings and such, or for not wanting to visit their wonderful gardens. But I simply don't feel like it, and aside from me, it seems no one else feels this way. Everyone else is in a good mood and can't understand me.

However, I am a winter person. That's my season. I start feeling really good in the fall, and I come alive in winter. All this spring magic actually makes me sad. Is that perhaps not normal? Aside from the mentioned acquaintance, nobody understands me.

Answer

I suspect there are many people who have mixed feelings about spring. You are not alone, it's just that few talk about it. Spring is also a symbol of the never-ending vitality of life, of renewal, growth, and becoming. It reminds us of our own growth, and naturally, of our non-growth. When everything outside is green and blooming, and we feel internally withered, spring is unbearable.

Most suicides happen during this season. The suicide rate starts to rise in March, peaks in June, and then declines. If spring makes you sad, you are feeling some of the pain of your own missed opportunities for growth; if it annoys you because you find the fuss around it ridiculous, you are fending off this sorrow. This is as normal as many other strategies we use to ward off unpleasant feelings and insights.

But if you feel really good in the fall and winter without a trace of doubt, then you are perfectly fine. There are no pollen flying around in winter. Hay fever can severely limit one's quality of life and increasingly spoil the spring for more people.

Perhaps next winter you can plant a seed that will sprout in the spring to help you better cope with this challenging season for you. It could be an exciting project, a trip, an important visit, a new plan—whatever appears desirable to you in winter when you are in a good mood.

I Was Really Nervous

Something strange happened to me, and I'd like to know what to make of it. I've been married for twelve years, fully employed the entire time, with two small children. Things are often quite hectic for us, I must say. To get through my day, I've been waking up at 5:30 AM for years. Even on Sundays, because my husband and I used to be competitive athletes, and we can't find any other time for some training if we don't want to get completely rusty.

I always talk about wanting to go somewhere without my family. Then I would sleep in, laze around all day, and just do what I enjoy. Miraculously, I was almost home alone for a week. My husband took the kids to visit his parents, and I was on sick leave but already felt quite alright. I thought it would be a great week for me—but it was the opposite.

There was no question of sleeping in; at 5:30 AM, I was as awake as ever. Even sleeping pills didn't change that. Everything I could finally do for myself didn't bring me any real joy. Inside, I was really nervous and couldn't enjoy anything.

One afternoon, I made myself really comfortable on the couch when the phone rang twice and then stopped. I got so terribly scared, I don't really know of what, that I couldn't stay alone and went to my neighbor's house. That night, I became convinced that something had happened to the children.

I called first thing in the morning, and of course, everything was fine. All my imaginings! I was really happy when everyone was back home, and we returned to our normal lives. I'm annoyed that I made so little of that week and don't want that to happen again.

Answer

An organism that has been running at full speed for months needs a transition period to adjust to a slower pace. Humans are not machines that respond at the push of a button. Those who apply relaxation and disengagement techniques, such as autogenic training or meditation, even in daily stress, find it generally easier to switch. But you obviously belong to those people who work restlessly from early morning to late evening and even have to accomplish something in sports on Sundays.

With so much activity, your passive desires have certainly been neglected for years. You have arranged your life in this way for some conscious or unconscious reasons to suppress these passive wishes. Maybe in the family where you grew up, it was dangerous to be lazy, to let go, to enjoy or just have fun because you always had to achieve something to be loved. Then you would have the desire for it but no practice in living it out, and when you try, you become afraid.

Perhaps, when the family demands nothing from you, desires arise that do not fit into your orderly family life, and would disrupt it, thus making you anxious. What you have experienced is a real anxiety attack. The fear was there first, triggered by suppressed desires surfacing from the unconscious due to the unfamiliar situation. You perceived this as nervousness. The ringing of the phone is merely a random hook for the fear; the thought about the children is an attempt to find some reasonable reason for the anxiety.

I would advise you to tackle the problem in small doses: First, create a small niche for fulfilling personal wishes every day. Second, learn to take breaks for relaxation even in everyday stress. Third, plan the next holiday situation not completely alone but perhaps with a friend. Then this should not happen to you again.

I Want to Study

I've always done what my father wanted. After completing my secondary education, I did an apprenticeship that my father chose for me, even though I would have much preferred to continue going to school. Now, I've earned my high school diploma through night school, and I could be happy if my father weren't against it. He's told me that I would no longer be his daughter if I dared to study. He himself is just a laborer, but he has a leadership role in his company and earns so much that I wouldn't qualify for financial aid.

I want to study, but I can't without his financial support. I've already checked: if he doesn't voluntarily support me, I'd have to sue him. I can't even bear to think about it. By the way, my mother shares his opinion. I can't go against my parents' wishes anyway. They've done so much for me. My biological mother died giving birth to me. I lived with an aunt for two years until my father created a proper home for me and immediately brought me back. He had a hard time with my stepmother; she's quite strict, but fair.

I've always tried to please them, so all their efforts wouldn't be in vain. Now I'd have to stand against them, and that's very hard for me. On the other hand, I feel like I can't continue living like this. Everything I do has so little connection with me. I need to find a purpose that really belongs to me. The conflict with my parents makes everything much harder because everything is so unclear inside me, and I don't know what I actually want or am looking for.

My parents don't understand me when I talk about this; neither of them can deal with emotions. Sometimes I think about my deceased mother and wonder if she would have understood me better. I had to pray for her my entire childhood, but that hasn't helped me either. I'm very lost. Do you have any advice for me?

Answer

By mentioning a few facts, you describe a tragic childhood story, and a significant part of your agonizing inner insecurity is certainly related to it. You have probably been doing what your father wanted since you were two years old, and that meant: to be a normal, happy child in a seemingly intact family. However, you had already experienced separation, were a sad, distressed child who had lost their familiar environment and their mother, as for your emotional life, your aunt was your mother during those important first two years.

These early roots are where your perception begins, that you don't understand yourself, and that your parents can't engage with your emotions. The beloved real mother (aunt) disappears overnight, you pray for the supposedly true but deceased mother that you can only imagine, and you must love the new (step) mother that you don't know. How is a small child supposed to cope with that internally!

You have become the daughter your father wanted, but where are you? Like him, you have suppressed all the feelings that would disturb the apparent harmony; and now, inside you where a core should be, there is only emptiness, from which no echo comes for everything you do, so you could also leave it. Psychologists call this a false self.

You must search for your true self. Conflicts with parents, which must now finally be openly addressed, cannot be avoided and are an important part of self-discovery. The high school diploma, the desire to study, are certainly also part of it, but you probably have to embark on an inner process that takes you back to the point where you lost yourself. You need psychotherapeutic help for that.

Is My Childhood to Blame?

My life situation is actually good, yet I'm often sad or simply discontent. Then I feel empty and eat too much. My husband, with whom I can discuss a lot, thinks that there must be something underlying my mood. He's also surprised by my exaggerated reactions to praise. I'm always moved. As soon as someone is nice to me, even if they are a complete stranger, I burst into tears. I can quickly compose myself again, but people close to me like my husband and my children notice that Mom is moved once again.

I'm actually a strong person. I've never been really sick; my household of five people, complete with pets and garden, runs perfectly, and for many friends, I'm a stable anchor in their lives, at least they say so. My husband, who has participated in various psychological seminars at his company, believes that my sensitivity and my cloudy moods are the fault of my childhood. I would like to know if you see it that way as well.

I'm the only child of my parents. Four months after my birth, my mother fell seriously ill. Until her death four years later, she was only home for short periods of time. My grandma took care of me, and when I was seven, I got a very loving stepmother. She is my mother today. I don't remember much from my early childhood, only the hospital visits are crystal clear in my memory.

I was dressed up especially nicely for the visit to my mother and was warned only to tell her cheerful things. In the last months before her death, she didn't want to see me anymore, and I was glad that I didn't have to go anymore. Can these memories really be the reason for my problems?

Answer

Your husband is right. It's highly likely that the experiences from your childhood are still affecting you in the way described. What you can still remember is probably just a small part of the whole picture; most of it is unconscious and, like all repressed emotions, strives to return to consciousness. The most important imprints a person receives are in the first four years of life, and your first four years were overshadowed by your mother's severe illness. It's easy to imagine that none of the people who cared for you could be genuinely happy. They all carried the worry about your mother.

Her short stays at home were probably more damaging to you as a small child because you couldn't emotionally settle into a reliable situation. No sooner had you gotten used to your mother again, you lost her. It is very difficult for a child to build inner stability and trust in the world in such conditions. You were probably a very sad little girl. The less your important caregivers addressed your sadness back then, the more you had to repress it.

The hospital visits were especially bad for your development. You were actually sad and depressed, but you had to be cheerful so as not to disturb your sick mother further. Back then, you learned to pull yourself together and be strong. You are strong as an adult woman, but behind that strength cries the little unconsolable girl you once were. That's why tears come to you as soon as someone pays attention to you.

Perhaps you should talk to a psychotherapist about this. The decision for therapy means confronting yourself with all the old pain. You need to find out whether you want this and whether you have the strength for it.

I Am Being Sexually Harassed

I have a problem that I can't handle alone; and I can't talk about it with anyone either (I wouldn't know who to talk to), because I feel so stupid. I am being sexually harassed at work. I am twenty-one years old, and I've been at a new office job for six months, which I really like, and the colleagues are very nice – except for this one, slightly older colleague...

From the beginning, I got along very well with him, he is fundamentally nice; and since he is a person who apparently has no issues with personal space, I didn't think anything of it when he occasionally hugged me, or massaged my back. He also did that with other female colleagues. However, gradually he has been using every situation to be alone with me. He has become increasingly pushy. While he's never really brutal, I now truly feel harassed and used. He touches my buttocks, strokes my back; he constantly tries to grope my breasts.

He is very tall and strong, and if he really had malicious intentions, I would have no chance against him. I already try to avoid him as much as possible, or never to be alone with him in a room, but unfortunately, I can't always do that, and then the drama starts again. I do push him away, but he is, as mentioned, much stronger than me. I also don't dare to say anything to him; I wouldn't know what to say because he somehow disguises it all under the pretense of friendship.

Besides, I am not particularly pretty, I am rather overweight, not a beauty. I would simply feel stupid if I told someone that I am being sexually harassed. But I really don't know how much longer I can endure this. I can't go on much longer. I finally want peace! Please don't say that I should talk to colleagues or superiors. I could never do that, not even with my parents or friends. I don't have the courage. But what else should I do?

Answer

Sometimes you really do need external help, and often seeking advice from an anonymous source is much easier than talking with familiar people. You've become so internally pressured that you can't find solutions for yourself anymore. Contact local women's organizations, where you can find competent people to talk to about sexual harassment. You shouldn't feel stupid; you are not the only one this happens to. Church counseling services should also be able to help you.

Furthermore, you mainly need help to boost your low self-esteem! As long as you're so unsure of yourself that you can't clearly show this colleague your boundaries, he will continue and possibly even revel in your confusion and fear. But I think you urgently need someone who helps you sort out your feelings. You actually find the colleague "nice". However, he chooses absolutely the wrong way to show that he finds you attractive through his physical assaults. The fact that you otherwise get along well with him makes it even harder for you to speak up.

Only when you take a clear internal position will you become capable of taking action. At the moment, you have a turmoil of emotions and can neither completely write him off due to his sexist advances nor believe that he might – albeit in a macho way – be serious about you. The pivot for possible future behavior will be your self-esteem as a woman. You have to do something about it. Take the colleague's boundary violations as an opportunity for self-development!

No One Likes Me

I am twenty-one years old and study with three other girls. We talk a lot about personal things. But I notice that I can't keep up. I don't have a boyfriend like the others, and otherwise, I'm somehow out of place. We are now in our second year of training. When we all started together, I initially felt like I belonged, but that has changed a lot. I think they laugh behind my back, and sometimes they stop talking when I come in. Then I have this terrible feeling that I'm just a nuisance.

Unpleasant tasks are often dumped on me. The boss doesn't even ask anymore, she just says that I should do it. I'm also not necessarily stupider or uglier than the others, but somehow it has always been like this, that nobody likes me. I would also like to have a boyfriend, but it doesn't work out. I have three brothers who have many friends, but they always act as if they don't see me.

It was always like this at home. The men, that is my brothers and my father, set the tone, my mother went along, and I was always somehow left over, and nobody believed me about anything. When I once wrote the best German essay in school, the teacher had to write it down specially because otherwise nobody would have believed it at home.

There must be something different about me than the others. Recently I took a train to Munich. Everyone in the compartment was talking to each other, but nobody spoke to me. I am slowly becoming very unhappy about this. What is it about me that others reject me?

Answer

You are reliving in all contexts of your adult life today your childhood family situation from back then. Whether you are with work colleagues or sitting on the train, you feel among people like the small, unnoticed girl at home. Your mother, who apparently as a woman could not take herself seriously and sought the approval of men, did not understand how to protect her daughter and strengthen her back. As a non-boy, you simply had no place and no love in this family. These experiences have shaped you.

Certainly, you are not less intelligent and less pretty than the others, but you are certainly less self-confident, less demanding, less carefree, and less active than the others. In the train compartment, for example, you wait to be spoken to and do not have the internal possibility to simply join in. Unloved children have a hard time as adults. Unconsciously, they display behavior that almost challenges the others to reject them or to burden them further.

Without outside help, you will hardly succeed in changing yourself and your life because most of your experiential and behavioral patterns are unconscious, that is, they cannot even be consciously noticed by you. I would suggest that you seek psychotherapy. In a therapeutic situation, you can correct your old emotional experiences: you will be taken seriously, you will be understood, and what you say is important. Gradually, you will learn to take yourself seriously and to like yourself. Only when you consider yourself a valuable person and behave accordingly will you also be accepted and loved by others.

The Lost Twin

I hope you don't laugh at me, but I am very preoccupied with a subject that won't let me go. I would like to know what you think about it. The situation is that I've always been a bit melancholic. At least that's what my husband calls this mood in me. Nowadays, it's probably called depressive. Since I'm going through menopause and both of my sons are studying, it has gotten worse. I think a lot about death, although I am otherwise healthy and at fifty-six, probably don't have to worry about it yet. The subject draws me in magnetically; I've read many relevant books, and I am considering joining the hospice movement.

My husband is not at all pleased with this development in me. At his urging, I have consulted various natural medicine doctors and also naturopaths with the question of whether I am missing some vital substance. Since then, I've been taking a lot of good stuff and dietary supplements; I feel stronger than before, but my mood hasn't changed much.

Now, on recommendation, I saw a woman who practices Bodytalk. This is a method where you can ask your body and soul what they lack. At first, the session seemed rather strange to me. The Bodytalk woman always asked something and moved my arm. If the muscles reacted strongly, it meant "yes", if they were weak, "no". I couldn't take it all seriously. But then she said something that immediately aroused me greatly. That was three weeks ago, and not a day goes by that I don't think about it.

She said that I had not been alone in the uterus but had had a twin until the fourth month before birth. I had experienced his death, so death is my topic. She also thought that my melancholic condition might come from still being sad about this loss, and also I might have guilt feelings that this twin had to die so I could live, and these guilt feelings are also spoiling my enjoyment of life.

My husband says it's all hocus-pocus. My mother knows nothing about it. But I waver. Sometimes I'm quite sure she's right and feel quite relieved; then it all seems totally crazy to me. Please tell me if something like this is possible.

Answer

This may sound very fantastical at first, but it is not mere hocus-pocus, especially because you react so strongly to this idea. This is a serious indication that the idea of having had a twin has triggered significant emotional patterns for you. Whether the Bodytalk woman is objectively correct or not is not so important in this context; in any case, she has hit something unconscious in you that is causing arousal. That's much more than what all the other visits to experts have achieved. In psychotherapy, one could work very well with such an image and see what it means for the soul.

However, you want to know how I assess the truth content of such a statement. First of all, Bodytalk is a serious method where you can learn a lot about yourself when it is done professionally. The lost twin idea is not new; there is some literature on it. What is certain is that multiple embryos are formed more often at conception than are later born. In the first months of pregnancy, the non-viable fetuses die off and are completely absorbed by the placenta. But sometimes one finds hairs or teeth from a twin that indicate that he once existed.

In later months of pregnancy, the traces are clearer. Pregnant women rarely know anything about it. What such a twin means for the emotional development of the surviving child, I can't tell you either. You can only speculate, and each scientific and/or philosophical position will develop its own interpretation. We know from prenatal psychology that children react very early in the womb.

My advice would be for you to deal with the topic fully and without any ifs or buts, because it probably won't settle down otherwise. Maybe you'll find a key to your lifelong melancholy, or maybe you'll discover something completely different that becomes a new meaning in the changed life situation. There are books on the subject of the lost twin, and seminars are also held on it. Involvement in the hospice movement is always meaningful and can also lead to important insights.

I'm Afraid of Failing

I've been unemployed for almost three years, and now I've found a new job after retraining. My new job starts on January 1st. The closer the date gets, the more afraid I become of failing. When I first heard about this opportunity two months ago, I was initially delighted. I then met my future boss and two colleagues and immediately felt that I would get along well with them. Everyone was nice to me. That was in early August.

I then went on a two-week vacation with my girlfriend, but I didn't sleep well and didn't relax at all during that time. Then I started having severe stomach pains, and the doctor diagnosed me with gastritis. He also told me that the condition might be related to my new job. I now have medication for the pain and am following a diet, but I still feel like I'm getting sicker.

I know it's probably just nerves, but that doesn't help me. I can't sleep at all without beer and sleeping pills. I keep thinking about what the right answer or behavior would be in certain situations. Then my heart starts pounding because I can't think of the right thing. What will it be like in reality!

The new job is crucial for me as my entire future depends on it. My girlfriend is pushing for marriage, and I also have plans that involve my parents, which I can only carry out if I have a regular income. No one understands my condition. Everyone says, "You'll be fine!" But I'm not at all sure if my training is sufficient for the challenges that lie ahead. Is everyone like this in such a situation, or am I a unique case?

Answer

You're certainly not a unique case. New, unfamiliar situations make most people nervous. However, you may be reacting a bit more sensitively than average. There are also complicating factors for you: the long period of unemployment, the entirely new job, and high expectations from your environment. Therefore, I can understand why you're afraid of starting work.

What you're missing most urgently at the moment is someone you trust who understands you and with whom you can openly discuss your emotional state. Your fears are also increasing because your environment downplays them. Your stomach speaks a clear (body) language: it's upset. You're annoyed that nobody really understands you, and everyone expects so much from you.

You would probably prefer a warm, nurturing environment where nobody expects anything from you. If you admit these feelings to yourself, your stomach doesn't have to express them and can heal, even if you're burdening it with sleeping pills and beer. However, I think you're torturing yourself the most by setting performance expectations for yourself that you can't meet.

Your fear fantasies about work situations always involve an all-or-nothing scenario. If you make a single mistake, you feel worthless. Fortunately, reality is not always like that. You don't have to be perfect on the first day. Everyone will give you a settling-in period. You're allowed to make mistakes.

Fear always arises when we leave the here and now and venture into the future. Fantasies about future situations are often worse than the real situations themselves because we can relieve ourselves in the real situations through actions, and the reactions from our environment often turn out quite differently than we had imagined based on past bad experiences.

Try to live in the here and now and forbid yourself from fantasizing about a future you can't yet know for sure. Maybe you can also have an open conversation about your feelings with your girlfriend; that could relieve you.

Everything Has Gone Wrong

What do you do with a pile of broken pieces? My entire life is a chain of failures. I just had my thirty-fifth birthday. I had to cry a lot because I realized that, apart from my mother, I have nobody. I took stock of my life. Everything has gone wrong. I got married at twenty-four. Back then, everything seemed like a great adventure. Due to marriage, I converted to Catholicism. My husband is Spanish, and we lived in Spain. I couldn't get along with his family, nor could I learn the language fast enough.

Then I had twins, and my migraines became worse and more frequent than ever before. I became addicted to pills. Combined with the challenges in a foreign country, it was hell. Eventually, I separated from my husband and returned to Germany – but the children stayed there. To me, they are lost. They are now eight years old, and I haven't seen them in the last four years. I do have visitation rights, but I can't afford the long trip, and I'm afraid of the Spanish family. In their eyes, I am worthless.

I also can't seem to build a new, good life here. Although I went through rehab for my pill addiction, the migraines have improved significantly, but professionally, I have failed. I have dreamt of becoming a pianist since childhood. After three years of music studies, I became an assistant organist and had to admit that my talent or courage is not enough for more, especially since I have great exam anxiety.

I don't understand why I've become such a failure. My parents have done everything for me. Being the youngest after three boys, I was the princess. I was often sick as a child, and the entire family took care of me. My mother is always there for me even now. Imagining that this is how my life is supposed to be makes me cry even more.

Answer

You're wallowing in self-pity. The birthday is over; dry your tears and take a critical look at your broken pieces: whether they belong entirely in the trash or whether some pieces could form a beautiful whole depends solely on your evaluation. If you looked at yourself and your life a bit more kindly, you'd undoubtedly find comfort and hope for the future.

You evidently had a difficult start in life. As the pampered and sick youngest, you couldn't learn self-sufficiency or assertiveness. You've learned to rely on stronger others. When these others are no longer there, you feel helpless and worthless.

Your pile of broken pieces consists of old shards that demonstrate this learned helplessness and new pieces that offer new forms of life. An old shard is certainly the Spanish extended family, where you hoped to repeat your princess-like childhood; the pill addiction also belongs here. In both cases, you expected external help instead of relying on yourself. Other old shards include that you did not fight for your children and generally gave up too quickly. You prefer to dream instead of facing reality.

Among the new pieces in your pile are two separations you managed: from your husband and his Spanish family and from your pills. Both are essential steps on the way to freeing yourself from inner dependency on your family and from the behavior patterns you've learned. Other precious pieces in your pile are your career wishes, even if you've realized only a few of them so far.

Desires are the harbingers of our abilities. How your life will look in the future depends largely on you! Not on your mother, not on your Spanish husband, not on uncontrollable powers. Take your life into your hands and do something, instead of sitting down and crying.

I'm Always Late

Punctuality is the courtesy of kings, my father always said, and we four children adopted that. It became second nature for us to be punctual everywhere and always. He was a public servant and always set a good example for us. He never even made us children wait. Now he has been dead for six years, and I've noticed that I've become increasingly careless about punctuality. At first, this didn't bother me because I thought it was just freedom from my father's strict rules. But now it's bothering me because I'm always late despite my best intentions.

I work as a senior employee in a large government office, and I'm late for every meeting. My poor reputation precedes me, so much so that my employees joke about it and even come in late because they know nothing will start on time with me. This led to us starting a meeting almost an hour late because employees were dawdling. I find it unacceptable and condemn myself for setting such a poor example, but I can't change it. I'm not open to criticism from subordinates, but in committees with people in my position or higher, and even in private circles, I'm heavily criticized.

A friend accused me of showing a lack of respect for others. This hurt me because I always try to treat everyone with respect. This friend, for example, is essential to me, and I always look forward to meeting her, but she still has to wait for me and then gets angry. I don't want that; I don't understand myself. I always resolve to be punctual this time. I prepare everything, avoid scheduling other meetings two hours before, etc., and yet it still happens. Something comes up that seems so important at the moment that I forget my resolutions. Can you help me understand my behavior and, more importantly, how can I change it?

Answer

When you began breaking your father's ironclad rule, it was liberating. But now, being late has become a compulsion that no longer falls under your conscious control. It seems as if your subconscious has turned the rule on its head: Instead of always being punctual without exception, you're now always late without exception. The external pressure from your father has turned into internal pressure from yourself, against which it's much harder to rebel because such compulsions are often maintained in the subconscious by several significant motives.

So, even if people around you react critically and your private relationships suffer due to your tardiness, you must gain some hidden benefits from it. Many possible explanations exist. One could be that your chronic lateness is your last small refuge that your soul takes because it can't breathe due to constant adaptation and external control. At the same time, it subtly expresses anger towards others who always want something from you. Your friend is right; you're not expressing respect for others and their time.

There are certainly other possible explanations as well, but since they largely lie in the subconscious, you'll need professional help to bring them to light. Short-term therapy would undoubtedly help you dissolve this compulsion. Perhaps you might gain even more from it than you now suspect. Going into psychotherapy is not a sign of weakness. Nowadays, it's a privilege.

Problems in Relationships

*The art of a relationship
is not in finding the right partner,
but in being the right partner.*

—Brigitte Halenta

My Husband Is Unresponsive

I'm at a loss and already consider my fourteen-year marriage a failure. What do you think? My husband has a very demanding job at a government agency. With increasing staff shortages, he faces many challenges and often feels overwhelmed. I understand that he needs rest during his free time, but some time must be left for the family. Moreover, I believe I am entitled to some of his help. I don't have a driver's license, and weekend grocery shopping is much easier by car. But he grumbles every Friday evening, and in the supermarket, he stands around as if it's none of his business. If I complain, he says, "See, this is why I don't want to do it, because you're just nagging."

When I try to explain to him that I just want to share a piece of life with him, he doesn't listen. At home, there's only one thing he's interested in: his computer. He used to read to the children (ages twelve and nine), but now you're lucky if he even says goodnight to them. Before I even get a chance to talk to him, he's already disappeared into the basement. Once he's in front of the computer, I can give up hope. He's not responsive. He's networked with colleagues from work and plays a game with them involving knights, fairies, and such. Once he sat in front of the computer for eighteen hours straight (true story!) and afterward told me he won for his team. I find that childish.

I don't have a partner, and the children don't have a father, and I can't stand it in the long run, and I don't want to live like this. Don't say I should talk to him. You can't talk to this man.

Answer

Talking would indeed be good; at the very least, your husband should know that you consider the marriage to be a failure under these circumstances. If you can operate his computer, you could write him a letter there; otherwise, the traditional way. However, the question you should also ask yourself is when did you stop talking to each other. The situation was not always like this. Your husband's retreat to the basement is probably also a response to something that has gone wrong in the relationship. It's not about blame. Usually, the motives for specific behavior in a partnership are circularly intertwined in such a way that one can neither discern a beginning nor an end. Both are to blame, if one wants to talk about blame at all.

In your case, there is something else. It seems to me that your husband is addicted to gaming. Gaming addiction also fulfills the criteria of a disease. This means your husband would need help to even realize he is addicted. As a wife, you are probably the last person who could successfully confront him about it. Consider whom among your friends you could approach and ask for help. Besides groups for Alcoholics Anonymous, there are also ones for gamblers and their relatives. There, you will learn which approaches have proven successful. Help for your husband will only be possible once he recognizes he needs it.

Before you can see your marriage as definitively failed, you first have to overcome this crisis. If you understand that your husband is ill, it will probably be easier for you to endure the situation. Don't give up hope. The status of your marriage can only be assessed once your husband frees himself from the clutches of addiction; then, he should be responsive again.

Is There a Way Out?

For a long time, we've been following your cases and admire your analyses and solutions. Can you find one for me too? Around the age of fifty, I met a very pretty, intelligent woman who is more than twenty years younger than me. Within six months, we were married. My first marriage at a young age was relatively short-lived and ended in divorce. This time it was serious: for better or for worse.

The "worse" started after three years. Severe stroke, a major operation every year. Almost nothing remains of the man my wife married. Her affection seems unaffected. I love her and trust her more than ever. Occasionally, her helper syndrome bubbles over. Her helper syndrome—her term—is further amplified by her career and youthful conditioning. Recently, my inner "HB man" has been taking on a life of its own and has become self-destructive.

My search for causes leads to my mother, a remarkable independent, intelligent, and dominant woman, to whom I owe my life but who could not let go. Due to the resulting conflicts, I had extensive talk therapy before the stroke and the current marriage. Generally speaking, I feel good, we feel good. Although I often have severe pain and am extremely disabled, these uncontrollable outbursts of rage and anger are incomprehensible and very self-destructive. They rob me of my last autonomy. Is there a way out of this?

Answer

Your illness and its associated consequences for yourself and your relationship with your wife are unfortunately facts that cannot be shaken. When you can't change anything externally, you're left with altering your internal attitude. And that's exactly where your conflict seems to begin: you are struggling with fate.

This is very understandable. Coming to terms with such a life-altering blow is very difficult. It's generally a process that extends over a longer period and goes through multiple phases. You are clearly still in the phase of protest, where impotent rage over-whelms you from time to time.

Unfortunately, you do not write whether the "HB man" in you emerged only after the illness or whether you knew it from earlier as well. Since you label your current bouts of rage with the name of an advertising character from the fifties, I assume you have known this aspect of yourself for a long time—also from the time when you were in full possession of your faculties and could con-trol yourself better than now. These fits of rage would then be a trait of your character, the earliest cause of which might indeed be found in your relationship with your dominant mother.

I see two other possible causes, with the named cause and the next one not being so easily distinguishable. Such a tragic event, as you have to suffer, of course, changes a person. You are reacting to all the many losses that come with the illness with anger. This is better for your inner vitality than if you were to have a severe depressive reaction now. Then you would really be lost to your wife.

The third cause could be purely medical, which you should discuss with your doctor. The stroke could have caused organic brain changes that lead to these uncontrollable impulse out-bursts. A psychological fight against it would then be absolutely senseless because medication might help in that case. Either way, psychotherapeutic support would effectively help you cope with this crisis. There are also psychological strategies for pain that make it easier to bear the pain.

My Husband Doesn't Want to Leave

I am forty-four years old and have three children. A son from my first marriage who has already moved out, and two daughters from my current marriage who are thirteen and eleven. Three years ago, I tried to separate because I felt the marriage was empty, but I failed due to my husband's stubbornness. He simply ignored my wishes for separation. At that time, I was financially completely dependent on him, or at least I thought I was, and I had no job. Now, I've completed a one-year course to become a childminder, learned a lot about myself, and also how a single mother can get support from government offices.

With the help of the Youth Welfare Office, I have set up childcare for children under three with two other women from the course and have been working there for a few months with great pleasure. So far everything is fine, but the situation at home is becoming increasingly unbearable. For over six months, it has been decided that my husband should move out. The apartment is ideal for me and the children, and I can also finance it, which my husband could not do from his income if I moved out. He is now unemployed, has a few small jobs that don't bring in much, mainly sits in front of the TV and pretends he has taken on the role of a houseman. Meanwhile, I still do most of the work.

I urge him daily to look for an apartment, but he doesn't budge. Occasionally, he looks in the newspaper and then says there's nothing. That's it. Twice, I took the initiative and visited an apartment with him, but he didn't like either one. He also wants an apartment nearby because the girls are very attached to him and he to them. I'm quite at a loss. I can hardly bear the sight of him anymore and constantly imagine how I would rearrange the apartment for us. I can't take this situation much longer. My colleague says I should set a deadline, but whether I do that or a bucket falls over in China, it all bounces off my husband. He simply doesn't want to go. What should I do?

Answer

In your marriage, you were apparently always the stronger one, actively and prudently managing life for the family. Perhaps your husband was like a fourth child and never really took responsibility for the relationship next to you. You probably have to take action along these lines one last time: find him an apartment, drag him to sign, organize his move and help him set up.

You cannot wait for him to like an apartment. He doesn't want to move out; it's too comfortable as it is. Why should he like an apartment! Moreover, he has experienced with you that problems can be endured and that he doesn't have to worry about your complaints because they have no consequences.

Your everyday life probably still goes on as usual. You'll say it's because of the children, but as preparation for a separation, you should have already started not to think for him. You don't behave like someone who wants the separation, so your husband doesn't take you seriously and boycotts all agreements. Setting a deadline along with filing for divorce might shake him up. You probably haven't even considered this step because you seem to be someone who wants to avoid open confrontation. But if you want to get your husband moving, that's probably necessary. You can get the necessary information from a women's counseling center.

Perhaps your husband is also depressed and without any motivation. But even then, separation is advisable if you don't want to spend your life as a nurse. A drastic change in his circumstances would be a chance for your husband to overcome such an emotional disorder. As a last resort, you and the children would have to move out, even if it means losing the ideal apartment.

We Live in an Open Marriage

We are a young married couple and have been married for nearly six years. We got married very quickly under the pressure of our parents because my wife was expecting our daughter. Our marriage became quite boring fairly quickly. Especially in bed, there was no excitement between us, although we can generally get along well in life. For this reason, we agreed to have an open marriage based on my suggestion. The only condition is no secrecy; instead, we openly tell each other about our relationships.

The last two years have gone very well. My wife had a relationship with a colleague from her office; I had various flings. But now, we suddenly only have conflict at home because my wife is not sticking to the rules. She has a new boyfriend but refuses to say who he is. She tells me almost nothing about this relationship. She hardly even tells me when she is going out and how long she will be gone. I try to explain to her that our marriage is based on openness, but she remains closed off.

In my anger, I looked for clues on her desk. There I found draft letters and couldn't believe it. She is writing things to this man that I would have never believed she could! Now that I roughly know what is going on, I can no longer stand her silence and her absence. I have all sorts of fantasies and can no longer sleep at night.

An icy atmosphere reigns between us. The good cohabitation is over. Our daughter is also suffering already. My wife does not respond to my requests. She walks through the apartment

like a sleepwalker. I am absolutely at a loss. What should hap-
pen next? Where is the mistake? Is it with her or with me?

Answer

If there is a mistake, it probably lies with both of you. In my opin-ion, the so-called open marriage is a very artificial and vulnerable construction. Nevertheless, it has allowed you and your wife to live peacefully for several years and kept the parents for your daugh-ter. The mistake is that, out of fear of separation, both of you did not want to see the actual conditions underlying your relationship.

Firstly, there was never a passionate love between you. That's why things you would have never expected from your wife could not happen between you.

Secondly, an open marriage satisfies the partners' thirst for experience but does not stabilize their relationship with each other. It only works if both partners are simultaneously engaged in other relationships of similar quality.

Behind your basic rule of openness is another hidden rule, which is: Only relatively harmless external relationships are al-lowed that do not really endanger the marriage. However, no one has control over this last point. It seems that exactly this has now happened. Your wife has seriously fallen in love. She remains silent because she cannot reveal her precious experiences. She would probably betray her feelings for this new love if she talked to you about it. And you yourself could not bear to hear the de-tails, just as you cannot bear her silence now.

A few lines in letters, of which you don't even know if they were sent, already deprive you of sleep. You are suffering now, as deeper feelings are obviously at play, just like the deceived partner in a conventional marriage. In my opinion, all people, even if they talk differently and have seemingly organized their lives differently, demand unconditional loyalty. We want to have at least one person entirely for ourselves.

But security and absolute trust in a relationship on the one hand, and freedom and adventure on the other, cannot be combined. Only as children can we expect that mother and father are an irreplaceable source of security while also rejoicing in our conquests in the world. As adults, we have to choose between commitment and freedom. All compromises here are bad compromises that cause a lot of suffering.

Now you are the one suffering. The problems that already existed at the forced marriage and then with the quick onset of boredom are resurfacing. Both you and your wife now probably have to make fundamental decisions. You may then discover that your marriage means more or less to you than both of you have thought so far.

Always Arguing While Driving

For ten years, I've had my driver's license, accident-free. But when I drive with my husband, I apparently become a novice. In his eyes, I don't even master basic operations like shifting gears at the right time. Either I don't properly use a gear, or I downshift too late and strain the engine. In any case, I have no understanding of cars and will never learn.

Meanwhile, my husband has had his driver's license only five years longer than I have. I'm quite irritated by my husband's attitude, which I can't seem to counter. Unfortunately, we currently have to drive frequently together because my husband has back issues. These drives involve longer private trips on weekends to my father's residence, who is critically ill.

We have a retail business, and during the week, each of us has our own area and car. My husband wouldn't even think of interfering with me. He had to work his way into our industry, whereas I learned it from scratch. Could it be that the visits to my father are getting on my husband's nerves, although he's the one who always insists on driving? The bickering in the car certainly spoils the mood, and the atmosphere at home is tense for the entire following week.

Answer

Shared car rides with a partner are a constant source of disputes and bad moods in many marriages. Trapped in a roughly 6 square meter space with no possibility of getting out, you are pretty much at each other's mercy. One person tolerates the closeness and intimacy poorly and becomes offensive; another enjoys this very fact that the partner must finally listen, initiating an argument.

In any case, the argument in the car about driving style indicates a conflict that is also simmering between partners otherwise. Even if you were to shift with the precision of an automatic transmission, your husband would not be satisfied. Your driving behavior is just a hook for his dissatisfaction.

What is your relationship like otherwise? If you don't have many points of contact in your separate work areas during the week or even avoid them, suppressed emotions may break out during the drives. Could it be that you are the dominant part in the business, and your husband doesn't feel important enough? Using his understanding of cars and technology against you would then be an attempt to demonstrate some form of male superiority. His back issues are surely bothering him more than he shows. The fact that you also have to take the wheel for him here is probably more than he can handle. He vents his tensions by criticizing you.

His relationship to your critically ill father-in-law may also play a role. You can better assess the significance of your father's life-threatening illness to your husband and why he insists on visiting him. Perhaps you can find someone else in your family who can drive your husband if you don't want to drive.

I would advise you to have an open conversation with your husband. Conflicts that are avoided tend to expand. Today you argue only in the car; tomorrow, perhaps, in the business. If you make an effort to understand his feelings and he gets a chance to speak his mind, he will probably be more inclined to stop his criticisms of your driving style.

My Wife Drinks Secretly

About three weeks ago, I made a discovery by chance on two consecutive days while looking for an old fishing rod. In a corner of the bathroom, a completely unusual place, stood a half-empty bottle of grain spirit. I just registered it, wondered about it, and then forgot it. When I wanted to fetch more gear for the fishing rod the next day, the bottle had been replaced with another full one. Now I became suspicious. In the evening, I asked my wife for a grain spirit and was told that only some Cognac was left, in the living room cabinet.

For a good ten days now, I have been observing the bottle in the corner; based on the different amounts and different brands, I have determined that grain spirit is being drunk every day. I then told my wife what I had noticed and asked if she drinks grain spirit and possibly has problems. I was quite factual and tried not to be angry. One can solve possible problems, and nothing is so bad that there is no way out.

I spoke of our daughter and the future. (I know the fate of a work colleague who was dismissed because of alcoholism.) To my great surprise, my wife denied hiding alcohol and drinking at all. She became as angry as I have never seen her before. She doesn't want to talk about alcohol, and the bottle in the corner is gone.

We are both in our late twenties, and our house is half paid for. Our daughter is eight years old, diligent, and neat. We have no more worries than anyone else. What should I do? Before I do anything, I would like your advice.

Answer

Unfortunately, I cannot offer you any comfort. You are rightly very concerned about your wife's behavior, but there are no simple solutions. Your observations suggest that your wife drinks regularly. She herself feels that her relationship with alcohol is no longer harmless; otherwise, she would not drink secretly and so categorically deny her alcohol consumption.

Both are typical for alcohol-dependent people. They don't want to acknowledge what's happening to them. Relatives and friends who try to talk to them about it run into a wall. Your wife is alcohol-dependent, making her one of an estimated two million alcoholics in Germany. One-third of them are women. Unlike men, women like your wife do not drink publicly but mostly secretly. The fact that your wife is an alcoholic is a shocking realization that you must first come to terms with.

You are probably now looking for reasons that can explain and excuse your wife's behavior. But do not deceive yourself. Problems and stress exist for each of us; however, not all of us resort to alcohol as an apparent problem solver. There is a rule of thumb that says, if alcohol causes problems, then alcohol is the problem. All other difficulties are secondary. Only when alcohol dependency is overcome can other problems in the relationship, at work, etc., be solved.

The affected alcohol-dependent individuals argue the opposite, blocking any change. In the end, alcohol destroys health, social relationships, and often the entire existence. As the partner of an alcohol-dependent person, you must continually review your own behavior. You can easily become an enabler who unconsciously provokes or supports the drinking.

I would advise you to turn to Alcoholics Anonymous. There are also groups specifically for relatives. You will meet people who have extensive experience with your problem. You will find understanding and empathy for your situation. You will be advised on what specific steps you can take to help both your wife and yourself.

My Boss Annoys Me

My problem is my boss, and it's getting worse every day. I'm a clerk in a fairly large company and have been working there for years. It's my first job, and I've always enjoyed working there. Recently, I was transferred to another department and now report to a new boss, along with an older colleague. I have quite a lot to do with him directly.

From the first day, I was annoyed by this man. He is only four years older than me (I'm twenty-five) and has a certain tone that leaves me helpless. He is very ironic and constantly makes jokes. Most of the time, I have to laugh, too, but my head is completely empty and I can't think of anything to say. My colleague easily jokes along. I stand there like a stick and feel awful.

Two weeks ago, all the employees were invited to his house. He has photography as a hobby and showed his pictures around; many were also hanging on the walls. All funny photos of people who look somehow weird. I actually liked the photos but couldn't say it when he asked me.

Since then, I keep thinking he's looking at me in the same way as the people in the photos and finds me strange. Just hearing his footsteps makes me turn red. It's obvious. He says nothing, but my colleague notices it too. The thought of bringing him documents makes my blood rush to my head. It's like a disease, and I'm suffering terribly from it. I can barely do my work properly, and in the evening, I'm completely exhausted.

The worst thing is yet to come. Next week my colleague is going on vacation for three weeks, and I'll be alone with him. If I don't find a solution, I think I'll go crazy.

Answer

You can't work properly anymore, you spend the whole day battling blushing, and in the evening, you're completely exhausted from the day's efforts. The whole thing feels like a disease to you, and you can't do anything about it. Perhaps it's really something like an illness, but I dare say you certainly won't become so ill that you have to stay at home during your colleague's absence. And you certainly won't go crazy.

On the contrary: You feel a tension growing within you, and something has to happen during the time you're alone with your boss. This new boss has set something in motion inside you from the beginning. He's witty, you like his pictures. Do you actually like the man himself?

Because you don't want to admit your feelings of attraction and are ashamed in front of yourself, you turn red and feel helpless in his presence. Of course, he also notices that you're blushing and wonders why. Your great fear and tension come from your inner question of whether he also thinks and especially does the right thing: Namely, showing that he likes you too and doesn't find you strange.

You haven't mentioned anything about your boss's family situation. But even if your love should be completely hopeless, it would be very important for you to admit and accept your feelings. We can only deal with our feelings in a realistic way if we fully recognize and accept them.

I'm Afraid of Losing My Boyfriend

I think I have problems with men. Something usually goes wrong after a short acquaintance. My longest friendship lasted just under a year, and then I was really glad to be rid of the guy. I'm twenty-four and have now met a man who is just super. Everything about him is just right.

Despite that, things are difficult between us. We don't argue, but there are often misunderstandings. For example, whenever he says he finds me pretty. When I laugh at him because it's simply not true, he gets angry. I can't stand his sweet talk; it makes me sick. I've never been pretty; I'm just average, but I'm good at my job. My two older sisters and my youngest brother, who look like my mother, I would describe as beautiful, but I, like my other brother, take after my father.

My boyfriend is almost not interested in what I can do but always talks about my appearance. How can I make it clear to him that I have other qualities? If he doesn't see who I really am, things can't work out between us in the long run.

Answer

I understand your concern and think you are rightfully worried about losing this boyfriend after a short time as well. However, the problem is probably not with your boyfriend, who is blind to your true qualities, nor with your lack of persuasive power, but with your insecurity as a woman.

It appears there were sides in your family of origin: the beautiful ones and the capable ones. Some were loved for their beauty, others for their capability. You belonged to the capable ones and, thus, couldn't develop self-esteem concerning your appearance. (When was the last time you looked at yourself in the mirror with kind eyes?) Your deep inner belief is that you can only be accepted or even loved if you achieve something. If someone praises your beauty instead of your capabilities, it can only mean to you that you are not loved, causing you to react hurt rather than flattered.

Initially, your boyfriend fell in love with your appearance. He tells you what he finds delightful and captivating about you. To him, you are beautiful. If you laugh at him and contradict him, you wound his feelings and reject his love. No wonder misunderstandings arise.

His compliments are difficult for you to bear because they provoke an internal conflict within you. After all, you would have preferred to be loved the way your beautiful sisters were loved. The boyfriend who finds you pretty reminds you of old sorrows that you overcame by forgoing the possibility of ever being beautiful.

Accept his love, meaning relish the fact that, for him, you are a beautiful and desirable woman. Your boyfriend is giving you exactly what you missed so bitterly in your childhood. If you can find joy in that, it will positively impact your relationship, clearing the misunderstandings.

My Wife Is a Domestic Tyrant

My problem is already two years old, and it's getting worse. Unless something significant happens, I'm slowly but surely going to hit rock bottom. I suffer from my wife's nature, which people colloquially call a domestic tyrant. Main features: complaining, yelling, fighting with neighbors, tensions with her own relatives, and the worst: sulking and self-righteousness!

My wife manages not to talk to me for weeks over the smallest transgressions. The longest period of sulking lasted over four months. Any appeal from my side for reconciliation failed. Until one day she started talking again. She's doing the same thing now with our sons, who are eighteen and twenty-one. I feel like I'm in a madhouse.

My circle of acquaintances keeps urging me to get a divorce. But I shy away from that. My wife understands some aspects of my nature. I am very soft-hearted and have no assertiveness when it comes to her. I am secure in my career.

All in all, my joy for life is at rock bottom. You can surely understand why I increasingly take to drinking. How should I behave? My wife refuses marriage counseling.

Answer

I understand very well that your joy for life is at rock bottom, and that you seek relief and forgetfulness in drinking. But alcohol doesn't solve problems; it actually makes them worse. It's very easy for relief drinking to turn into dependent drinking, and in the end, you also risk your job security and health.

You haven't mentioned your age, but judging by your sons' ages, I'd estimate you to be between forty and fifty. This is an age where one takes stock. Could it be that after twenty years of being distracted by job security, child-rearing problems, and the like, you are now agonizingly experiencing the poor relationship with your wife?

All the slights, all the unfulfilled wishes in this relationship are now accumulating, plunging you emotionally into a crisis. It's always relieving to shift the blame for a conflict onto someone else. But it's not that simple in relationships. Fundamentally, you can assume that both parties are "to blame," even if it doesn't look like it at first glance.

Imagine a relationship like a scale. Your wife is so tough because you are so soft. She has to be so loud because you are so quiet. She can be silent for months because you can endure it. If you were to finally slam the table, she would certainly pull back. But for twenty years, you've had a set role distribution: your wife is the tyrant, and you are the victim.

You have endured this marriage for twenty years. There has also been some hidden benefit for you – and there still is, otherwise you would have separated long ago. Sometimes the idea of being alone in the world is such a horrifying thought that you'd rather have a bad relationship than none at all. But what about the next twenty or thirty years? Your wife probably won't change!

Rethink your life! If you don't want to continue living like this, you have to make decisions. The amount of joy you have in life solely depends on how you shape your life for yourself.

His Jealousy Is Destroying Me

I am quite desperate and don't know what to do anymore. I've only been married for two years and I love my husband very much. It was love at first sight for me when I saw him at a party with friends, because he looks incredibly good. For him, it took a bit longer, but now his constant jealousy is destroying me. Not a day goes by without such an event. I'll give you just a few examples from the last week:

He secretly watched me park the car in the city and claimed that I had arranged a meeting for later with a man who got out of his car next to me at the same time. After an invitation to my sister's house, he raged at home because I had allegedly held hands with my brother-in-law under the tablecloth. A dress that my brother brought me from Turkey, I'm not allowed to wear because, in his opinion, it still smells like my brother's things even after being washed.

I'm also not allowed to go to the sports club I've been a member of for years, because according to him, I always behave provocatively there. If I try to justify myself, he only gets angrier. What can I do to convince him of my absolute love and loyalty?

Answer

I'm sorry to have to tell you this, but this form of jealousy is an illness. Your husband has lost touch with reality. His jealousy has nothing to do with your behavior anymore but originates from his own, tormenting fantasies. It's not in your power to convince your husband of the baselessness of his jealousy through your behavior and explanations. He needs psychotherapeutic help.

It's a part of this illness that the patient cannot recognize that he produces all these jealousy fantasies himself. He is rather firmly convinced that only the behavior of the other person is the cause of his jealousy. Therefore, your husband will also reject the idea that he could be ill and will instead demand that you change. However, do not try to satisfy your husband any longer through increasing compliance. It's a task without any prospect of success!

As harsh as it will sound to you, your relationship only has a chance if the situation becomes so acute that your husband, under the pressure of his suffering, wishes for help and treatment for himself.

Why Is My Girlfriend Risking Our Relationship?

I would like to hear your opinion on the following problem. I am twenty-eight and about to finish my studies. My girlfriend is twenty-six and works as a waitress. We have been together for four years, the last two in a shared apartment. I think our relationship is good, but from time to time, about once a month, my girlfriend loses it. She then makes nonsensical accusations, cries around, and is unapproachable for days.

I tell her every time that this can't continue, that she has to change. I've already sent her to the doctor, but she is physically fine. I've already made her two appointments with a psychologist to start therapy, but she refuses to go. I am pretty angry. I've given her an ultimatum. Either she goes to the psychologist or the relationship is over.

My girlfriend finds my behavior iron-hard and does nothing. How can I still bring her to reason? She has to realize that it's about our relationship. What do you think?

Answer

You have the wrong idea about what psychologists and therapy can achieve. If it were up to you, you'd drop your girlfriend off at the psychologist who would then set her straight so that she functions without unpleasant disruptions for you in the future.

Change through therapy is only possible if the person themselves decides that they need to do something about their suffering. So, the person has to find a therapist for themselves and take responsibility for their own well-being. That means you can't send your girlfriend. She can only go to a therapist of her choice of her own accord.

You are correct in believing that it's about your relationship. But a relationship involves two people. You are behaving as if your girlfriend's conflicts have nothing to do with you. The opposite is likely the case. Your girlfriend is suffering in this relationship with you, but you don't take her complaints and her tears seriously and only make your own wishes the benchmark for whether the relationship is okay or not. Maybe you are not just in this case so iron-hard and authoritarian.

If therapy or counseling, then for both of you. I could imagine that your girlfriend would also be willing under such conditions. If she sees that you no longer shirk and solely blame her for a shared problem, then the derailed dialogue between you can get back on track.

Am I Prudish?

We have a persistent problem. Every time we've been to a party, there's a big fight afterward. I accuse my husband of acting like a stray dog that has to lick every female dog. He tells me I'm prudish, uptight, and petty. I swear to myself every time that I won't go with him again. But since my husband is determined to have fun without me, I go along anyway because I want to at least know what he's up to.

Being home alone would be even worse. He says it's all harmless. But I can't believe that. I find this party kissing, everyone with everyone, simply disgusting, and I act accordingly. As a result, I'm increasingly cornered in our circle of friends. My husband boasts that Mr. X and Mrs. Y also said that I'm somehow uptight.

I don't know how to behave. On the one hand, I don't want to lose contact with the others, and the constant argument also gets on my nerves, but on the other hand, I can't get over myself. Am I really prudish and old-fashioned, as my husband thinks, or is this party kissing not also excessive and tasteless?

Answer

You're looking for a referee in a marital dispute and, of course, one who agrees with you. But it's not that simple. What is objectively exaggerated and what is appropriate can't be determined. Every group of people, whether at work or in leisure, develops its own norms. The individual must always decide whether or not they can accept the norms of a group they want to belong to.

In your case, your norms don't match those in your circle of friends. If you want to belong to this group, you need to figure out how much adjustment is possible for you and how much resistance you can put up without becoming an outsider. The key point seems to me to be that it's only superficially about the party kissing. Behind it is probably a deeper sexual problem between you and your husband.

The arguments about behavior at parties are actually about sexual behavior in the marital bed. It's likely that your husband has desires that you don't want or can't fulfill. In his disappointment, he calls you prudish and uptight. You are hurt and retaliate by belittling his sexuality. Many couples find it very difficult to talk openly about their sexual problems. Mutual disappointment and the resulting anger at each other are then carried out on secondary battlefields.

It is always better to talk openly about the basic problem. This is easiest where they arise: in bed.

Take courage and talk to your husband at the next opportunity. But try not to accuse him. All sentences that start with: "You have, you are, you should know, etc.," fuel the argument. If you want understanding, better make "I" statements. Tell him something about your experiences and desires. Then both of you have a chance for reconciliation, and the next party doesn't have to serve as a welcome occasion to fight over conflicts.

My Husband Left Us

After twenty years of marriage, my husband left me (forty-one) and the children (sixteen, twelve, and eight) overnight and moved to another city. Financially, he had arranged everything for us, so we are not in need. On the contrary, he was very generous, probably out of guilt, but I am completely shattered because his departure came like a bolt from the blue for all of us.

We never had secrets from each other, and we had never talked about separation or divorce before. I don't know what to think anymore. He has been gone for eight months now. He refuses any discussion. When I call him, he hangs up as soon as he recognizes my voice; he does not reply to letters. I feel that he has not only left me physically but also left me alone with all thoughts and possible explanations for this drastic change in my life.

The children are asking, and I don't know what to tell them. Is Dad coming back or not? For the entire initial period when I myself could not believe that my husband was serious, I kept putting them off somehow, but I can't keep doing that forever. My eldest daughter already sees the bigger picture and says terrible things about her father. I have nothing to refute her. She also mocks me and calls me naive because I still believe he will come back.

Somehow I still love my husband despite everything he has done to us, and hope that he will show up at the door one day. Should I wait? I could also file for divorce, but the thought terrifies me. What do you advise me?

Answer

Separations, especially sudden ones, only appear to come out of the blue. They usually have a long backstory, and both partners contribute to that backstory. What I want to say is, don't see yourself only as a victim, but also as a player in your marital drama.

The fact that your husband suddenly gives up everything shows that you were deceived, and that there were secrets between you after all. Apparently, your husband had serious reasons to avoid a discussion. These reasons could lie in his personality, in the nature of your relationship to each other, or in circumstances you are unaware of. In any case, such a breakout has the character of an escape, so one can be sure that he was very afraid of something.

However much understanding you have for him, the fact remains, he has left you in every respect; the good financial provision is just a consolation. You have every reason to be not just deeply hurt but also furious at him. Your eldest daughter seems to be angry on your behalf. She's right, it's naive to think he'll show up at the door one day.

If you just wait and hope, you'll miss your chance to learn and change. During this entire waiting time, your husband is experiencing something new. If he really came back, he'd come back changed, and you'd still be the same. If the marriage were to resume, it could only be a whole new beginning under new conditions on both sides.

You will certainly need a lot of time to get over the shock, but as soon as possible, you should take control of your life and your children's lives. Then you'll also have to decide whether you want to get divorced.

A Slap in the Face

For twelve years, I believed that my wife and I were on the same wavelength, that we could tell each other everything and trust each other completely. It's the second marriage for both of us, and we had vowed never to repeat the old mistakes, meaning, above all, to always be honest with each other. I relied on that, but now everything is shattered, and I don't know what to do. I see myself at a dead-end, and my life plans have fallen apart. I'm forty and work as a physical therapist; my dream was to have my own house where I could work independently in my own practice. Ever since we've known each other, I've talked about it. My wife works as an occupational therapist; it would have been a perfect complement. We've been saving for years for this, and I've continually taken further training.

Then, two years ago, the perfect property presented itself—an older house that needed a lot of work but was affordable with a lot of our own effort. No sooner had we begun to build the house than my wife fell ill. In retrospect, I have to say that she's been unwell for the past two years, always having something that hindered her from fully engaging in the work. I've done most of the work myself, after work and on weekends. It's not perfect yet, but we can move in. We've terminated the lease on our old apartment. Then, after a protracted bronchitis, my wife got pneumonia and was sent to a spa clinic after her hospital stay. I've been working like a maniac to make everything beautiful for our move-in, which is supposed to happen in three weeks when she's back home.

Now, I was called in for a family discussion at the spa clinic, and my wife tells me, in the presence of the doctor, that she doesn't want to move at all, that she's attached to the old apartment and wants to reverse the termination, and that the idea of becoming self-employed scares her. It was like a slap in the face. Having the strange doctor there only made it worse; why couldn't she tell me this privately? She cried and said she was sorry for hurting me, but that doesn't buy me anything; she knows how important the house and being self-employed are to me. I'm sitting here, numbed at home. My wife will be discharged in two weeks. I don't know what to do.

Answer

You've been hit twice, and one blow is as bad as the other. First, your wife's revelation brutally shatters the illusion that you and your wife are a fused entity that always thinks and feels the same and has the same perceptions. On this account, you feel deceived, if not outright betrayed, certainly abandoned and alone. Secondly, with her veto, your future plans, into which you've poured so much effort, are called into question. You're immensely disappointed and frustrated that your hard work is not being recognized. Once you've recovered from the initial shock, you may be able to see things more realistically. As bad as it feels right now, as if your entire happiness is shattered, it's really not that grim. It's about finding new solutions, both at the level of marital relationship and future planning.

You have to learn that your wife is a separate individual with her own point of view, which does not automatically align with yours. You've been so dominant in the relationship that your wife has always just agreed to everything you wanted. The moment the dream becomes a reality, and you buy the house, your wife can only express her resistance to the house subconsciously through illness, out of fear of disappointing you. At the clinic, she must have realized the deeper reason for her illness and been encouraged to tell you. But she still didn't dare to do so without the support of the doctor. This should give you pause. You have to pay much more attention to your wife in the future and ask her what she envisions. Definitely listen more, rather than talking as you have been.

If your wife experiences that her wishes and ideas, even if they differ from her husband's, are taken seriously, she won't have to become sick to express her resistance. Then both of you can find real solutions that are livable for both. In the current situation, there are certainly also interim solutions that, on the one hand, alleviate your wife's fear of being discharged and, on the other hand, offer you opportunities to approach the future, and thus your life dream, optimistically.

A Big Family

I would like to hear a neutral opinion because I don't know what to think anymore. My acquaintances just shake their heads when I tell them about it. I am a widower, sixty-six years old, and have been involved with a woman fourteen years younger than me for almost a year. That is, we don't live together, although that would actually be my wish, but we spend a lot of time together, either at my place or also traveling. Now my girlfriend has a large family to which she is very attached. Since her divorce, she has been living with her elderly mother; sometimes her daughter, who is actually married in France, also spends a lot of time here. She has an eight-year-old daughter who was even enrolled in school here for a while. The son-in-law, an innkeeper, only makes short visits. The ex-husband, who is terminally ill, also plays a role.

When I met my girlfriend, I was warmly welcomed into the family. Since I have no immediate family myself, I was very happy about it. In the first summer, I went with her to her daughter in France and got along very well with the French son-in-law. I also had a good connection with her mother; since I am older, I could understand many things, such as war experiences, much better than my girlfriend. The worries then came with the illness of the ex-husband, whose end was foreseeable. My girlfriend took care of him tenderly because he had no one else. She visited him daily in the hospital. As for our plans to move in together, it was always said, please wait, I don't have the head for that now. The funeral was eight weeks ago, and there is still no talk of moving in together because new things are always happening in the family.

First, my girlfriend quarreled so violently with her daughter that she swore never to speak to her again. My girlfriend's mother then tried to mediate because of the granddaughter, which soon led to a rapprochement. But now my girlfriend was angry with the mother because she had said something she shouldn't have. I was forbidden to contact the mother because I had allegedly hurt her very much. I still don't know what with. Then they both went to France, but I was not supposed to go. Meanwhile, I have the impression that our relationship is also shaky, as my girlfriend no longer tells me anything, makes completely untenable accusations against me, and compares me to her ex. Can you help me understand what is going on here?

Answer

You have gotten into a family dynamic that has it all. One thing is certain, it will never be boring in this family, but you will also not come to rest. Fights, intrigues, manipulations, and temporary reconciliations are part of the program. The most powerful person directs, and that is your girlfriend here. Unconsciously, this family is probably held together by aggression rather than love. All injured parties who don't want to admit their anger at each other and therefore stage a happy family with the corresponding feelings. However, this only works if the underground aggression is stored somewhere, and for that, you either need an external enemy or a scapegoat in the family.

The sick ex-husband was a good object for this for a long time. Half still belonging to the family, half already outside, all negative feelings could be projected onto him. With his death, a new solution is needed. Now the daughter gets the short end of the stick, which is then passed on to the mother. I venture to predict that the family will soon agree that you are the troublemaker. You already feel that a different wind is blowing against you. How long you will be out of favor is not foreseeable, but at some point, the tide will turn again, and then perhaps the son-in-law is the one everyone must rally against, including you.

This is a family dynamic that will not change. You have to decide if you want to join in. By the way, I don't think anything will come of moving in together. For your girlfriend as the director, the figures on her game board are much more variable. She will not want to commit.

The Dog Is More Important Than Me

I am fifty-five and have been a widow for ten years. I lost my husband, unfortunately, quite early due to an accident. Since I have recovered from the shock, I have been longing for a new partnership, but it never really worked out. Now, through the newspaper, I have met a sixty-year-old widower who I immediately liked. His wife has also been dead for eleven years. We immediately liked each other, and everything was so harmonious that I have already dreamed of a future together. But there is a problem. The problem is named Senta. Senta is his dog, a mix between a hunting dog and a German Shepherd. He got her from the animal shelter eight years ago when she was just one year old. My friend is utterly enamored with the animal.

At first, I found it touching how caring and gentle he is with the animal, but now it's starting to make me really angry. I now have the feeling that the dog stands between us and prevents us from being happy. I would have loved to fly with him to Mallorca, but due to Senta, only destinations accessible by car are possible. It's entirely out of the question for someone else to take care of her. If we are at the theater in the evening, we can't go for a drink afterward because the dog is waiting at home and has already been alone for too long. Supposedly she goes crazy if she's alone for more than four hours. It's worse than with toddlers. Whatever comes up, the first question is always how it fits in with Senta's needs.

The tone in which he talks to Senta is more tender than with me, and gradually, I also believe that she is petted more often than I am. I am writing to you because I am really in doubt whether I should hold on to my friend any longer. When it comes down to it, the dog is always more important than me, and I don't think that's okay. It's just an animal. What would you advise me?

Answer

You have probably already noticed while writing how you evaluate the situation, and my answer will only confirm your slowly maturing decision to separate. The man is unfortunately married to his dog, and his ability to bond with a woman and thus give her importance in his life is very limited. Many people living alone make their pets their partner substitute, or the animal is credited with aspects of their own being, which are then pampered and sometimes fought against. Your friend can only tolerate a woman by his side who consistently joins him and makes Senta the focus of life together.

If you can't or don't want to do this, it's probably better to say goodbye soon before you have invested too many feelings in this man. It's not just the dog that stands between you. That's too short-sighted. It's the very special condition of this man who has given his heart to a dog. You can't actively change that, and it doesn't change by itself over time.

You are probably very hesitant, now that you have finally found someone you like, to break off the relationship, but perhaps lovable men are not as rare as you think. It could be that you just needed ten years to approach the world of men with an open heart again.

I Have No Future Anymore

At sixteen, I had a relationship that lasted for half a year. It was a wonderful time for both of us and left a lasting impression on me. I experienced so much love, got so much from him that I hadn't even dared to wish for. He was a few years older than me and had big plans, which he later fulfilled. He wanted us to move in together. I had to decline that idea because it didn't fit with my plans, and my parents would never allow it. He was very disappointed. We broke up later, the reason for which I still don't understand to this day. After a year, we met again. He wanted to start everything anew, but I turned him down this time.

A few years later, I got married and had a child. Our relationship was reasonably good for as long as I adapted, because I was so in need of love and harmony. I fought for a long time and have now given up. We haven't spoken to each other for about four years. He doesn't care about his child. There is no room for feelings in our marriage. The only thing that holds us together is duty.

A few months ago, I saw my ex-boyfriend again. He has separated from his wife and confided a lot about his past to me. He called me "my girl," as he used to, and said he could imagine a future together with me. This offer threw me off track because tender feelings were awakened in me after so many years.

I was both happy and afraid but still said no. I couldn't count on his memories of our early happiness being as strong as mine. I didn't want to hurt him or myself. He was my soul-mate; we understood each other on an unconscious level.

I'm searching in vain for a solution, but I know there isn't one. My eyes are empty and full of pain. The days on which I no longer "exist" are piling up. I only live in the loving past because tomorrow offers me no future anymore.

Answer

You need to change your life quickly; otherwise, you'll make yourself unhappy and sick for the rest of your life. You already have depression as a reaction to your unhappy marriage, but that could change quickly if you take action and take control of your life. No dark fate rules over us; it's us who set the course for a good or bad life. Take responsibility for yourself!

You've always made decisions with your head and not your heart. It seems you didn't learn to allow feelings in your parental home, and beliefs such as "Life is hard," or "One must do their duty" prevailed. But life can also be light and beautiful (like when you were sixteen), and everyone has a right to happiness.

You reject all the good offers that life makes to you because you don't listen to your feelings and don't dare to be happy. Finding someone who makes you feel the way you describe - at sixteen and again now - is a great fortune and doesn't repeat itself often in life. Why, in God's name, do you always say no?

You should bring about the separation from your husband as quickly as possible. Don't ask him if you may, but act! At the same time, you should give your ex-boyfriend a sign. Relationships of such intensity as you have experienced usually rely on reciprocity. He probably dreams of you just as much as you dream of him.

My Wife Refuses

I think a lot about life and what it should be like. Lately, I have doubts about whether our marriage is as good as my wife always claims. I used to think the same way. Everything works for us, except for sexuality.

Before we were married, our sexual relationship was good and even enjoyable. Almost from our wedding date, she started refusing. She was always tired or otherwise busy. I felt dirty, like a beggar, whenever I had sexual needs. But that is entirely normal. We also didn't have any children, although I wanted some.

Our marriage is harmonious. We have many shared interests, and I can't imagine a life without my wife. However, I've met a woman who would be willing to sleep with me, and I am full of desire for that. At the same time, I feel guilty towards my wife. I will soon turn sixty and fear that I have missed something important in my life.

I think my feelings tell me to follow my desires. But then again, it's the opposite, and I find everything good with my wife and don't want to spoil anything. What do you think I should do?

Answer

No one can tell you what you should do and thus take the responsibility for your actions. The decision is solely yours, and you will have to face the consequences. I understand that this conflict, exacerbated by thoughts of nearing old age, is tormenting you. It seems sexuality has been a lifelong issue for you. On the one hand, you feel your needs; on the other, you fear them.

You apparently solved your problem by marrying a woman who is sexually inactive. This way, you don't have to feel your fear of sexuality. Your wife took the blame when no sexuality was involved, and you could feel your desire for it without being disturbed by the fears within you.

If your sexual desires had been clear, you wouldn't have spent so many years in a marriage without satisfying sexuality. Your marriage is thus an exact reflection of your emotional possibilities, and in that sense, you haven't missed out on anything. The part of your being that longs for security has been very satisfied in this marriage. Perhaps you had to gather enough courage in this security to be able to live the other part of your being, which includes dangerous sexuality.

Now you're at a crossroads in your life. Whether everything continues as before or you take a step into new territory probably doesn't depend on your conscious decision, even if you experience it that way, but on the strength and direction of your desires.

My Husband Talks About Divorce

For months, my emotions have been like a hot and cold bath, alternating. This is all due to my husband, who loses his cool every four weeks and thinks he should get a divorce. It's been a terrible back-and-forth since the birth of our youngest son. One day he wants a divorce, and the next day he doesn't. I no longer know where I stand. I am twenty-five and married my husband right after my apprenticeship. It was a great love for both of us. Then our three boys (four and two years old and seven months) came quite quickly. I enjoy being a housewife and mother; I breastfed the children for a long time, and I'm still breastfeeding the youngest.

My husband seems to be quite successful and satisfied in his job, but at home, he's not happy with anything. Nevertheless, I love him and can't imagine life without him. But my husband keeps talking about divorce, especially when we argue about the children. He thinks I spoil them. Yet, I often find that the oldest is somewhat neglected. I have to take care of so many things; sometimes, I'm exhausted. The youngest has asthma, and to avoid having to get up at night, he sleeps in our bed. My husband is furious about this and doesn't understand that it's more convenient for me.

He has packed his bags twice to leave. When I cry, he comforts me and says we should keep trying. He is then also very kind to me. But after a while, everything starts all over again. I don't understand what's happening anymore. What is true?

Answer

The apparent back-and-forth of your husband is easier to understand when you see it as the expression of his conflicting feelings: on the one hand, he loves you; on the other hand, he finds the family situation unbearable. He wants to stay, and he wants to leave; both are true. Your husband not feeling comfortable at home has several reasons, one of which is quite evident: he is overwhelmed by the role of a family father. You don't write how old your husband is, but if he's not much older than you, he may have imagined his life quite differently than it turned out after the birth of the children.

On the other hand, you seem to thrive in your new role. But aren't you perhaps a little too much of a mother and housewife and too little of a partner? For nearly five years, you have been fully occupied with the children. Pregnancy, childbirth, breastfeeding, taking care of the young children are all important experiences for you and also an aspect of female sexuality. Perhaps this satisfies you to such an extent that you no longer have sexual desires for your husband and can't meet his needs sufficiently.

Having the child in the marital bed, regardless of the reasons, is always a sign of a disturbance in the sexual relationship between spouses. Your husband probably feels that next to the children, he doesn't count for you anymore. His threats of divorce may be a call to you: pay more attention to me; I'm still here. Maybe his discontent would already improve if you could be more attentive to him.

Perhaps you also need to involve him more in family work. It doesn't sound like your husband feels paternal responsibility for his children. Sometimes, hand over the care of the children to him.

If he also gets up at night to care for the youngest who has asthma, then the little one can sleep in his bed again, and intimacy between husband and wife is possible again in your marital bed. You are both too young to live only as parents.

Always the Same Game

I'm twenty-seven, so as they say, of marriageable age, but a husband, something long-term, is not on the table for me. It's always just fleeting encounters. Just now, a new guy has appeared in my department: Cool, casual, quite attractive, but he totally overlooks me. I can already predict what will happen next, as it's been happening to me for years.

It's always the same game! A great guy shows up, and I'm invisible to him. I instantly fall for him, do all sorts of crazy things to get his attention. It works, we sleep together, and within three months at most, he leaves, and I'm utterly miserable. Until the next time.

Somehow, I must have a glitch in the system, because I never learn. My girlfriends have much better luck with their guys than I do. With so many men around my workplace, I should be able to find someone more attached at some point. But how? Don't think that I'm some wallflower. Quite a few people turn around to look at me. By the way, everything else is fine. Only my love life is a constant rollercoaster.

Answer

Your love life suffers from what's known as repetition compulsion, meaning that despite better judgment, you unconsciously make the same mistakes over and over again. You've already recognized this pattern. Two conditions trigger your infatuation:

First, he has to appeal to you; second, he has to overlook you, with the latter being the more critical condition.

Perhaps you fall for every man who treats you like you're invisible. The fact that he's not interested in you makes him attractive in your eyes. Tragically, the opposite also holds true. Men who fall for you become uninteresting and dull because they do. This cycle repeats itself over and over because you're always driven by the deep hope that once, just once, you'd be able to sustain the interest of a man who initially ignores you.

Usually behind this lies an unconscious, unknown factor, often an absent father, and the little girl in every grown woman still hopes for a correction of that rejection. That's why only the aloof, cold men are so attractive to you. They fulfill the old relationship pattern with your father. You probably made great efforts as a child to get your father's attention, and for a short while, you may have succeeded, only to be disappointed again.

For your current situation, this means that you choose the wrong men from the start, setting the stage for the relationship's eventual end. You should talk about this glitch in your system with a psychologist or psychotherapist. If this answer motivates you to have such a conversation, that's already the first step towards change. To your comfort: We all live under repetition compulsion, both in everyday situations and in matters of love. If the suffering becomes too great, we need to seek clarification and change.

My Husband Patronizes Me

We've been married for over thirty years now. My husband has been retired for four years, and since then, things have been tense between us. He has always had a tendency to be opinionated, but now that he no longer has apprentices to guide, he's started instructing me. Things in my household, which I've done a certain way for over twenty years, should now, according to him, be done differently. He has all sorts of reasons for this, which I either can't or don't want to see. This naturally leads to arguments, as he also checks whether I've done everything as he wishes.

The problem is likely that he has nothing to do. We unfortunately sold our small garden because he thought he couldn't maintain it anymore due to his slipped disc, but that was premature. In the house, he now takes over everything without any issues. He interferes in everything and takes work away from me, or even wants to dictate when things should be done. For example, I like to lie down for an hour after lunch and then tidy up the kitchen before bed. Now, he insists that the kitchen should be tidied up at noon and complains if I don't do it. I feel patronized. But when I say this, he doesn't address it but gives me a hundred reasons why it's better this way.

Initially, for the sake of peace, I gave in quite a bit, but if you give my husband an inch, he takes a mile. I now get the impression that it's getting worse and soon I won't have any say in our home. What can I do to make things better?

Answer

Entering retirement is a critical situation for many couples. If things are not working out, it's sensible to schedule an appointment for counseling. The advisors there deal with these problems daily and can offer effective help. In your case, both of you first need to learn to listen to each other. Your husband is not hearing how badly you feel with his constant interference and patronization, and you are not hearing how much he's suffering from a loss of significance and feeling needed. Only when you both better understand each other's needs can you satisfactorily organize the new situation for both of you.

It's important to set the right course from the beginning. The sooner, the better. If there have already been mutual injuries, the fronts harden. You've identified the basic problem: your husband needs a new field of activity. He must find this outside the home, and the counseling center can also help with this. The quarreling over domestic work must stop. If your husband wants to take over some of it, the areas must be clearly discussed. But in his area, only one person gets to have the say. Interference is not allowed. This requires respect for the other's personality. This way, more freedom could also emerge for you, in which you can either do something together or find new tasks for yourself.

Her Kids Reject Me

I became a widower early in life and have found a woman I love after eleven years of being alone, whom I actually want to marry—if it weren't for her kids. She is divorced and has been living alone with her two children (ages twelve and thirteen) for years. I also have a son from my marriage, but he is already in college. That's why I understand focusing a lot on the kids when there is no partner. My girlfriend has lived only for her children so far. She has few friends, rarely left the house, and didn't have a relationship with a man.

Since we got to know and love each other, she also wants to have time for herself, i.e., for activities together, but her children do not allow her to have her own life. Whenever my girlfriend has been with me, she finds some disaster waiting for her when she returns, so she hardly dares to leave.

I would gladly come to her apartment, but her children reject me so openly that it becomes unbearable for both of us. I have nothing against the children and initially approached them kindly. I fear that the relationship I care about may fail due to the kids' behavior. I see little hope that anything will change. In the six months we've known each other, the kids' hostility toward me has gotten worse rather than better. What should I do?

Answer

Patience, patience, and more patience is required, as everyone needs a lot of time to adjust to the new living situation. The easiest adjustment is for you. Your son no longer needs you; you are independent and mentally prepared to fully commit to a new relationship after eleven years of being alone. It's different for your girlfriend. She has to balance between the demands of her children and her own desires, which she has suppressed until now. She probably pays for her happiness with you by feeling extremely guilty towards her children.

She first needs to find a new balance in distributing her time and emotions. In the end, this will benefit everyone, because it's not healthy for the kids to be the sole focus of their parents. The hardest adjustment is for the children, which is why they need the most patience and understanding. Do not overanalyze every statement and action from the kids! Right now, they can do nothing other than misbehave. A totally available mother was their norm. All the new, unwelcome changes hurt and shake the children.

If they don't want to direct their anger towards their mother, whom they need, you are left as the one to blame. You experience this as rejection and hostility. You are not so much rejected as an individual, but as the evil intruder who changes everything. The intensity of rejection increases as the children sense their mother is serious about the new relationship. After six months, the peak of hostility may not even have been reached yet.

However, that doesn't mean you should let the children intimidate you. On the contrary: openly showing and confessing the relationship helps the children to accept the new reality. So, do not avoid your girlfriend's apartment; be present and keep making offers that include the children. There will be struggles, but if the relationship is right, it won't fail due to the children who are growing older and thus becoming more independent.

The First Birthday After the Separation

About a year ago, I separated from my husband. I couldn't stand it anymore in this marriage, where my whole life was dictated by my husband and his career. Our four-year-old daughter lives with me. Now, her first birthday after the separation is coming up, and I dread it. My daughter looks forward to spending time with her father. He has promised to pick her up the day before, and they plan to do fantastic things together, he tells her on the phone. But in the entire year after the separation, he has only managed to find time for her once, for three hours.

There are always important work commitments. It was the same during our marriage. I would sit there and wait, sometimes for days with packed bags because we were supposed to go on a trip. Now, I'm afraid that my daughter will experience the same disappointment. I'm also frustrated that I can't properly plan for these days because I can't rely on my husband to even show up, let alone keep our daughter for the promised two days.

I'm very doubtful whether I should talk to my daughter about this. After all, he might keep his promise, and then I would look foolish. So far, I haven't said anything to my daughter.

Answer

Your fear of your daughter's fifth birthday is mixed with many feelings, not just anger about your husband's unreliability. Certainly, you feel the pain of the separation more acutely during such a family celebration. Behind the worries about your little daughter, who could be disappointed by her father, are your own injuries from the marriage.

You have been living alone for a year and have therefore faced the external consequences, but emotionally, you have not let go of your husband. You still hope that if he cannot be a reliable partner, he might at least be a reliable father. From your many bitter experiences, you should learn that you cannot count on your husband and that you should rely more on yourself. This now includes your little daughter. Yet emotionally, you still behave post-separation as you did during the marriage, making yourself dependent on his promises or cancellations.

Make your own schedule. It's important for both you and your daughter to plan this first birthday according to your own wishes and needs. Do you want to program feelings of abandonment for both of you by possibly waiting in vain for the father? In the future, you should offer possible visiting dates in a way that won't affect your own planning if the father is once again unavailable.

In the long run, you won't be able to protect your daughter from disappointments with her father, whether you talk to her about it or not. But don't mix your feelings with those of your daughter. If she leads a fulfilling life with you, she doesn't necessarily have to suffer from the absent father. The occasionally appearing father is then a visit she can look forward to, instead of suffering from it.

My Husband Only Thinks About Himself

For the first time in our eight-year marriage, I was really sick. For almost two weeks, I was bedridden and had to rely on my husband's help. That's when I fully realized how selfish my husband is. I received just the bare necessities from him, and even that I had to ask for. He doesn't mean it badly; he is just so self-centered. When he drives, he complains about the stupid pedestrians who don't pay attention; when he walks, he gets angry at the inconsiderate drivers. Our overgrown garden is now a beautiful nature garden because he doesn't feel like taking care of it; but because of the lime tree growing from the neighboring property into our garden, we almost ended up in a lawsuit with the neighbor. He always talks about environmental protection, but for his own car wash, he uses more chemicals than I think are necessary.

I get upset at every news story about environmental pollution; he just shrugs it off. Ever since this issue has come between us, we've been constantly arguing. For the sake of peace, I should keep my mouth shut, but it's hard for me.

I've gotten used to taking care of my needs myself; I've stopped making a fuss about it with him, but with all the everyday stuff, we are constantly at odds; it seems my tolerance for him has reached its limit, or how should I understand this? I actually don't like to argue.

Answer

You are still disappointed and hurt by his neglect during your illness. In your arguments with him, all your suppressed anger comes out. If you tell your husband clearly what has hurt you, you may be able to give up the small battles over all the other things. Your husband didn't become this difficult person just during your illness. You wanted exactly this man when you married him. Now you have to either make it work with him or separate.

Your husband shows—extremely pronounced—traits that sadly are fundamental to human nature and are responsible for the fact that many problems of humanity, such as world hunger, cannot be solved. Our ability to react emotionally, accomplish great things, or take responsibility depends on our selfish interests and our limited perception. When it comes to boosting our self-esteem and our social standing, or about power, money, or being loved, we can muster a lot of emotional and physical energy.

When thousands are starving in a distant, foreign country, as long as we ourselves are full and don't have to see and experience the suffering of others with our own eyes, it doesn't elicit much more than fleeting concern. Chernobyl was the best example. If radioactivity hurt, i.e., if it were perceptible to us, there probably would have been an uprising in the country. As it was, after the initial concern, we went on living as if nothing had happened.

Because disasters in a distant country seemingly do not affect our daily self-centered needs, we must learn to look beyond the edge of our own small circle of life. Our children must learn through education, where immediate experience fails, that it is a great task for everyone to keep our planet habitable. Your husband, unfortunately, is one of the unteachable. If the drinking water that flows from your faucet were chemically contaminated, even your husband would stop shrugging his shoulders. By then, it might be too late for many things that could still be done today.

How Can I Find My Peace Again?

In August, I caught my husband with my best friend. Since then, I can't find peace. They had been in a relationship for almost a year and three quarters, and now I keep pondering why I didn't notice anything and why my friend could do this to me. We've been married for thirty-five years and had a normal marriage. Three and a half years ago, our son left his wife and child for a younger woman. I couldn't understand it and didn't want to. That's why my husband and I had a lot of arguments because I didn't want to accept this younger woman. Our sex life was never very active, but from that point on, it became almost non-existent.

I confronted my friend and told her that I had confided in her in full trust about the state of our marriage, and she had exploited it. She only repeated what she had said when caught, that she likes me and loves him. She would take him if she could get him, and she could still look me in the eye. That grinds me down! How can one look someone in the eyes after such betrayal? My husband chose me, and I forgave him, believing that I was partly to blame. I didn't give him what he needed in bed. My friend is a widow and took advantage of the situation.

In hindsight, many things have come to light. He got into her car, which he also admitted. But he says it wasn't that often, and he doesn't tell me how many times they were intimate. When he had been drinking, he would stroke her back and thighs; this I hear now.

What's very difficult for me is that she sat in our apartment with my husband and me, drinking coffee just a day before the discovery, as if nothing had happened. I had confided a lot in such a cold, ruthless person, and she still brazenly tells me she can look me in the eyes.

I've already written her letters, pouring out my rage. But I still can't find peace. My first thought in the morning and last thought at night is: why did she do this? She is so devout; this doesn't match her beliefs. Can you tell me what to do to find my peace again?

Answer

You're hurt on two fronts: first by your husband's infidelity and second by your friend's betrayal. Such deep wounds take time to heal. One or two years is a realistic time frame for healing from such a profound injury. Right now, you're in the first phase of processing this, struggling with what has happened and asking yourself how it could have occurred. Other phases will come, ones where you're just sad and others where you're preoccupied with changes in your relationship with your husband. That he chose you and you forgave him means little more right now than that you'll continue life as before.

You're channeling all your anger and resentment onto your friend, but I believe she's interchangeable in your husband's affair. Given the state of your marriage, it could have been any other woman; it just happened to be your friend.

Your husband sought in another woman what he didn't get from you. If you can separate the two issues—the marital infidelity and the breach of trust—the whole situation becomes clearer and more manageable. If you mix them, you can ponder endlessly and still find no solution.

Give yourself time to process these two blows of fate. Divert your thoughts with pleasant things to stop brooding. Inner peace cannot be forced; it will come naturally when you've reconciled with yourself.

I Am Extremely Disappointed by Women

I am twenty-eight years old, and for the third time now, a woman has severely disappointed me. Are all women like this? At the moment, I'm in a mood where I could strangle every woman I see. I don't trust any of them anymore. I'm actually a stranger here, but I chose to take a job in this miserable little town because of this woman, a decision I now deeply regret.

I met her seven weeks ago through a friend with whom I am now living. I immediately fell head over heels in love with her. An incredible woman, truly my dream woman! Blonde hair like an angel and a fantastic figure. She showed me that she liked me too. Unfortunately, I lived two hundred kilometers away at that time, so we could only see each other on weekends. I didn't quite realize then that she had other irons in the fire besides me.

After I finally moved—because of her—she never had time for me. When I confronted her, it turned out she has a steady boyfriend, an older coworker who wants to marry her, and the worst part: She already has an illegitimate child living with her mother. It was a shock from which I have not yet recovered. After that, the magic was gone. But I can't forget her. All I can think about is her and how she deceived me. Are all women so false and deceitful? And how do I stop falling for their sweet faces again and again?

Answer

Your question is difficult to answer because many issues are hidden in your seemingly simple story. First of all, I think you're writing to me—a woman—because you can't easily bear your anger toward women and are looking for a way to quickly regain your faith in them. You don't want to hate women; on the contrary, you have a deep longing to love them.

This strong need clouds your perception of reality! Women, like men, have both good and bad sides. But you divide your perception and feelings of this mixture. When you're in love, you only see the angel; when you're disappointed, only the wicked witch. To be as disappointed as you are, you must have been heavily deceived before. It wasn't the woman who deceived you; you deceived yourself.

You've imposed your idealized image of your dream woman on a stranger without asking who she really is. Thus, you fantasized a relationship that never existed in reality. Even if you now say she clearly showed that she liked me too, that's still just a beginning. But you've already committed yourself, even moved for her. Reality's intrusion can then only shock you.

To make matters worse, it seems you're clearly afraid of competition. You never even consider that you could try to win the woman against the claim of her steady boyfriend. You immediately feel like the weak third party with no chance. That, too, can be a fantasy, the reality of which you should check.

Real relationships are characterized by not forming instantly at first glance but need time to develop. If you don't want to experience such disappointment for the fourth time, take time next time to explore the reality of your partner. Look closely! Blonde hair and a fantastic figure are a little less than the basis for a relationship. Be curious: What does she think, what does she do, how does she live, what does she feel, what are her life perspectives? Only in this way can you save yourself from deceptions and thus disappointments that hurt.

I Would Do Everything Differently Today

A year ago, my boyfriend left me. We were together for two years, some of which were terrible, but some were also very happy. I now realize that I was incredibly selfish and jealous, demanding unreasonable things from him and generally behaving like a crazy person. I was very unhappy after the breakup and thought for a while that my whole life had fallen apart. Without my best friend, who comforted me, I would not have survived this period. But I also learned a lot during this time. I think I've changed, and I can see the mistakes I made back then.

I haven't started a new relationship and still think about my ex-boyfriend. He has had different girlfriends since us, and he's been with the current one for six months. I often see him with her at the disco. We greet each other but don't talk. I keep racking my brain about how to get into a conversation with him alone.

I really want to tell him that I see my mistakes and that I would do everything differently today. But I don't dare to approach him. I am also afraid that I won't be able to open my mouth. I don't know what to do. I constantly dream of this conversation, but when I actually see him and he hardly notices me, I'm paralyzed.

Answer

Dream and reality are far apart. The reality is that you were friends with this man for two years and had to realize that you couldn't live well together, and that he is clearly maintaining a distance from you a year after the breakup.

In your daydreaming, you separate the unpleasant reality and only imagine the good side: In a conversation, he will be touched by your confessions of guilt and turn back to you; you wouldn't make the old mistakes again, so you could only be happy together now.

The paralysis in the real situation is a protective reaction out of fear because, subconsciously, you know exactly that your dream has nothing to do with reality. If you manage to approach him, you would probably be rejected and thus be very hurt and injured. Even if a resumption of the relationship were to be initiated, it's very unlikely that the old ups and downs would not return. You haven't changed as much as you dream in the past year. You have just become wiser and more insightful.

Different partners bring out different qualities in us. Perhaps you are naturally less selfish and less jealous with a different man, and you develop entirely new sides to your own surprise. You should better say goodbye to this love story and keep your wishes and good insights for a new partnership.

Excessive Self-Congratulation

I am a divorced retiree and live alone. A few weeks ago, I met a woman who would be a very welcome fit for cohabitation. She is employed and certainly contributes a lot in her work. She works from early in the morning until literally the early hours. In addition, she is intelligent, clever, creative, attractive, educated, athletic, eloquent, extraordinarily multifaceted... I list all this because it is inexplicable to me how a woman with such attributes can occasionally say such strange things. I notice that she sometimes exaggerates—so, technically speaking, she lies.

She says she takes care of her elderly aunt "every" day, but this aunt lives sixty kilometers away from her home. I would notice if she were actually away for 2 hours every day. She doesn't have the time for that. She talks about an older gentleman she met a few months ago who has written to her "every" day since then—I would also notice that. She says she takes care of over a thousand clients, some of whom are executives in large companies, whom she "controls." She says she moved to a village months ago and is now "tremendously popular" there. What should I make of such self-congratulation, noting that I tend to use understatement?

It is part of the overall picture that she has been divorced for many years but was humiliated by her husband for almost thirty years, was treated miserably, and remained without recognition, for example, for her performance as a housewife and mother of her well-raised, now almost adult, children. She says she felt very oppressed during this time and suffered from feelings of inferiority.

It also belongs here that she now has to earn her living after all her life's work. My questions are: Is the excessive self-congratulation related to her past? Is this an attempt to get some recognition (from me) at least now? How do I deal with it? What do I need to learn? Am I too sensitive? Can I contribute to her balance?

Answer

This fantastic woman has certainly turned your head. However, some doubt seems to nag at you, otherwise, you wouldn't be writing to me. I can't explain why your friend is the way she is; I know too little about her, but your discomfort is valid. You probably want me to alleviate your irritation with plausible explanations for your girlfriend's peculiarities and with prescriptions for your own behavior, but the opposite is the case. I would urgently recommend comprehensive reality checks. Especially if you plan to move in with this woman, you should know what you're getting into.

So: Visit her in her village and verify her tremendous popularity. It's part of the process of getting to know each other that you form an image of the other person's life and also participate in it. Ask to see the letters from the older gentleman and accompany her to the elderly aunt once. Ask her to explain in detail by what means she "controls" the gentlemen from the large companies, and so on.

To an outsider like me, everything you report appears a bit disturbed, as if your girlfriend is building up a world in her head that does not exist in reality. The excessive self-congratulation is certainly related to her past, but that does not make it any less strange.

I think you should learn in this situation to pay more attention to your own feelings and be less fascinated by your girlfriend. You are primarily responsible for your own balance, and that can be quickly damaged with such a dazzling woman.

The Neighbor Is Making Eyes at My Husband

We live in a row house. Until now, we've always loved our neighborhood—full of young families like us. The children play together, and we help each other out. At least twice a year, we all celebrate a big street party with music and dance. Since last year, a band has formed; my husband is on the keyboard, and my neighbor sings. When he went to practice, I never thought anything of it, but now I accidentally observed how my husband and the neighbor were talking in the garden at the fence. He was on our side, she was on hers. I became attentive because my husband was laughing so loudly, which he never does otherwise. Then I watched them.

They talked with each other for over an hour; I couldn't understand what about, but I saw enough. The neighbor really posed and flirted with my husband to such an extent that I almost felt ashamed for her. This made me vividly imagine what goes on during their practices. When I confronted my husband, he initially wanted to deny it but then admitted that he has fallen for the neighbor. However, he keeps assuring me that nothing has happened between them; it's just a spark. And he is now avoiding her. Even if I wanted to believe that, it's too much for me that there is a spark between them.

My husband keeps telling me he knows exactly where he belongs and that he won't risk anything. But my suspicion has been aroused, and I can no longer easily believe him when he leaves. Because I couldn't bear the tension any longer, I gathered my courage and talked to the neighbor about how she sees the situation. The woman has no morals at all. She openly admits that she's fallen for my husband. Her own husband works in outside sales and is often not at home. But that doesn't mean she can now snatch my husband! I ran home crying and don't know what to do. What should I do now?

Answer

Apparently, this conversation with the neighbor turned out quite differently than you had imagined, and that's why you are so confused now. You probably hoped that the neighbor would promise to leave your husband alone. Unfortunately, the opposite was the case. Your unscrupulous neighbor confirms her interest in your husband and openly competes with you. This has hit your weak spot. Your female self-confidence does not seem to be well-developed. You quickly find other women prettier and more attractive than yourself, and that's why you're feeling bad now. You fear losing your husband. According to your unconscious inner calculation, you stand no chance against other, more attractive women.

If you had more female self-confidence, you would have already interrupted the scene at the garden fence, and most importantly, you could have believed your husband that he knows where his place is—namely with you.

Love relationships are based on trust, which the partners grant each other like an advance. At the moment, you're trying to control instead, and that will ruin any relationship in the long run. The fact that your husband reacts to the neighbor's flirting is not unusual; few men would be completely indifferent. What is unusual is that he is honest with you about it and admits it. At the same time, he knows exactly what he wants, which is you, and he wants to avoid the neighbor. There's not much more he can do.

Perhaps more women will make eyes at your husband in the future. The crucial thing is whether you can believe that your husband loves you, and that, in turn, depends on how valuable and attractive you consider yourself to be. All the male love vows in the world won't convince you if you secretly consider yourself a Cinderella. Do something for your self-confidence as a woman!

He Is Too Young for Me

For seventeen years, I've been a widow. It was a very, very hard blow for me at the time. I thought my life was over. With the help of good friends and also through my two daughters, sons-in-law, and grandchildren, life somehow went on. At one point, I even had another relationship, which I ended after three years because the right love wasn't there. Now I'm fifty-eight, thought I was quite content in my life, everything was peaceful and calm—until three months ago. A new junior boss, thirty-six years young, came into our company.

To make a long story short: From the beginning, he showed that he was interested in me, launched a full-fledged seduction campaign, managed to overcome all my concerns and fears, and now we've had an intimate relationship for four weeks. He says he loves me, which I can hardly believe, but slowly must start to believe. The worst part, however, is that I've now also fallen in love with him! I'm completely off balance, act like I'm eighteen, can't sleep or eat from longing for him.

Sometimes I see the whole thing from the outside, for example, through the eyes of colleagues who suspect nothing, then I panic. He's much too young for me. I can already see that he'll lose interest in me quickly, and I'll be left broken. However, he's making plans for the future, wants to make our relationship public, an idea that fills me only with horror. My eldest daughter is older than he is, how will she react? What will the colleagues say?

Reason tells me I should end the story quickly, but I can't do that anymore. Or go on a long journey in the hope that I can forget him—and he can forget me. Do you have advice for me? I can't talk to anyone about it.

Answer

Congratulations! This is actually a wonderful story you're telling, showing how young and lively you've remained at fifty-eight. I think fate is giving you a great gift, which you should gratefully accept. You have already experienced in the other relationship after the death of your husband that without the "right love" everything is worthless. Be happy about your ability to love! Your feelings have lain dormant for a long time, and you probably have a lot to catch up on.

Your friend seems to be very serious, and in your heart you also know this and are opening up to him; it is your head, your reason, that produces all the scruples and fears. Listen more to your heart and enjoy the present. There are never any guarantees; even with a man your own age, you'd run the risk that love won't last. But you should really wait to make your relationship public until you feel entirely secure in your feelings, and your familiarity with each other offers enough protection against critical remarks from the environment.

If you're convinced by your own feelings for this man and your mutual happiness, you'll also convince everyone who really loves and appreciates you, and your children will be happy with you. Colleagues and other acquaintances will surely say things that you'd better not take note of. Remember that envy often plays a significant role, and many people who have closed off their emotional world can't understand it anyway.

Why can't a younger man also love an older woman? The reverse is fully accepted in society: We had a chancellor whose wife is in a similar age difference to him as you are to your young friend. Enjoy what life gives you!

My Husband Is a Hindrance

I am becoming increasingly dissatisfied because I can't do what I want to do. I am thirty-six years old and completely frustrated with my existence as a housewife and mother (one son, fourteen). I've been married for fifteen years, and from the beginning, my husband's concerns have determined our lives in all areas. When I was younger and the child was still smaller, I submitted to his ideas, but now I am just annoyed. For the sake of peace, I still try not to antagonize my husband, but I feel that I can't do this much longer and don't know what to do.

We live in a small town, where people know each other in certain circles. We have a watch shop, and my husband always argues with customers, wondering what they would think if either our son or I were to attract public attention. Of course, he expects good grades from our boy at school, but I had to fight for any other activity that is normal for his friends. My husband found soccer primitive; now my son does karate, but a public appearance at an open house at his club is already a problem again. My husband wouldn't go; he finds such a display embarrassing. Now a catastrophe is looming: my son wants to act in a school performance.

As for me, I have completed vocal training, but I'm not allowed to perform. My husband has now gotten used to my choir, but I have to turn down offers for solo performances. I now secretly rehearse with a small ensemble with old instruments. Slowly the others find themselves ready for concerts. I break into a sweat when I think about what my husband will say; on the other hand, I can't let my ensemble members down. In all my other interests like painting, interior design, and garden design, I have always let myself be determined by my husband, even if I have often experienced him as a hindrance, but somehow it's enough now. What should I do?

Answer

You have unconsciously maneuvered yourself into a dilemma. Your self-restraint has reached a limit where you have to become active if you don't want to get sick. The fact that such a marital situation could arise at all has to do with your excessive need for harmony. That's your share of the misery. Too much harmony always comes at the expense of autonomy. Conflicts are a part of life, and you are not really capable of handling them; you have to learn this now. It's often easier for others, especially for children, to take on conflicts, but now it's also about you and your life satisfaction.

Apparently, you and your son, unlike your husband, have distinctly artistic inclinations. The resulting publicity scares your husband. He devalues creative expressions because they are unreachable for him. Overall, his various "concerns" and consideration for customers are no longer in the realm of normality; some aspects of your account suggest that your husband suffers from an anxiety disorder.

But as long as you don't defend yourself, he cannot realize that he has a problem. Like all anxious people, he believes that he and his family are constantly being critically observed. So far, you have played his game. In the interest of your mental health and your son's good development, you must exit this situation. Only that can motivate your husband to change.

We Are Living Parallel Lives

For two years, after a long period of solitude, I have been living with a partner again. My wife passed away after almost thirty years of marriage, and it took me a long time to recover from the loss. Then I met an old school friend by chance at an event. Like me, she was widowed, and we were both happy to see each other again. A good relationship quickly developed, so we decided to move in together. She was living on a small pension, so it was only natural that she moved into my home. I still live in my big house, which became much too large for me after my son moved out with his family.

We've made some changes to the house, and at first, everything was wonderful. Even intimacy resumed. I was very happy because I thought I had found a life partner with whom I could grow old. But gradually our life has changed for the worse. I find that we are now just living parallel lives.

This is particularly evident in the fact that my partner is hardly ever at home. I've been accustomed for many years to being at my company by nine in the morning. But that's too early for her; she likes to sleep late, so I have to have breakfast alone. Because she has a late breakfast, she doesn't need lunch, so we can't even meet somewhere for lunch. She allegedly spends most of the day with her over eighty-year-old mother, who cannot manage without her, and in the evenings she has courses. When she finally comes home late, she is tired and just wants to watch TV.

Weekends are not much different. Initially, she took me along to her mother on Sundays. I found her mother quite fit and don't understand why she needs so much help now. But after an argument with her mother about a political topic, my partner prohibits any contact as it could overly excite her mother. I'm also annoyed with her handling of money.

In my opinion, she receives a not insignificant sum from me each month for household expenses. But she doesn't take care of the household at all. The cleaning lady is paid by the company, and someone from the company also does the shopping because she can't carry anything heavy anymore. When I make accusations, she brushes it off and insists that she loves me, and that her mother is just a bottleneck at the moment. However, I don't see it that way. Am I wrongfully dissatisfied?

Answer

Your partner can consider herself lucky; she's found a fool who allows her a comfortable life without expecting much in return. You urgently need to decide whether you want to continue playing this game. I suspect that you don't put your foot down because you're afraid of being alone again. But you're already alone!

What you had hoped for, namely closeness and being there for each other, hasn't been happening for a long time. When you met your current partner, you were both probably lonely, and maybe that feeling was your only common ground, as subsequent events show that you don't have further mutual interests, and love is also lacking.

Affection cannot be demanded; it's a gift. Your partner's behavior clearly shows that you're not important to her. It seems that after securing her position with you, she's established a second, separate life without you. Your doubts about whether she's really spending all her time with her mother are justified. Also, her cutting off contact points in that direction. If you could talk to her mother, you might discover the truth. However painful it might be, this woman is shamelessly taking advantage of you. Your dissatisfaction is more than justified. The sooner you end this unsatisfactory relationship, the better for you.

My Husband Is Working Himself to Death

We are a young married couple, both of us employed and without children yet. I'm worried about how our personal life is suffering, as my husband practically has no free time left. Any activities we plan to do together need to be scheduled weeks in advance; otherwise, they don't happen. I often complain about this, and my husband is then willing to make more time for us, but usually, something else comes up last minute and takes precedence. When we met at a sports club, it was precisely this quality of commitment and responsibility that attracted me to him, but now I sometimes think it can also be too much of a good thing. I would like to know your opinion.

My husband is heavily burdened at his company. He's constantly required to work overtime, and he even takes work home. I recently found out from one of his colleagues, who made a comment not meant for me, that people at his company consider him career-obsessed. I can't judge that; my husband would deny it and say he is just normally ambitious, and that others are simply jealous of his success.

However, I'm slowly starting to have doubts. He's not just heavily involved in his work; he is also active in other areas. He has been elected as the chair of our club and has immediately launched a campaign to attract new members. If there's a neighborhood barbecue being organized, it's definitely my husband who is doing it. Now, he even wants to join a political party. I can already foresee what's coming our way.

I am the one who entirely organizes our daily life, even though I don't get home until around six in the evening. Help from him is not an option. When he is home, he's at the computer preparing documents for his various tasks. I think it's also affecting his health. During his last run training, he collapsed; he, of course, didn't take it seriously and shrugged off all my concerns. He is literally working himself to death. What do you think about this situation, and how should I behave?

Answer

You are understandably frustrated; this is not how you envisioned your young marriage. The comment from his colleague has made you wary, as it aligns with your own secret fears. Perhaps your husband is more ambitious than others; whether his ambition has reached unhealthy levels, I can't easily judge. If he is successful at work, it naturally invites jealousy, but it's not just at work. What you describe raises suspicions that your husband may be suffering from a compulsion to always be important. Such people usually suffer from an inferiority complex, which they try to hide from themselves and others through their accomplishments.

This happens more or less unconsciously, so confronting them about it is useless. They also can't easily change their behavior, as an inner necessity drives them to put themselves in the spotlight. This often comes at the expense of health. Such restless individuals are prime candidates for heart attacks.

As the partner of such a man, you need to decide whether you can accept this and adapt to life beside him, or if you can't live like this. In the latter case, you should present him with the alternative of either changing or separating. Change can only come through a therapeutic process, which he should willingly undertake, not to do you a favor, but because he also wants a different kind of life.

Perhaps there is also another reason your husband works so much, which you should consider at least once. Could it be that he is escaping into work because your relationship is no longer satisfying? If your husband agrees to speak with a couple's counselor, you should have a three-way conversation about your expectations for your shared future.

Visit to the Parents

I've been dating a girl for half a year now; I'm twenty-three and we get along really well. She's twenty-one. Now I want to introduce her to my parents. My parents are very conservative and don't have a taste for unconventional clothing, for example. My girlfriend, however, is more of the extravagant type. She works in the big city and is heavily influenced by the scene there.

I'm trying to convince her to buy something decent for this visit, not just in terms of style, but also quality, as my parents value that. She usually wears a lot of cheap stuff, which only looks funny in her circle.

I also find that many aspects of her lean towards the vulgar, such as her flashy makeup. It's only a show in her circles, but among us, she makes herself look ridiculous. My friends also share my opinion. However, my girlfriend is incorrigible. She won't even make concessions for my sake. I care a lot about her making a good impression on my parents.

If she would change on this issue, I could imagine us staying together. What can I tell her so that she realizes she's only hurting herself?

Answer

Many problems arise from the way one dresses. The fact is that clothing is not just a matter of taste, which can be debated, but also an expression and self-presentation through which messages are sent to the environment: For example, "I am shy," or "I want to be someone special," or "I am an important person," and so on. Whether the environment decodes these messages as the sender intends is another question. A flashy outfit that looks great in the city can lose its luster in a rural setting and be perceived as ridiculous.

Your girlfriend, at first glance, shows remarkable self-confidence when she disregards the reactions of others to her appearance. Maybe her exterior accurately reflects her inner feeling of herself, and she can thus handle the fact that some people reject her.

Alternatively, her refusal might be an expression of unconscious conflicts in her relationship with you. For example, she might be protesting against your pressure for her to conform. Or she might be trying to provoke you into making a clear commitment to her. Your feelings for her are actually quite ambivalent. On the one hand, you find her great and can even imagine staying with her; on the other, you find her vulgar. Given your description, one might even say she seems somewhat trashy to you.

But isn't it precisely this vulgar, extravagant side that also attracts you? You fight against it externally because you don't want to admit its appeal to yourself. She doesn't fit into the world you come from. If your girlfriend were to become completely demure, both outwardly and inwardly, she would probably lose all her appeal to you.

Delay the visit to the parents as long as you cannot openly stand by your girlfriend as she is; otherwise, you'll only harm both her and yourself. Your girlfriend must fully appeal to you, not your parents. If you primarily want to satisfy your parents because you still urgently need their love and recognition, you probably need to find another girlfriend.

I Still Have a Debt to Pay

I have always tried to be a good person. On the whole, I think I've succeeded. I have built a life that would be pleasing to God, if it weren't for a debt in my past. Thirty-two years ago, as a young man, I had a friendship with a girl my age. My big mistake was not realizing how deeply she loved me. After I broke up with her, she attempted suicide because of me. I heard about it a year later from a friend.

Thus, the tragic fate of this woman took its course. She quickly married another man whom she did not love. I did not dare to approach her again. From this marriage, two children were born. The second child has Down syndrome. When I heard about this new blow to her fate, I was deeply moved. I lost touch with her because she moved away with her family. But now she's been living near us for almost two years. I've always been afraid to meet her because I think her life would have been different if I hadn't caused her that pain back then. I see this as my fault.

But as fate would have it, we have now met. We were both suddenly sitting next to each other in a government office. At first, I was completely surprised by her kindness, which I had not expected. Then she told me a lot about her life, and I was shocked. She had been operated on for cancer, and her husband had since found another woman. I felt she urgently needed help and human understanding, and I promised her that I would be there for her. After all, I still have a debt to pay.

When I told my wife about this encounter and my intentions, she was absolutely against it. She does not understand that I now have a chance to make amends for my wrongdoing. How should I behave?

Answer

Listen to your wife! If you value your marriage, try to understand your wife's arguments. She represents the claim of reality, while you are somewhat lost in fantasies. We cannot talk about guilt or wrongdoing here. As a young man, you acted according to your own feelings; that others get hurt is inevitable in the way the world is designed.

One can't even walk across a meadow without trampling flowers and animals. So you have no debt to pay or wrong to right. But the fact that you have such thoughts, and that you feel such strong emotional attachment to the life of this woman, shows how important she was and is to you.

You overestimate your significance in her life because she means so much to you. You fantasize that she would have been happy with you, without a child with disabilities and without cancer. But you are not so powerful as to steer other people's lives. You are actually dreaming secretly of your own happiness. You didn't play fate in this woman's life; she seems to be your fate, from which you ran away as a young man.

These unconscious feelings of having missed something important are the source of your feelings of guilt and your desire to make amends. I suspect your wife feels more clearly that your intentions to right a wrong are more about a longing for love and perhaps also sexuality. Deal with your wife and your feelings for her. Evaluate the worth of the life you've built. You can't avoid making a decision. Advice to behave one way or the other won't help you.

My Boyfriend Hates Children

I never thought I would find myself in such a conflict as I am now. I feel torn apart! It's a terrible dilemma. Maybe you have some advice. More and more second marriages are taking place these days, so my problem can't be unique.

I am thirty-three years old, have been living alone for four years, and have a seven-year-old daughter from my first marriage. I met a man through an ad who said right away on the phone that he didn't want a woman with a child. But we met anyway. My daughter was with her father on vacation at the time. We hit it off over the phone, and sparks flew at our first meeting. Everything would be incredibly wonderful with this man, just as I have always wished, if I didn't have a child!

My boyfriend is increasingly sensitive to my daughter, although I always try to keep them apart. Just her presence is enough to put him in a foul mood. He has even said that he wouldn't move in with me; he would rather break off the relationship than put up with a child in the apartment.

He hates children in general and can't deal with them. In practice, he is making me choose between him and my child. But that's impossible! Can he demand this of me? I see no solution and am very unhappy.

Answer

What your boyfriend can demand from you depends on how much you're willing to allow, meaning where your boundaries are. If your relationship with your daughter has always been somewhat ambivalent, his demand will find an echo in you, and you will seek a solution to accommodate your daughter, perhaps with her father, grandparents, a boarding school, or the like.

If your child is an integral part of you and your life, such a decision for you is, just as you say, impossible. Your boyfriend is selfish and a dreamer; he doesn't properly recognize reality. Despite all contrary statements, he fell in love with a woman who has a child, meaning he must decide what to do about it, not you.

He seems to be the type who operates on an "all or nothing" principle. This is always somewhat risky because reasonable and realistic solutions are thereby excluded. One such reasonable solution could be to maintain separate apartments and spend the time you don't need for your daughter in his apartment. However, he would have to accept that he's not the only important person in your life.

This would be a practical solution that also allows your relationship to grow. If your boyfriend continuously experiences that you and your daughter are inseparable, that you essentially come as a package or not at all, he will have to change or leave.

But you also have to ask yourself what it means for your affection toward this man that he puts you in such emotional distress. If he really loved you, he would see how you are suffering and try to alleviate it.

Problems With Family

> *Every family has its difficulties. The key is not in avoiding them, but in going through them together.*
>
> —Brigitte Halenta

Is My Mother a Hypochondriac?

I live near my eighty-two-year-old mother with my two sisters, who like me, have their own families. My mother takes care of herself in her apartment; we only assist her with major shopping. The three of us sisters always coordinate who does what for her. We completely renovated her apartment two years ago. She is mentally very sharp, but her physical strength is gradually diminishing. While one expects this at her age, what increasingly bothers us are the games she plays with us. At least once a month, she urgently needs to be driven to the doctor or even to the emergency room. Usually, the emergency call comes late in the evening or on weekends. Thankfully, so far, it has never been anything serious.

Our husbands are becoming increasingly annoyed and refuse to support us. For instance, my husband only makes jokes about her and claims she's a hypochondriac. However, I know from my childhood how she never spared herself and thought of her health last. Now, in her old age, things may have changed. She watches all health-related shows on TV and reads pharmacy magazines from cover to cover. She also asks us concerned questions about our health and has a thousand good pieces of advice for the children, which of course, no one follows.

I feel sorry that no one takes her seriously anymore, but these never-ending health debates are also bothering me. I'm not sure how to behave. My two older sisters are increasingly refusing to cooperate, thinking it's just another false alarm. This leaves me to handle everything, and it's causing disputes between us. What do you think I should do?

Answer

You find yourself between a rock and a hard place. On one hand, you don't know how to interpret your mother's behavior and don't want to hurt her; on the other hand, you don't want to strain your relationship with your sisters. However, each of the three daughters has a different relationship with their mother, making it unrealistic for you to always be of the same opinion. This means you have to find and hold your own standpoint, even if your sisters don't share it. Clearly, among the three of you, you're either the most compassionate or have the closest emotional relationship with your mother.

Your mother has changed over the years, but even if health issues are now her main concern, it doesn't necessarily make her a hypochondriac, someone who continually imagines illnesses. Health becomes the most important topic for most older people. Your mother apparently lacks age-appropriate friends with whom she can discuss this. You should speak to her about it calmly.

Probably, her family has always been her focal point, and it never occurs to her to seek friends of her own age. Point out the various offerings for seniors. Perhaps more distractions would ease her heightened body awareness. The frequent false alarms might also be a cry for help for her children to take more interest. General fears of aging and dying could also be factors. Many older people feel this way. A large number of people who visit doctors do so for emotional reasons.

Whatever the case, conversation is not only useful but vital. It would probably be good if you openly talked to your mother before suppressed anger strains the relationships. In the future, when she has complaints, she could consult with medical emergency services first or exchange experiences with other older people. Some uncertainty will remain because, at eighty-two, it could be a real alarm instead of a false one, which you should not ignore.

Taking Time Off as a Family Man

For 30 years, I considered myself to be someone with strong nerves and good health. In my job, I've worked my way up to a leadership position, and my word is respected among colleagues. None of them know how I really feel, only my wife does. A year ago, I suffered a heart attack at work, at least I thought it was one. I was terrified and was rushed to the clinic. There it turned out that my heart is in perfect health and that I had "only" suffered a panic attack. I was given sedatives and sent back home. The next attack came a week later; it lasted about four hours. After that, the image I had of myself was shattered. From then on, I was afraid of fear itself and didn't leave the house without my pills.

I then underwent behavioral therapy and learned that fear comes from confinement, and that my life had become pretty confined. Work and then home with my wife and two children, everything on a set track, and free time spent in front of the computer. On the therapist's advice, I changed some things, also learned autogenic training, and now I'm off medication again. But the fear that it could happen again remains. I feel that I should be doing a lot more new things than I currently am. I am very interested in foreign cultures and would like to travel, but as long as the children (12 and 14) are so young, it doesn't seem appropriate, my wife thinks the same. But when I think that I have to wait until retirement, the fear rises again.

Now I have very concrete travel plans that don't cost much except time, but I don't dare to talk to my wife about it because I already anticipate her negative reaction. Unfortunately, my therapist has moved to another city, and I don't feel like my therapy is really over. Therefore, I want to ask you whether you think it is right for a family man to take some time off alone, without any family, for several weeks. Or do you think that is too selfish?

Answer

You are correct; your therapy was not really finished, otherwise, you would have also learned that every person needs a balanced equilibrium between pursuing their own interests and fulfilling the obligations they have taken on. Like all anxiety patients, you got sick because you have always tried to meet others' expectations and thus have neglected your own needs. This is how the internal tightness arises, which eventually manifests itself in states of anxiety, suggesting that the soul is no longer getting enough of what it needs for nourishment. Joy and real satisfaction only come when you wholeheartedly do things for yourself and others; what you half-heartedly do for others, just to please and avoid conflicts, doesn't satisfy you. The hoped-for love for bending over backwards usually remains absent as well. It is especially bad when you almost always suppress your own impulses to fit in, and then it's not even acknowledged.

A marriage should not be a prison but a life community that also provides both partners with the space to develop their own personalities. A partner plagued by anxiety attacks is certainly not a joy to your wife either. Your feeling that you need more freedom is likely correct. Taking a trip alone once a year, if it doesn't strain the family budget too much, doesn't seem like an excessive demand. You should negotiate this with your wife and, in return, offer to take care of the kids on weekends or during vacation times, so she can also do something for herself that solely satisfies her needs. Once this right is fundamentally recognized in a partnership, the rest is just a question of organization.

The Lost Daughter

The family Christmas celebration, which I organized with a lot of love and commitment, left me with a bad feeling and the question of whether I should do it a second time. We celebrated at my mother's place because she has the biggest apartment, but I did all the preparations, from shopping to decorating the Christmas tree, because I live nearby. My three children helped, but most of the work fell on me. My younger brother and his family (two children) arrived on Christmas Eve and loved everything. He's not the problem; it's my older sister. She's always been the enfant terrible of the family, moved out at seventeen after a fight with our father, made a living from street music, became pregnant without a husband two years later, and now lives on welfare with her 16-year-old daughter. She arrived the day before Christmas with her daughter after we hadn't seen her for four years.

My mother had hidden from my brother and me that she had been writing to her since my father's death two years ago and had invited her for Christmas. That was my first irritation when I suddenly found myself facing my sister unexpectedly. We got along well as children, but when she caused all these family problems, I distanced myself from her. I didn't want to cause our parents as much grief as she did. Also, I could see from her example where that leads. So far, we've always had very harmonious family Christmases, but this time it immediately became complicated because of her presence.

She wanted to get involved right away, couldn't accept anything as it was but had to always somehow judge it, mostly negatively. The worst part, however, was her daughter, who at sixteen spent most of her time smoking on the balcony and eventually left the dinner she had earlier insisted on, even before dessert, because she had to go to a Christmas party. My mother didn't seem to mind at all; her joy that her lost daughter was back seemed to be enough for her. I think I'm pretty angry. What do you think?

Answer

I think it was good for you to get your frustration off your chest by writing it down. Apparently, you only realized while writing that you're angry. And you have good reason to be. You're upset about your mother's secrecy, about not informing you that your sister would also be coming, especially since you were the one who planned everything. And it infuriates you to see how your mother forms an alliance with the lost daughter against the rest of the family. Your anger is mostly directed at your mother, and you urgently need to have a clarifying conversation with her.

Given that I don't know much about your relationship with your mother, I can only make some general remarks here. It seems that during your father's lifetime, a split occurred in your family. There was a 'bad' child (your older sister) and two 'good' children who met their parents' expectations. But families are systems, so the 'bad' child is really just the child who took on all the family's problems so that the rest could live relatively conflict-free.

With your father's death, your family system has fundamentally changed and now needs to rebalance. Many conflicts that have always existed become visible again with your sister's return. To give just one example: The mother's preference for the eldest.

Be careful not to make your big sister the scapegoat again. She has probably gone through a lot in that role.

Christmas, with all its expectations of harmony, was probably the worst time for the return of the lost daughter. But now that contact has been re-established, you can take your time and see how relationships develop. Eventually, a conversation with your sister will be due. And how the next Christmas will be celebrated will probably have to be decided by the new family council. Things won't be as they were before.

Who Owns the Money?

I grew up with constant money worries. Only after I had moved out did the situation stabilize for my parents. I myself came to my profession as a civil servant in the administrative service through a circuitous route. The financial security for years has been good for me. We built a house, and we have lived there— my wife and our two daughters—for over ten years, very happily. My wife is also a civil servant and has been working part-time since the children were born. So, of course, she earns less than I do. We have financially arranged that all fixed costs come from my account, and the daily needs are covered by hers. At the end of the month, we pool what is left.

This arrangement worked smoothly for many years, until inheritances disrupted the peace. First, I inherited a large sum from my father. At that time, it was a given that the money would be invested in our house. It was our money, which naturally benefited the whole family. The emphasis is on "our" because now, six years later, my wife has inherited a comparable sum, and suddenly "our" is no longer the case. From the first news, she speaks of "my money". She wants to invest it in her retirement savings and maybe go on a trip with our older daughter. I see red when I hear this. She doesn't even consider doing something with this money that would benefit the whole family. It's all about her selfishness.

Now we have a problem with our flat roof. Naturally, I will cover the costs for the repair, as anything that concerns the house is my responsibility, and payment also naturally comes from my account. However, there isn't enough money available for the repair, so I'm considering selling some investment papers. On the other hand, my wife does have the money.

Answer

A lot seems to be going wrong for you. The times when you had less and were quite in agreement about what to spend money on are over. Your marriage was still intact back then. The way you handle the available funds today reflects the disruption in the relationship. Such disruptions are never the fault of just one person; the actions and reactions of the partners are mutually conditional. Doing nothing and staying silent, as you do, is also an action. You can't not behave. One way or another, you are always part of the system in which you live. At first glance, the fact that your wife doesn't even think of sharing some of her inheritance seems very selfish, and I can very well understand that you are extremely annoyed about this double standard for dealing with an inheritance.

But there are likely motives behind your wife's actions that come from an imbalance in the relationship. Perhaps you dominate her in other areas, and this is her subtle revenge. Or you have always said "my house," and now she retaliates with "my money." Many other motives are conceivable, which I can only speculate on since you don't write anything about your relationship with your wife. But it becomes clear that you don't speak up and tell your wife what you think. You are apparently one of those people who avoid conflict because they can't stand disharmony. Silence and swallowing it down, however, is the surest way to undermine harmony and get sick yourself.

If your daughters are older than ten, you should call a family meeting and openly discuss the family's financial situation and look for solutions. If that doesn't work, you should consider financial counseling as a couple. Consumer advice centers can provide addresses. That will surely lead to a workable solution on the financial level. If you then notice how little practical sensible solutions are, it will be time to also consider the possibility of marriage counseling.

The Injustice Is Robbing Me of Sleep

I have come to understand in my fifty-four years that the world is not a fair place, but sometimes it's more than one can bear. Since the will was read, I can't sleep anymore, and the doctor has diagnosed me with heart arrhythmias. My father died five weeks ago; he had left a will that, over and above the obligatory portions, specified how his considerable assets should be distributed. We are three children: an older half-brother who my mother brought into the marriage, myself as the eldest from this marriage, and my sister who is three years younger. My father was a passionate innkeeper, and my mother was just as committed. We children were taught that the business and guests always take priority.

However, my older half-brother wouldn't accept this. Our entire childhood is marred by the constant fighting surrounding him. When he hit puberty, things got really bad. He and his friends would break into cars, repeatedly steal money from our cash register, get into fights constantly, drawing frequent police visits to our home. I think the sorrow caused by him drove my mother to an early grave. Despite their best efforts, nothing worked. While my sister and I have turned out well, he lives on social assistance, claiming to be unfit to work due to asthma and diabetes.

Now, the reading of the will reveals that my father didn't just financially support him for years but also essentially provided him with an annuity from his estate, which considerably reduces our share of the inheritance. I had expected that we could finally pay off the debts on our house, but the money isn't sufficient. My wife takes it calmly, but this injustice is robbing me of sleep. What do you think?

Answer

I can certainly understand why you are deeply disappointed that the size of your inheritance does not meet your expectations. But your emotions go deeper and are probably also being fueled by ancient feelings of childhood envy and helpless rage. In your eyes as a child, the older brother was not just a disruptor but also the one who received much more attention—even negative attention is a form of attention. It's easier for your wife to remain calm; she doesn't have a painful history with this brother like you do. Now you have to experience that this unfair preference for the older brother continues even after your parents' death.

If you stop viewing your father's legacy through the eyes of the hurt child, you might discover some truths that help you accept your father's decisions. There is not just your version of the truth. Everyone who has lived in the family system has their own perspective and thus their own truth. Perhaps your viewpoint aligns somewhat with your sister's, but your older brother likely has a truth that is diametrically opposed to yours.

He was the black sheep of the family and possibly suffered so much in his development that he was doomed to fail in shaping his adult life. Overall, there was too little love and time for the children in this family, so it's even more bitter for you that this deficiency is now not even compensated for by money. But your father apparently saw that of all the children, the stepson had suffered the most. He may have also had guilt feelings about it. His will attempts to make amends. You should respect his view of things.

My Mother Has a Dark Secret

Two weeks ago, my father passed away at the age of 75. My parents divorced 45 years ago when I was five, and I was raised by my mother. Later, she found a new life partner and moved to Spain. I regularly visited my father until his death and took care of his personal affairs. So it was natural for me to sort out his estate after his death. In the process, I came across a folder containing about fifty love letters from the time my parents were engaged. The letters are arranged chronologically and end about six months before my birth, when my parents had to get married. One letter was not properly filed; it was loosely in the collection and had been taped back together after being torn into several pieces. It was written by my mother a year before my birth, at a time when my father was undergoing training in another city for several months.

After reading it, nothing was the same for me as it had been before. My mother writes about the birth of her first child, the pain, the complications, and how she had only seen her child briefly because its new adoptive parents were already waiting in the hospital corridor. She writes about the relief of finally being free of the child, and about the freedom to finally do everything and determine her life herself.

So I have an older sister. I am now fifty—this has been kept from me all my life. It took me a while to come to terms with this, and I debated whether it made sense to go to my mother to find out the whole truth about this story. On one hand, I want to know what happened back then and possibly look for my big sister; on the other hand, such a sensitive topic can't be discussed over the phone—I would have to travel to Spain, and—what's more—my mother is already 72 and has a weak heart. I just don't know what to do—what do you advise?

Answer

First of all, it's naturally a shock for you to learn this way about the existence of a sister. The first question that comes to my mind is, why did your parents keep this a secret? It doesn't necessarily have to be the case that your father was also the father of this child, or that your sister was an "accident" in a very young love relationship. Isn't it also possible that your mother associates painful experiences with this child, which she does not want to be reminded of, and which she has kept under wraps for over fifty years now? That could range from an unhappy previous relationship to a "one-night stand" to rape. If so, would it really be good to confront an old woman against her will?

The second question is, what would you personally gain from learning the truth? A sister is a sister because you spend your childhood with her and share many memories. In your case, it's a stranger; you also don't know what emotional chaos you might plunge her into with your revelation. If your sole aim is to take revenge on your mother for withheld secrets, then you must immediately travel to Spain and confront her.

However, I suggest another option: Try to find people who were close to your parents and could know about the story. Gather facts from friends, relatives, and confidants of your mother. If after your research you still feel you need to question your mother, go to her and try to find out more in a careful conversation. Perhaps you will come to the conclusion that it's good to let the past rest and to respect the decision of a then very young woman never to be reminded of this event again.

I Am At a Crossroads

For nearly two years, I've had a very responsible job. The well-being of many people depends on me. Considering my background, I've achieved a lot with this position. Now I am at a crossroads.

I have been toying with the idea of making painting, which has so far been a hobby, the focus of my life. I have to decide now whether to accept a place at a private art school or not—and possibly quit my job. Everything is pushing me towards it, but my family is in uproar. They all think I'm totally crazy. The fact that I'm not married at 35, as one ought to be, is one thing; but no one understands why I would give up such a successful and secure job.

I completed my high school diploma as an adult and then studied social pedagogy. I'm the only one in my family who has studied, and I already feel like nobody really understands me there. At home, everything revolves around farming and my disabled sister.

We were four girls. The oldest sister has always looked after the disabled sister. My youngest sister is like a boy and wants to take over the farm. My interests have never mattered to my family. I would have liked to go to a more advanced school, but I never dared express that. Still, can I ignore their warnings and do what I think is right? It feels like I would be risking a break.

Answer

After completing your high school diploma and studying social pedagogy, going into art studies would be the third break from your family's traditions! You've demonstrated so much independence up to this point. Why shouldn't you continue on this path? Breaking the pattern of one's family of origin is not easy for anyone, but if you manage it, it will also release a lot of energy.

Your family thinks in traditional patterns, in which permanence and security are important values. You too grew up with these values and have internalized them. The break you fear might be more of an internal one, conflicting with deeply rooted beliefs about what is right and important in life, rather than an external break with the actual members of your family.

Taking the step into art studies with the aim of making a living from painting is a step out of bourgeois lifestyles. This could make you anxious. From that point on, you have to rely entirely on your artistic talent, your creativity, and originality. Perhaps you are not entirely sure what you can trust yourself with. Your family will accept you, as they have always done, if you are convinced of your own path.

Before making your decision, you should get acquainted with freelance painters. Show them your work, make personal contact, and see if you feel comfortable with these people and can imagine belonging to them.

Don't let yourself be pressured by a deadline. Such a decision must mature and should not be rushed. Once you are completely sure, the decision for art is not a turn away from the family, but a turn towards yourself and your own unique life plan.

Dog in Bed

My husband gave our seven-year-old daughter a Cocker Spaniel for Christmas, which she had been longing for. I was against it because we live in a two-room apartment and I believe that a dog needs more space to run around. This problem has not really arisen as our daughter spends a lot of time outside with the animal. However, we now have another problem that is causing me great stress. Our daughter takes the dog into bed with her.

I am strictly against the dog being in bed for hygiene reasons, but I can't enforce it. No command works. Sooner or later, the dog jumps back onto the bed because he is used to it. My daughter simply ignores my instructions. As soon as I turn my back, the dog is in bed with her during the day. She tells him hypocritically when I suddenly come in, "Get down, Mom doesn't want you there!" But of course, she lured him onto the bed beforehand.

The whole room smells like a dog. The bed should be stripped every other day because the dog brings in enough dirt even if we wipe his paws. Also, such an animal sniffs at thousands of unappetizing things outside. The thought of how many bacteria she might be in contact with through the dog makes me sick. My husband doesn't support me at all, but rather undermines me. Sometimes I catch him sitting next to our daughter's bed while the dog is there. I'm slowly becoming so angry at the animal that I've even threatened to get rid of it. But even that doesn't help.

Answer

People's notions of hygiene differ and can also vary depending on cultural background. Generally, people who are in close contact with animals are not more at risk for health problems than those who are not. One could even argue that moderate contact with dirt boosts the immune system. Your husband may assess the situation less strictly than you do, particularly since he doesn't feel responsible for keeping the apartment clean.

However, your issue seems to me not only about hygiene but deeper relational conflicts. The dog is becoming a bone of contention in a relationship problem between the father, mother, and daughter. Your daughter felt lonely and wanted a playmate, something to cuddle. She might have felt lonely not just because she is an only child, but because she lacked affection in general. The presence of the dog in the bed fulfills such vital needs for closeness and warmth that hygiene and maternal authority become meaningless.

Your husband seems to understand the emotional needs of your daughter better than you do. He gave her the dog and now allows the dog in the bed, forming a united front against you. Perhaps it's a front of emotions against you as the representative of reason and order. You feel doubly threatened: firstly, because they can allow themselves something you can't, and secondly, because you are isolated: husband, child, and dog against you.

Your anger, mainly at your husband for not standing by you, is being displaced onto the dog. Even if you got rid of the dog, the core issue would remain. The best thing for everyone, including you, would be if you could move out of your opposing position and join them on the bed. This scene would symbolically mean a lot and could probably lead to some changes in your family life.

The Wrong Son-in-Law

I am the only daughter and it seems to me that my parents have had high expectations of me from an early age. I won't even talk about good school performance; that was simply a given. But my behavior, my appearance, and my interests should be as my parents envisioned them.

In addition, it was a foregone conclusion that I would take over my parents' textile business. It has been in the family for three generations. When I dared to say at the age of thirteen that I find fabrics boring, my mother did not speak to me for three weeks. If there's any matter or subject she doesn't like, she always says, "it's not up for discussion." In this case, I was the one who was not up for discussion.

Now I'm twenty-eight and have taken over the damn business. I studied business administration, at least I could assert myself there, and now the battle is about my parents resisting all modern concepts of business management. I was close to quitting it all, but the economic crisis came to my aid. There were simply constraints that I could use to my advantage so that they had to grudgingly give in.

But now, according to them, if I continue like this, I will send them to an early grave because I want to marry the wrong man. He is a literary scholar, so he has no idea about real life; he is not Catholic, so he's godless; he's only as tall as I am, so we don't make a proper couple; and he has been married before, which is somehow immoral, especially since he still has to pay for a child who lives with his ex. In summary, he is the wrong son-in-law.

We've been living together for a year already. I'm sure he's the right one for me, but the fact that my parents won't acknowledge him wears me down. What should I do?

Answer

Worse than your parents not recognizing the son-in-law is their refusal to accept your choice. But this is characteristic of how your parents treat you. If they ever claimed to love their daughter, it was a very selfish love that did not care about the daughter's well-being. It was always about satisfying their own visions, never about the needs of their child. You probably have a lot of emotional scars and offenses from your upbringing. Subconsciously, you are far angrier with your parents than you can admit to yourself. And rightfully so. This is called narcissistic exploitation in technical terms.

If you can feel a little of what your parents have done to you, then you can also mobilize aggressive feelings that you urgently need to emotionally separate from your parents. Only when you have gained some distance from them will their actions no longer directly hit your heart, as is currently the case. You may need psychotherapeutic help for this, as the next steps are clear. You need to emotionally detach and establish clear boundaries.

Regarding the business, you either have control or you don't. If you do, you must set clear boundaries for your parents on how much say they still have. If they threaten with their early death, that is blackmail you must reject. As for your boyfriend, hopefully, love will give you enough courage and determination to finally make your own decisions against your parents' wishes. There is no wrong son-in-law, just the right one whom you choose. Your happiness lies solely in your own hands.

Secret Visits

I am a divorced grandmother and have issues with my only grandchild. My son was married for seven years. From this marriage comes Timmie, whom I practically raised during these years. My daughter-in-law was happy back then that she had me to look after the child. She returned to her bank job six months after Timmie's birth. I have to say, I was happy with the little boy. To experience everything again—the first steps, the first words, and all that—I had no objection to her leaving the child increasingly in my care because she wanted to go on training courses. Her career was always more impor- tant to her than the child. But since she needed me, she was always very nice to me.

Then their marriage hit a rough patch. My son was quite unhappy, which led him to start an affair. I didn't approve, but I understood him. When it came out, she terminated the rela- tionship instantly. It was clear that he was the guilty one. She took the child and left overnight. Terrible times followed. It took a year and a half for my son to win visitation rights. By then, she was in another relationship and had a paid nanny. She did not want the boy to come to me at all. Now she was full of hate to- wards me, as if I were to blame for the separation.

However, my son still brought Timmie to me on his visiting weekends, and the joy was mutual. Timmie never spoke about his visits to me at home. He was nine at the time and knew how to keep quiet. Now Timmie is almost fifteen and comes to see me more often. He tells his mother he's staying overnight with friends. We always have a great time together, even when his father, my son, is not around. Sometimes he comes unannounced for two hours, just because he wants to tell me something.

I enjoy seeing his development, but the situation is getting a bit tricky. Now Timmie wants to have a fifteenth birthday party at my place. I don't mind, but won't that cause trouble with his mother? She mustn't know about these secret visits, and now a party? That can't end well. My question is whether I should take the initiative and inform her of the situation. But I am also afraid that Timmie would suffer. Can you give me some advice?

Answer

Your grandson is now fifteen, so I don't think you need to worry about him. He managed to handle the complicated family situation when he was much younger. I also suspect that his mother has suspected something for some time but doesn't ask because it's easier. She'll also realize that she can't regulate a fifteen-year-old anymore. She may continue to accept further lies—why, one can only guess—but there's probably an unspoken agreement between Timmie and his mother.

As a grandmother, you should not interfere. If anyone is in a position to speak openly, it's your son. But he's the one who started with the secrets. He probably still fears the aggression of his ex-wife and therefore will not take action.

Timmie is at an age where any family court would listen to his arguments. No one can forbid him from visiting his grandma anymore. You can simply enjoy your time with your grandson and let him handle things at home.

Eventually, everything will come out because Timmie is growing up and wants more freedom. His emotional attachment is clearly to you and not to his mother. No wonder, considering you filled the mother's role for the first seven years of his life. Be happy that you haven't lost Timmie despite the divorce.

My Daughter-in-law Hates Me

For weeks I've been racking my brain because I can't accept that I'm no longer able to see my two grandchildren, ages five and three. There's been silence between my only son's family and me for months. I tried one last time on my five-year-old grandson's birthday by leaving gifts at their door. My daughter-in-law took them to my 88-year-old mother in the nursing home, saying they don't want gifts from me. This hurt me deeply.

The conflict happened on my son's birthday, over putting the children to bed. This led to an argument with my daughter-in-law, while my son didn't get involved. I mentioned she was quite strict with the children; she became angry and verbally abused me. My son told me to leave.

Before meeting his current wife, my son was open with me. His various girlfriends were always welcome. His demeanor changed upon meeting his current wife. I helped him set up his physiotherapy practice, but haven't set foot there since they married. He says his wife doesn't want me there. I believe my daughter-in-law hates me and has turned my son against me. What should I do?

Answer

I understand that this is a difficult situation. However, it might be helpful to shift your perspective. Right now, you're focusing on your daughter-in-law as the cause of all the trouble. But the central person in this family drama is likely your son. If you blame everything on your daughter-in-law, you're oversimplifying things.

The real conflict seems to be between you and your son. He was an only child raised by a single mom, and his attachment to you was probably too strong and lasted too long. He seems to have distanced himself only after meeting his future wife. He avoids open conflicts, possibly because he's afraid of you. Instead of confronting you, he hides behind his wife.

Your daughter-in-law is to be pitied; she's being used by both her husband and you. If your son truly cared about maintaining contact with you, his wife would act differently. Your point of contact should be your son, not your daughter-in-law. Try to talk to him; he's your only avenue for reconnecting with your grandchildren.

My Father Is Stubborn

Ever since my mother died six years ago, my father has been living alone in the same apartment, which is sixty kilometers away from us. He is now eighty-four years old and is increasingly a concern for me due to his declining health. He smokes too much and has a very unbalanced diet. I visit him once a week, do his laundry, and try to clean up.

I say "try" because he only lets me do the bare minimum and gets annoyed if I so much as move a newspaper. Every visit becomes a battle over whether or not I can vacuum. My mother had a hard time with him too. I remember them always fighting over cleaning his workspace. I am the only child, and now he is directing this behavior towards me. He sees cleaning merely as a disturbance, which frustrates me because I have good intentions.

His clutter and the accumulated dust are indescribable. I've often threatened not to return if he won't let me clean, but I can't bring myself to leave him in his mess. He also doesn't see well; when he does the dishes, half of the food remains stuck. My husband and I think he's no longer capable of taking care of himself. We've offered for him to move in with us, where I could better care for him. But my father is stubborn and refuses to discuss the matter.

Answer

Even the most beautiful south-facing room in a daughter's house is worse than one's own four walls and independence. Your father feels that he is still quite capable of managing his life on his own. What looks like stubbornness to you is his justified claim to shape his life according to his own needs and capabilities. It seems your standards for order and cleanliness are not his. After all, he has lived this way for eighty-four years.

As long as he feels comfortable in his environment and doesn't ask for help, you should respect his lifestyle. Could it be that you have unresolved issues with your father, and now want to make him as dependent on you as you once were on him? If so, then moving him to your house would be more important for you than for him.

The time-consuming driving is surely inconvenient, but is that really your primary reason? Relocating him can only occur with his full consent; otherwise, cohabitation will quickly become a burden. If you want to do something for your father now, arrange for a mobile meal service to deliver a daily meal tailored to the needs of elderly people; he'll appreciate it. Pay for weekly cleaning help and visit him just for enjoyment.

Every Year Again

Every Christmas we have the same trouble. We are a young family with three small preschool-aged children. Ever since our now five-year-old daughter was born, our parents—both mine and my husband's—assume they have the right to celebrate Christmas with us. We are both only children. No one ever asked us if we wanted this. To make matters worse, the two sets of grandparents do not get along at all. They come from differ- ent worlds and have practically no common topics for discus- sion. However, they both know exactly how to raise small chil- dren, constantly offering contradictory advice that doesn't fit our parenting style. I find myself caught in the middle, trying to keep everyone happy amidst the chaos.

This year, we have another problem: I would like to invite my friend, who became a widow just three months ago, and her son. I don't want her to feel lonely at home after this devastating life event. My husband also likes her, and the kids get along well, but my mother can't stand her. She's an actress and, in my mother's eyes, leads a superficial lifestyle. Furthermore, adding two more people would make our space cramped. Without the four grandparents, everything would be easier. We have wished for years to be able to celebrate just as a family.

I want to uninvite both sets of grandparents by telling them that we want to celebrate alone this time. Even though it's very last minute, I stand by it, but my husband keeps holding me back. He is particularly afraid that his mother will be deeply offended. As an alternative, I would offer the grandparents Christmas coffee on the second holiday, after which they can return home. Both don't live far away. Since my husband opposes this idea, I keep wondering if I'm doing the right thing. What do you think?

Answer

You clearly know what you want, but you don't want to risk a conflict with your husband. He seems to still be very attached to his mother, which suggests that there are likely more conflicts between you and him of the same nature. So, take courage. Adding one more conflict to the mix won't make much difference. Maybe you'll get lucky, and he'll actually enjoy Christmas Eve without his mother. But he'll have to experience it to know. Children definitely need a relaxed atmosphere, and that's not possible when so many different personalities are clashing in a confined space.

You are obviously the one who feels responsible for the Christmas harmony, and therefore your decisions carry the most weight. If everything falls on your shoulders, you need to ensure that you don't feel overwhelmed and still have the energy to enjoy the festivities with your small children.

The understandable desire to include your recently widowed friend simply brings the recurring Christmas problem to a head, forcing you to finally take action. Even without your friend's situation, you have the right to enjoy your family life undisturbed on Christmas Eve. The grandparents, who so casually assume they belong, are asserting outdated parental rights.

Use this Christmas as an opportunity to settle the matter once and for all. Make it clear to the older generation that they need to ask, and that there are years when a visit just doesn't work. You can't avoid a conflict with your husband; he needs to learn to prioritize his wife and children. An offended grandma is not the end of the world.

Reconciliation Would Be My Downfall

I am in great inner turmoil and do not know how to behave. My body is going crazy, and if I don't find a solution soon, I'll become ill. I am forty-six years old, and up until 2 months ago, I felt healthy and was very satisfied with my life. Now everything is being questioned. My mother, from whom I've had sixteen years of peace, is back and pressuring me. We have four children, and the eldest daughter is in college. My mother has found out her address and written to her, saying she is old now and regrets the estrangement with her family. Just her calling us "her family" makes me extremely angry; she treated us like dirt. Now she allegedly has her life under control, would love to see her grandchildren, and has invited the eldest on a trip to Sweden for which she has won two tickets.

My mother was heavily dependent on alcohol when I was a child. At ten years old, I practically organized life for myself, my brother, and her, and in return, she physically abused me. She scared away my first friends, needing me for herself because she had no one else. She waged a veritable war against my later husband, costing us two years that could have been happy. We married anyway, and she tried for years to ruin my husband's career with anonymous letters. She almost succeeded. When we found out she was behind all these vile acts, we completely broke off contact. But before that, I had been running after her for years, begging for her love, as I know now after therapy.

The last sixteen years without her, with my husband and my children, were peaceful and beautiful. I almost forgot her and everything she did to us. I never thought she would show any interest in us. My absolute nightmare is that she will show up here unexpectedly when my husband is not around. She has already spoken twice on the phone with our eldest daughter, who sees no problem with it and would like to get to know her grandmother.

Since my mother found out about the existence of the two younger children and their birth dates, she has been sending them postcard greetings and even a birthday package for the youngest. I would have preferred to burn it immediately. Through my eldest daughter, she has let me know that reconciliation for her 75th birthday would make her happy. My husband says no, that's out of the question, but he's not upset. I am horrified. A reconciliation with her would be my downfall. What should I do?

Answer

Take your physical and emotional condition seriously! This mother has not done you any good and is still harming you today. Calm down by making it clear to yourself that you are the one making the decisions. You have your husband's support. On a realistic level, you have nothing to fear. It's different on your inner stage. While you may have essentially buried your desires for this un-motherly woman, you have not buried your fears of her. Your childlike fears and pains have reawakened, and from this perspective, your mother still appears as a powerful woman against whom you stand no chance. But today you are an adult and no longer at her mercy.

Sit down with your husband and discuss all measures. The best course of action would be for both of you to send a jointly signed statement to your mother, without explanations, stating that you do not wish to have any contact. Regarding the children, you need to distinguish between the eldest daughter and the children who still live at home. The eldest has every freedom to make her own decision, but she should know her parents' stance on the matter. The other children live in the family, and the parents decide for them. Explain the situation to the children objectively and send back all mailings.

If your mother really does show up unannounced at your door and does not leave, you will need to call the police. You might also have friendly neighbors with whom you can make arrangements. But your mother is probably just an old woman now who realistically has no power over you anymore.

My In-laws Reject Me

I have a big problem with my in-laws. They have been against me from the start, I think it's because my parents are divorced. If their rejection only affected me, I could still cope with it, but it also involves my eight-year-old daughter. I have been working part-time since my daughter was one year old, so I have always relied on help. My mother, who lives near me, has regularly looked after the child during my working hours. My in-laws, on the other hand, only occasionally look after my daughter when I specifically ask and bring her to them.

From the start, my in-laws have said that they can't watch the child as much as my parents can, so I have always been prepared for that. But for four years, I have had to watch as my in-laws have time every Saturday to look after their other grandchild. They love that child, and my daughter has to watch as the other child is favored. When we meet, they only talk about the other granddaughter, and my daughter, my husband, and I are ignored.

Even when my daughter has a birthday, these grandparents ignore it. This is already noticed by strangers. Even the neighbors are outraged and say: How can you be like that! My husband has already talked to his father about it, but it didn't help. I suffer greatly under these circumstances. What can be done?

Answer

There's not much you can do. People don't have levers that can be used to change them. You can only change your inner attitude so that the behavior of the in-laws no longer hurts you. The fact is, the in-laws are more fond of the other granddaughter and show it without regard for feelings. That both children are grandchildren doesn't matter; the world is not a fair place. Love cannot be demanded; you either get it as a gift or you don't.

You could talk to your mother-in-law again, as she is the one who makes the decisions about childcare, not the father-in-law. But I don't think much will change, and everything will continue as before. You suffer twice under this relationship with the in-laws, once as a rejected daughter-in-law and again by identifying with your daughter.

Perhaps there is already an old story in your life involving jealousy and rivalry, e.g., if you suffered as a child from a sister or brother being favored. Then these old injuries come to life again now and intensify your feelings about the situation.

The only thing that can help you and protect you from further injury is distance. Reduce your expectations of these in-laws and avoid contact. Childcare can be resolved differently. If the in-laws want to see their grandchild, they should reach out themselves. If asked why you're distancing yourself, you can give an evasive answer or, if you can manage it, kindly tell the truth. I would avoid a major confrontation, as it only hardens positions and possibly makes everything worse.

The decisive person will be your husband because it depends on his relationship with his parents whether he can support you.

If he still hopes that his parents will finally prove their love to him (or subsequently to his daughter), he will not maintain a distance from them. Then your strength is required, specifically if you can enforce your interests for your inner peace and that of your daughter, even on your own.

Looking for Convincing Arguments

Dancing has been my passion since I was little. I can't imagine my life without dancing at all. From age ten to sixteen, I had ballet lessons that my parents supported. It was very sad for me when I had to quit because of my asthma. But the desire for dancing has never ceased for me. I have read many books on it and also attend all adult education courses and similar events that are available here. Now I am quite excited because I have an offer to learn Flamenco in twelve weeks, spread over two years.

I would have to drive fifty kilometers each time and leave my family alone. It is also not cheap. But as far as my family is concerned, my children are ten and a half and twelve, and Grandma usually takes good care of them when my husband and I go on vacation or business trips. And I could cover the costs from my personal savings.

The bad thing is that everyone in the family thinks I am crazy for wanting to learn Flamenco at thirty-eight. They point out the costs, the children, the long journey, and my asthma, which is much better today than it was before. Especially my husband finds the whole thing completely ridiculous, saying that nothing comes out of it.

I rack my brain to find convincing arguments that would persuade everyone, but I can't think of anything sensible. I oscillate between discouragement and sometimes defiance. My family should understand how important dancing is to me and that this Flamenco course is something I have dreamed of for a long time.

Answer

It would certainly be nice for you if your family understood you and encouraged you to fulfill your long-desired wishes. But when we are adults, it is rare that our environment supports us in that way. Most of the time, we have to fight to fulfill our wishes. So there's only one person who really has to understand how important dancing is to you, and that is you yourself.

If you feel that dancing is a central life wish for you, then you have to make sure it is fulfilled. You are an adult; you decide for yourself about your life. Your family, your husband, cannot allow or forbid you anything. You have to represent and be responsible for your wishes yourself.

There are no factual arguments for Flamenco that could infallibly convince your family, your husband. There is only the intensity of your feelings. And feelings are an undeniable reality that rational arguments cannot reach. Try to talk to your husband about the not-so-factual world of your feelings, desires, and longings. Perhaps such conversations frighten him because they announce occasional separations and the growing independence of his wife, and he cannot and does not want to understand you. Then you have to decide whose wishes you want to fulfill: his or yours.

Your problem is not to be solved at the level of arguments. Behind the dispute about childcare, financing, asthma, and the usefulness of Flamenco courses, it is actually about questions relating to your relationship with your husband and your family and your attempts to assert your wishes. Only if you take yourself seriously will others also take you seriously.

The Little Brother Is Being Coddled

I would like to talk to you about a somewhat complicated family matter. It's about my parents and my little brother. I simply can't stand to watch how they coddle him and hover over him as if something terrible could happen to him at any moment. The situation is as follows: I am twenty-six and have been married for four years, my husband is the same age. We have two children, a three-year-old daughter and a son who has just turned one. I also have a sister who is two years younger and unmarried. My mother had another child two years ago at the age of forty-nine.

My little brother is now a year and a half old and therefore younger than my eldest daughter. My mother noticed her pregnancy quite late, and then she was very worried about whether the child would be healthy. I believe they were also embarrassed to have a child so late in life. My father still introduces the boy to strangers as "our slip-up," which I find terrible. Even if he looks more like a grandpa, he's sixty-one and an early retiree, it doesn't have to be expressed that way.

The little one is healthy, handsome, and incredibly lively. My mother and father never take their eyes off him. Sighing and whining, because the little one has come up with something new again, they spend the whole day fussing over the boy.

I'm not saying they don't love him, quite the opposite, they spoil him a lot, but they are so fearful that you can't help but feel sorry for them. I think my little brother is an absolutely normal

*child. I fear that he is not developing well under these circum-
stances.*

When all three young children of the family are together, he really lets loose, because I make sure that the children have more freedom. My mother sees this too, but says she just can't help it, especially because the father is so anxious. How can one help them?

Answer

You can't do more than you're already doing. Talking doesn't help much; a good example helps more. The more often your parents experience that their little one can try out many things without getting hurt when he is with you and the grandchildren, the more they might be able to relax and let their child be. Your little brother has these no longer young parents, that is his fate, which he could not choose.

From the outside, it is always very difficult to assess what ultimately connects with such and other configurations for later life, good and/or bad. Even younger parents can be overly anxious and overprotective. If mother and father always fear the worst for their child, it means that deep in the unconscious there are also feelings that are directed against the child and wish it would rather not be there. Children are also a tremendous obligation and bring great restrictions.

Your parents understandably have ambivalent feelings for this late child who has once again turned their lives upside down and will now demand their full attention for the next few years. As a daughter, you are certainly not the best person to talk to your mother about this matter. Subliminal feelings of competition may make any conversation more difficult than necessary. I think you should better hold back. Take care of your own children as best as you can and let your mother do the same.

I Can't Please Her

I am nineteen years old and am supposed to take over my parents' business someday. Because of the opportunity to do a commercial apprenticeship here, I left home.. My aunt, who had moved to the north because of her marriage and who runs a retail business here, offered me a job.

I was also happy about the distance to my parents because the atmosphere lately has not been particularly pleasant. My aunt has taken me in like a son in her house, and I enjoy all the comforts like at home. She has been a widow for a year and a half and, as she says, was pleased about my arrival because then she is less lonely.

At first, I was very pleased with my new situation, but now the drawbacks are showing, although I make an effort in every respect, my aunt is never satisfied with me!

Either she criticizes my alleged inability to take responsibility and that I don't see the work lying right in front of me, or she finds me arrogant because I have taken care of pending work without asking her, as she puts it. When she was down with the flu, I took care of many things independently and couldn't always ask her. Now, that was too much independence for her. I had expected her to be pleased with me, but instead, she complained, even though there were no mistakes in the process.

This continues in the private sphere. Either I should have washed the car by myself, or I should have asked her beforehand so that I'm not washing the car when she ur-gently needs it. I think she is unjust and disregards my good intentions. What should I do?

Answer

I can well imagine that the new living situation so far away from home is becoming increasingly uncomfortable after its promising start. The longer you live together with your aunt, the more entangled you will become with each other, and the worse the mutual dissatisfaction will become. You have fallen into what can be described as a relationship trap.

This means that you have absolutely no chance of doing anything right! Whatever you do, it's wrong! But it takes two to tango! One who sets the trap and one who keeps falling into it. The relationship trap occurs when two mutually exclusive wishes are both to be satisfied, and either one or the other wish is used to evaluate the situation. So your aunt apparently wants a son in her house, whom she can mother, and who therefore must be kept small. At the same time, she needs a partner to replace her deceased husband, who should relieve her of responsibility and therefore must be grown-up and independent.

If you act as a son, your aunt lacks the partner and feels overwhelmed; if you show yourself as an adult who takes action according to his own judgement, your aunt feels disempowered and wishes for the son who recognizes her authority. No matter what role you play, you can't satisfy your aunt.

But it's not just your aunt sending a double message; you are doing the same, otherwise, this game could not work so perfectly. You have to decide what kind of relationship you actually want to have with your aunt. Are you the pampered nephew who is like a child in the house but is thus also dependent on the aunt's ideas and goodwill, or are you a young independent man who is completing a vocational training in his aunt's business. In the second case, you should move out of your aunt's house. As long as you want both, the comforts like a son and the freedoms like an adult, you are playing your aunt's game, and the accusations will never end.

I Can't Stand Her Proximity

One problem that particularly occupies me at this time of the year is the loneliness of the elderly and the addiction to pills that is supposed to make this loneliness seem more bearable. My over seventy-year-old mother-in-law has been taking pills for her soul for decades. She claims to feel happy about it but is unable to truly empathize with others and their needs and act accordingly. I am the one who suffers the most under her because I am the only one taking care of her. My husband stays out of it.

Last year, when Grandma fell seriously ill multiple times, I stepped in each time. Once I even took care of her in her apartment and slept there, which ended in a row when she started bossing me around. In this twisted way, she apparently gets healthy. Now I can make a wish. She probably wants to buy her way out; she has nothing else but material things. I guess I have to accept that she is the way she is. However, I can't stand her proximity in the long run.

The elderly are always the older ones. Just being older does not entitle one to demand that younger people adjust to all the demands of the older ones. We learned to honor thy father and mother. Will the next generation still do that? Who will want to earn high pensions for elderly people who want to live selfishly for decades and then criticize the younger ones? What could I offer in old age if I still have a clear mind, I wonder. Understanding, affection, acceptance of the different other human beings. Here with my mother-in-law, I thought I could practice that, but it exceeds my abilities.

Answer

All human relationships are based on reciprocity. Where real power relations do not establish dependencies, relationships are formed according to individual attributions. This means: Your mother-in-law's demands are as important as you make them. For your husband, for example, although it's his mother, they are apparently much less important because he cares less about it than you do. You clearly write: I can't stand her proximity. If you were to follow your feelings, that would mean you should protect yourself.

You would have to strictly distance yourself, care less for her, and do more of your own things. But you don't allow yourself to do that. The idea of leaving your mother-in-law more to herself gives you feelings of guilt—also in connection with the thought of how will it happen to me when I am old. You are correct when you assume that your mother-in-law's behavior is also related to the psychotropic drugs. An already poor ability to handle conflict and contact is totally reduced by years of pill-taking.

Fortunately, not all elderly people are like this. Those who have led a fulfilling life at a younger age continue to be lively in old age, take an interest in their environment, and have understanding and love for others. Your mother-in-law is probably a deeply unhappy person not just today. You have to decide if you want to feel responsible for her.

The Family Is Malicious

I'm sick of my husband's family. Both his parents are still alive, as well as three sisters and one brother, all with families. There is at least one celebration every month that we are obligated to attend. No matter how I behave, they always find something to criticize about me afterward. If I inquire about others' circumstances, I am nosy; if I act as carefree as always, I'm presumptuous; if I hold back and say little, I'm sulky.

My husband says not to worry about it, they're just like that, and you have to take them as they are. But I can't. Nobody is sincere in this family; everyone talks behind each other's back; feelings don't matter, it's always just about material things. My husband has gotten used to it. Unfortunately, he decided eight years ago to return to the family business. We also benefit from it, living in a very nice, large house that belongs to his parents, but that shouldn't mean my husband has to put up with being treated like dirt and demeaned daily by his father.

His older brother, on the other hand, who also receives his salary for his work in the company, has an easy life in my eyes and cherry-picks the best for himself. He is never criticized; instead, everything he does is praised to the skies. His children also receive nothing but hymns of praise, while our children, no matter their achievements, are never even mentioned.

I am increasingly unable to cope with the situation. If there were less contact, it might be bearable, but there are daily touchpoints, even if it's just my husband's evening report from

Answer

Your situation is difficult. You didn't even mention that a conflict is building up between you and your husband. You are stifling everything you'd have to say about his family, knowing your husband will trivialize it all. His pacification strategy has deeper reasons. Since childhood, he's been repressing that his parents have divided feelings for their children. There's a good, idealized son, which is the older brother, and a bad, devalued son, which is your husband.

Your husband has been fighting against the devaluation and rejection of his person since his childhood; he has developed a strategy of apparent indifference to protect himself from lifelong injuries caused by his parents. When he says you have to take the family as they are, it shields him from pain. But this claim is only correct for childhood; as adults, we have the freedom to arrange our own lives.

As the wife of the 'bad son,' you naturally get some of the aggression aimed at your husband. That you don't want to accept this is only natural and, by the way, also healthier. Your husband is probably not even aware of the connections. He is trying to get recognition from his father through double the effort. But that will never happen! It's a misfortune programmed for years. If you don't want to separate from your husband, and I assume that you don't, then your husband has to separate from this family that does not love him—even if that means losing economic security.

You can help him by not avoiding the conflict and by mirroring exactly what you observe and experience. Painful insights, unfortunately, cannot be spared for him. The more conscious your husband becomes of the evil relationship structures, the more willing he will be to undergo psychotherapy to resolve the unhealthy bonds of his childhood. Only then is he free to establish a new, more loving life with his new family.

No One Helps Me
With Household Chores

I have problems with my family. After a long search, I have finally found a part-time job in my trained profession. I was home for twelve years due to my children, who are now ten and eleven years old. I love my job and was able to get back into it quickly. I could be completely satisfied—if it weren't for my family. Everyone agreed that I would go back to work, and it was also clear that my husband and the children would have to help out more with the household chores.

But the reality—after three months, I can say—looks very different! No one is really helping me; everything falls back on me. My husband might put some of his dress shirts in the machine on Saturday, but I have to hang them up again, otherwise they would still be in there on Monday; and he doesn't even think to check if anything from me or the kids also needs to be washed.

The kids were initially quite willing, but that has already waned. Essentially, everything is as it has always been—with the only difference being that I'm not home from eight to one in the afternoon. And only I notice this difference because I now have to accomplish in the afternoon what I would have spread out over the entire day.

I've become an endlessly nagging mother who chases after her family. I really don't want to be like that, but I see no way

*out if I don't want to suffer from the double burden. How can I
get my family to help me?*

Answer

Your problem is very familiar to me, but I think your question is framed incorrectly. It assumes that doing household chores is primarily your responsibility, and other family members should merely help out. This might have been true when you were not working, but with your re-entry into the workforce, a fundamentally new situation has arisen. This requires a complete redistribution of responsibility for household and lifestyle management. This calls for both you and your husband to be willing to rethink and change old habits.

Your husband needs to learn to take responsibility in the household. This probably starts with improving his awareness. Men who have never been responsible for household chores often simply don't notice things like dirty doors or other people's dirty laundry. These things simply do not prompt them to act. If that's to change, women need to give them the opportunity. For example, you should not complete all the chores before men are even motivated to act themselves.

This means that you have to learn to let go of responsibility. As long as you remain the boss in household matters, the others can only be helpers—a role that is no fun for anyone. However, you cannot expect the household to look the same as it has for the past twelve years. Therefore, you have to let go of your old image and be surprised by a new, shared way of running the household. This is probably as hard for you as it is for your husband when he should start caring about his children's dirty socks.

Call for a family conference. Distribute tasks proportionally according to time and abilities and document the agreements in writing. Then comes the most important and hardest part for you. Only do what's on your list and not a single task more! Practice looking away and being patient. Your husband and children need time to adjust.

Thoughtless Gifts

I'm annoyed with my sister. Since she got divorced and I became widowed, and our children have moved out, we've grown closer again. We often go to the movies, have taken weekend trips, and of course, we celebrate all holidays together. We have a large family, so quickly twenty people gather for Christmas or birthdays. I always put a lot of thought into gifts. Because I write down throughout the year what someone might need or enjoy, I always have good gift ideas ready.

My sister, on the other hand, doesn't think at all. Usually, she calls me the day before asking what I'm giving and if I have an idea for her. This frequency annoys me, which I've told her, but nothing has changed. If I don't advise her, she makes thoughtless gifts that nobody can really enjoy.

Another bad habit is that she doesn't unwrap the gifts she receives; she leaves them and later regifts them. I believe that one should unwrap a gift in the presence of the giver so that one can thank them appropriately. I find my sister's behavior rude.

The peak of this occurred last Christmas. I actually received the same six mulled wine glasses from her that I had given her for her birthday. Even the wrapping paper was the same, and she didn't notice! I haven't confronted her about it because it's embarrassing for her, but my anger is growing. What do you think I should do about my sister?

Answer

The fact that your sister's behavior is becoming a problem for you mainly shows how much you fear confrontation. What are you afraid of? Could your sister be so sensitive that she breaks off contact with you? Or is she perhaps someone who easily becomes aggressive and hurtful? Relationships between sisters are usually no less complicated—perhaps more so—than those between friends, often because they carry baggage from childhood. Nevertheless, you should talk to her; otherwise, your repressed anger will gradually affect what seems to be a satisfying relationship for both of you. This should not happen during a celebration but either before or after.

Your sister has a very different attitude towards giving than you do. Those who don't enjoy giving often find it awkward to receive gifts. It may be embarrassing for her to be gifted, so her way of dealing with it appears rude but may actually express a personal issue. It seems to me that your sister, unlike you, rejects the whole idea of gifting within the large family.

She probably doesn't dare to openly oppose the tradition. However, it could well be that other adults also find all the gifting burdensome. I know many families where only the children are gifted.

You might want to use the exchanged mulled wine glasses as an opportunity to discuss the family tradition of gifting, rather than getting angry about it. What appears thoughtless to you in your sister is likely the expression of deep-seated reluctance. If she can be loving in other contexts, there's no reason to be angry with her.

My Mother Doesn't Leave Her Apartment

I have a brief question concerning my mother. She has been a widow for seven years and lives alone in her apartment. After my father's death, she became very reclusive. We children took this as a reaction to her loss. My sister and I agreed that we should leave her alone for a while. She also didn't want us to visit her. Since both of us daughters are married and have enough to do with our own families, it was quite convenient for us to respect her wish.

However, we're starting to worry now. It's been seven years since my father passed away, and she practically never leaves her apartment. She has her neighbor do her shopping. She doesn't come to family gatherings because they are too "hectic" for her. On her own birthday or Christmas, we're allowed to come for an hour, and then she ushers us out again. She shows little interest in her three grandchildren, except for sending packages punctually for all holidays.

She is sixty-one and physically healthy. This can't be normal! How do you assess such behavior?

Answer

Unfortunately, your description of the situation is quite brief, and neither your feelings nor those of your mother are discussed, making it difficult to assess. It's also not clear what role you and your sister are playing and whether you are trying to encourage your mother to go out. If your mother is happy within her own four walls, receives occasional visits, and could leave the house without problems if really necessary—for a doctor's visit, for example—then no one has the right to disturb her lifestyle.

It's more likely, however, that your mother doesn't leave the apartment out of fear and is thus not free in her choices. She would then be suffering from a so-called phobia, which means that the very idea of having to walk alone across the street causes her fear because public spaces, streets, squares, etc., seem somehow dangerous to her.

In a phobia, the fear, which actually arises from suppressed inner wishes, is projected outward. Open streets and squares, or, conversely, confined spaces, as well as animals, great heights, or pointed objects, and many more can become triggers of fear. Avoiding them helps control the anxiety. Perhaps she keeps the visits with her daughters so brief because she fears you might try to coax her into going out.

This avoidance, however, often means that personal life possibilities become very limited. In your mother's case, this would mean that anything that happens outside her apartment becomes inaccessible to her, resulting in a significant loss of quality of life. You should find out how she internally feels about her reclusiveness through conversations. You can do absolutely nothing without your mother's willingness to change.

It's also possible that your mother has undergone a personality change following your father's death. You could only find this out by taking more interest in your mother and learning more about her current life, so that you can compare her behavior and reactions today with those from earlier times. If your mother reacts to such efforts with hostility or agitation, then this is likely the case. Even then, you have to respect her way of living as long as she is not harming herself or others.

I Am "Just" a Housewife

I am forty-one, married, and have four school-age children. I am a so-called "just" housewife, meaning I manage a household of six people, including a big dog, two budgerigars, and a hamster, as well as a rather large garden. In fourteen years, I've been off work for only three days due to the flu; otherwise, I am up and about from 6:30 a.m. to late at night. I take care of everything and everyone, but no one ever asks about me or how I'm holding up.

My husband comes home at very irregular times. Sometimes he wants a hot meal at one in the morning, and so far, I've made it for him no matter how tired I was. He's been quite successful in recent years but is always exhausted. I know he's working hard for us, which does soften my perspective. However, I don't think it's right that he takes everything I do for granted. I never hear a word of appreciation from him, let alone from the children.

I know other mothers who are much more selfish, and sometimes I wonder if I'm missing out. Besides family, I hardly have time for anything that interests me. I thought things would lessen as the children got older, but it feels like it's only increasing. I constantly have to chauffeur one of the kids around since we live in the countryside. They make plans without consulting me, and I have to figure out where to find the time to drive them.

How can I get my family to consider my needs too? I think about everyone, but nobody thinks about me.

Answer

Your situation is far from unique. Many other women, who are also "just" housewives, share it to varying degrees. Wanting recognition after fourteen years of complete dedication is completely understandable. However, you are unlikely to get that because the inner logic of such dynamics usually leads to the opposite: long-standing habits create a sense of entitlement to your services, which would be indignantly demanded if you suddenly stopped. Your family knows nothing other than you being there for everyone and always being available. That's their normality.

If you are falling short and others aren't noticing, it's because you haven't been vocal enough about your own needs. Or, to put it another way: you've failed to care for yourself as lovingly as you do for others, and to claim what you need. Paradoxically, our needs are taken seriously by others only when we take them seriously ourselves. Protests are of little use; action is needed.

Specifically, this means saying no more often! Your children will only consult you about their plans when they've experienced their mother rejecting their requests for rides. Your relationship with your children seems to be an extension of the relationship you have with your husband, and gaining his recognition is undoubtedly most important for you.

Being needed does not automatically mean you are loved as a person. What would happen in your relationship if you were no longer the perfect mother for him and the children? The shared—probably unconscious—dream of total security at the cost of your own needs is detrimental.

Behind most successful men in our society is, as is generally known, a woman like you who frees him to pursue his ambitions by taking care of all the everyday drudgeries. It's only half true that your husband is working so hard for the family. He's also doing it for his own life goals. What are your life's wishes? If you see your selfless devotion to your husband and children as your primary life goal, then the satisfaction comes directly from mastering this task, and you don't need external recognition.

Our Mother Suffers
Due to the Family Conditions

My mother just turned sixty, my father is sixty-three. My mother's recent birthday was yet another occasion for a meeting with my siblings, where we've urged her for the hundredth time to separate and live alone but peacefully. Living with my father is pure torment for her, and has been for thirty-eight years of marriage. He bullies her all day long. In his eyes, she can't even properly place a cup on the table.

He himself never lifts a finger to help with household chores. I can't remember a time when he ever praised anything she did, or even silently acknowledged it. He always has something to criticize, often completely out of the blue. My mother has virtually no life of her own. She exists only for him. He controls her money and scrutinizes her expenses. Once a year, at Christmas (which coincides with her birthday), he takes her clothes shopping; she has no money of her own to fulfill her own wishes.

Even a simple community college course is out of reach for her due to the inability to pay the fees. She knows no social life or variety, as my father disapproves and prefers to sit in front of the TV. Her only outside activity is walking the dog. My father is inherently anti-social and stubborn, but my mother is actually a cheerful woman, and she suffers under these conditions. However, she can't find the courage to leave, even though we would all support her.

She says she should have separated when she was younger; now she feels she can't do it anymore. But back then, she always said that separation was not an option because the children needed a family. It tortures me to see how she lives. But all our advice is in vain. Do we as children have any other options?

Answer

Unfortunately, no. You are not responsible for your parents' lives; they are adults and have made their decisions, whether consciously or unconsciously. As hard as it may be for you to bear this feeling of helplessness, the solutions you see, like separation, are your solutions and not your mother's. If separation had been an option for her, she would have pursued it, especially with so much support from her children.

It's often hard to see from the outside that people, despite all their suffering, also derive some hidden benefit from the situation. Your mother's inner life balance may not be as bad as you perceive it to be. Only when the pressure to suffer reaches unbearable limits will our will to change, at any cost, become strong enough to overcome our fear of the unknown.

Your parents, like many people, have settled into their everyday unhappiness because they fear taking the risk of trying something new, and because even the claim for more happiness and satisfaction in life makes them feel guilty. Practice serenity and accept your powerlessness in this case. The realization that we can achieve much less than we wish means that we become more modest and thus more mature and realistic. The only thing you can really do is not follow in your mother's footsteps and arrange your own life better.

How Can I Help My Sister?

My sister is in an unhappy marriage. She moved close to us a year ago with her husband and increasingly involves me in her marital drama. She is a trained bookseller but has quit her job for his sake and now runs a pub with him. Financially, they don't seem to have direct worries, but this kind of work, especially staying up late, is very stressful for my sister. The real problem, however, is her husband. In my eyes, he is an alcoholic, a reckless, unpredictable braggart who repeatedly manages to wrap my sister around his finger with theatrical scenes.

In my sister's eyes, the enormous alcohol consumption is part of everyday work life. Especially during periods when everything is supposedly going well, she idealizes him completely. Then he's an all-around great guy, looks fantastic in some new clothes, entertains the whole place with music and jokes, making the guests say there's no cozier pub anywhere else.

He's also allegedly an incredibly good lover, giving her gifts like no other man. If this view were consistent, I would just pity her for falling for this deceiver and wait quietly. But unfortunately, the situation flips entirely at shorter or longer intervals, and then my sister is just a pile of misery, clinging to me on the phone for hours.

She barricades herself in her room, has terrible anxiety attacks and fears that her husband will break into the room and kill her. I have repeatedly offered her to stay with me temporarily if she wants to leave. Sometimes we even discuss concrete

Answer

You probably have to come to terms with the fact that you can't really help your sister at the moment. She lives with her partner in a perpetual conflict situation, where the abrupt change of moods is a condition for the relative stability of this relationship. Like many people, your sister can't tolerate the coexistence of good and bad traits in her partner.

Ambivalence, which means that many things in the world are not only good but also bad at the same time and vice versa, is a fundamental feature of reality. Your sister escapes from reality by splitting her too painful perception that her husband is simultaneously a reckless drinker and an attractive, entertaining partner. This splitting corresponds to an early childhood stage of conflict processing, which means that the person always only sees one side of reality; the other is denied. In your sister's case, her partner is either the best man in the world for her or, on the contrary, a monster threatening her.

There is no connection between feelings and perception. Since, however, reality cannot be permanently rejected, you have the fluctuations you described. On the positive, wish-fulfilling side, one lives in illusions and idealizes everything, that is, sees everything more beautiful and more perfect than it actually is. On the negative side, everything is totally devalued and made worse than it is. The unconscious anger about this now perceived total inadequacy is perceived as an external threat and, of course, triggers great fear.

If your sister succeeds in splitting off all the negatives, especially the disappointment and anger about her husband, she feels temporarily omnipotent, has everything under control—if the split-off aggressions overwhelm her, she feels completely powerless. You can really do nothing more than be there when your sister calls for help. But prepare for the fact that your conversations with your sister will hardly have any real consequences, so you at least won't lose your footing in reality.

My Second Family Is More Important to Me.

I am somewhat in a predicament and was wondering what I could best do. I am twenty-four, male, and studying German and Music for teaching. My hometown is not too far from my place of study, so I can arrange to go back to my old home about twice a month. However, I do not visit my parents, but my second family, as I call them. I have been welcome in this family since I was ten years old. They lived two streets away from my parents' house, but the two families did not know each other. The man was my elementary school teacher, and we became friends.

Soon I was spending more time with them than at my own home. They had a piano, which I could play whenever I wanted. Although I managed to get my parents to pay for piano lessons, they never asked if I should practice at home; they were just content with me supposedly practicing at school. My parents have not heard me play until my graduation ceremony. My father then simply said that his years of investment in me had paid off.

My parents have no clue what really interests me. I found all the support and recognition I needed in my second family. For the children there, all of whom are much younger than I am, I am somewhat like the big brother. They are very happy when I visit. Both of my substitute parents are also interested in everything that happens in my studies. The same cannot be said for my parents' home. When I am there, which is rare enough, we usually quickly move on to the agenda.

Now, by some stupid coincidence, my mother has found out that I am "constantly" in town, just a few streets away, and don't think it's necessary to visit her. She is deeply hurt and blames me. I find this very uncomfortable and don't know how to behave now. The fact is that my second family is much more important to me than my real family, something my mother will never understand.

Answer

Actually, you have the same issue as always: your family does not understand you. The only new thing is the accusations from your mother. You have apparently successfully hidden from her for fourteen years where you hang out when you're not at home. Since the accusations do affect you, or are at least uncomfortable, this means that there is some bond with your original family, or maybe just with your mother. If that were not the case, you would be indifferent to your mother's reaction. It's understandable that she is hurt. Unlike children, whose bonds to the family change, mothers usually maintain their affection for their children for a lifetime.

For the first ten years, you only lived in your real family, and the love and care from your mother provided a basis for everything that was possible for you in life. Without this foundation, you could not have developed your musical talent, for example. Unfortunately, in relation to parents, we take everything that was good for granted and overemphasize the inevitable shortcomings.

Your parents were apparently not capable of supporting you musically as you would have wished. The fact that you found a second family is a tremendous stroke of luck but should not lead to devaluing your real parents. You should catch up as soon as possible on what you have missed so far, namely introducing your first and second families to each other. An external rapprochement between the two families would benefit your inner peace.

Practically, this means that you first have to talk to your parents and explain both the situation and your feelings to them. This will not go without hurt feelings, but if the relationship with the parents is no longer burdened by hidden hostilities and secrets, you may also find a new and now adult form of relationship with them.

As a Grandmother, I Am Not Accepted.

I only have a single son who, unfortunately, lives very far away from me. He is married, but until now, the marriage had been childless. After many years of waiting, I finally became a grandmother last year. My son, daughter-in-law, and I were filled with joy over the healthy baby girl. My problem now is as follows: I recently visited my children for the first time and was looking forward to it. I wanted to finally hold my grandchild in my arms. Unfortunately, the visit did not go well at all. I increasingly felt that I was being looked upon with rejection.

For example, when I wanted to pick up my grandchild in the morning (I heard her chatting in her room), my son took me aside and corrected me. His wife always wants to be the first to greet the child in the morning. And when I sneezed while looking at a flower with the little one, I was basically labeled as foolish. These are just two examples from a series of similar events.

I am so sad about it and sometimes have to cry. Then again, I am so angry that I never want to visit my children again. I can't be that bad of a mother; my son has become a successful and capable man, but as a grandmother, I am not accepted. What can I do so that my children are kinder to me and accept me?

Answer

Your children's behavior likely has a long backstory. The nature of the relationship you had with your son before he got married plays a role, as does your personal relationship with your daughter-in-law. The young mother herself might also be struggling with her new role, which has nothing to do with you, but your son naturally sides with his wife.

Regardless, your impression that you are not particularly welcome in the young family is probably accurate. The described small episodes indicate that beneath polite manners, a lot of aggression and rejection are lurking.

A good way to improve relationships is always to address such suppressed feelings. But this requires courage and a willingness to talk from both sides. You certainly won't come away unscathed in such a discussion. If you want to talk about your disappointments, you must also listen to what your children have against you. If such a conversation occurs, it would be good if you could simply listen to what the children say. Do not try to justify yourself, as both sides usually have their points. Mutual understanding is always better than defending one's own position.

Another way to cope with the situation is to come to terms with reality as it is. Clearly, you are just a visiting grandmother, and normally your son's family gets along well without you. If you fully accept your role as a visitor without having any expectations, the atmosphere might relax next time.

Entirely New Customs

We are an older married couple. Naturally, after thirty-seven years of marriage, we have many cherished, established habits. Our youngest son moved out eight years ago, so as retirees, we didn't have to accommodate anyone else. Now, a big change has occurred in our lives, and I dread what we've gotten ourselves into.

We've taken in my husband's older brother into our home. He is the only remaining relative from my husband's side, so it was especially my husband's wish to have him here. Until now, he lived in East Germany, childless, and very lonely after the death of his wife.

He accepted our tentative offer to move in with us with great enthusiasm. Sooner than we thought, he arrived and occupied a vacant attic room in our house. He is a pleasant person and very similar to my husband. However, entirely new customs now reign in our house.

For example, we used to go to bed early, as we are both early risers. Now, at least once a week, the two men have a long evening involving much alcohol, which is not good for my husband. Meals are skipped because the two are out and about, and lunchtime doesn't fit into their plans. Recently, they turned the living room into a crafting workshop for an entire weekend. According to a book, they were folding paper airplanes. I was near a nervous breakdown because there was nowhere left to sit.

My complaints fall on deaf ears. I dread thinking about this continuing. I already regret our decision to take in the brother.

Answer

You don't specify how long the brother has been living with you. In the first few weeks, the joy of reunion can disrupt the daily routine. When the brother is no longer seen as a guest, normality will return. However, if you want to treat the brother as more than just a renter, it's a significant change to move from living as a couple to living as a trio.

The old intimacy focused solely on each other is probably gone. This likely saddens you, even if you're not fully aware of it. Aren't you also jealous of the camaraderie between the brothers, which excludes you? Your husband has gained reinforcement in the form of his brother. Perhaps he's fulfilling desires he couldn't fulfill with you, making you both angry and helpless.

In any case, your husband seems to be enjoying himself, and you should allow him that pleasure. Unlike you, he doesn't question the decision to bring in his brother. Therefore, he won't be receptive to your complaints. He enjoys this new life.

Avoid creating divisions: you alone against the two men. Try to turn the adventurous duo into a cheerful trio instead. A power struggle is likely to be lost, and it would ruin everyone's joy for life. Join in the fun instead! Maybe you'll discover you also enjoy folding paper airplanes or other things that were not part of your routine.

Problems With Children

*Children are like little mirrors,
reflecting not just our strengths,
but also our weaknesses.
The true goal of parenting is not
perfection, but understanding.*

—Brigitte Halenta

Am I a Bad Mother?

I'm a forty-two-year-old full-time working mom with a thirteen-year-old son. We've been living without his father since he was two. We've had some really tough times. I'm self-employed and had to build my livelihood from scratch. His birthdays have always been special days. I've always taken extra time for him. It was very important to him because I've always pampered him on those days.

Now he's about to turn fourteen, and that's where my problem lies. The weekend when he has his birthday, I unknowingly scheduled work appointments, meaning I won't be able to see him until the evening of his birthday. It pains me that this has happened. I can't (and don't want to) back out of my work commitment for the day for financial reasons. Our financial security depends on it.

I know my son was very hurt when I explained my decision to him. However, he understood and consoled himself (and me) that we would celebrate in the evening.

So far, so good. What is absolutely unbearable for me, however, is the reaction in the house. The neighbors pity my son and give him the impression that he has a bad mother. Shouldn't I have tried to cancel my appointments no matter what the cost?

Answer

The judgments of the neighbors are so unbearable for you because they voice what you secretly fear yourself. You think you're failing your son, not just on his birthday, but maybe throughout all the years you've been living alone with him. But it's also an accomplishment to raise a child while being fully employed. If you were a single dad, people would admire how you manage everything. Mothers, however, are expected to be superhuman. Meeting all the needs of the children is seen as normal; disappointing them is a disaster. But children are, rightfully so, insatiable, and no mother in the world, not even the best, can fully satisfy the demands of her children. When the children later tally up what was missing or wrong, all mothers are bad mothers.

What's crucial for a child is having a good enough mother, so they can develop into a mentally and emotionally healthy individual with her help. The inevitable pains along the way also strengthen them and are part of life. Your son may certainly have it harder than children from complete families, but he might also learn to be independent and responsible in his situation.

What's most important, it seems to me, is letting him feel how important he is to you on this birthday and always, and that it pains you when you can't meet his needs. Stand by your decision! You didn't want to cancel the appointments. Your son is important to you. Both can't always go hand in hand. You, as a single mom, have probably already made many decisions favoring your son at the cost of career advancement.

Being in this conflict between child and job is your reality, which you have to negotiate over and over. You shouldn't feel guilty. Not just children and men, but mothers too have a right to their own lives.

The Youngest Is a Problem Child

We have four children. The three older ones have never given us much trouble, but our youngest daughter is becoming a problem child for me, and that's why I'm writing to you. I don't know how to behave anymore. I've tried both love and strictness, but nothing works.

I've probably made many mistakes. My husband is rarely home. I feel responsible for the children. Our youngest is eight years old and was finally the long-awaited daughter after three sons. She's in third grade with just average performance but has many big and small problems with her classmates. Until kindergarten, we only had joy with her. She really had everything a child could wish for. I stopped working altogether; I used to work part-time and now could take care of her around the clock. She was also the princess for her older brothers and my husband.

Maybe we spoiled her too much because difficulties started in kindergarten. She couldn't adjust, and we eventually had to take her out because she only cried there. Even today, she hardly plays with other children and prefers to stay at home. She's the sweetest child as long as you don't ask anything of her. As soon as I ask something of her, scenes ensue. Almost nothing goes smoothly in our house anymore without major drama.

This is already irritating, but now she's also starting to blackmail us with alleged illnesses. In the mornings, she feels so sick that she can hardly speak, but by late morning, she's already chipper and enjoys the school-free morning. Recently, we didn't go on an urgent family visit to the Rhineland because she was sick again on the day of departure. But the next day, her illness seemed to have vanished. Although I no longer believe her performances, I can't counter her, and there might really be something serious one time. I'm worried about how this will continue.

Answer

I assume you've consulted your pediatrician to rule out anything serious, so we can exclude possible medical reasons for your daughter's behavior. All that remains to be said is that your eight-year-old daughter firmly has the entire family in her grip. You're rightly concerned about the future. These are the methods of an eight-year-old, which will escalate as she gets older.

As always in interpersonal relationships, no one is solely to blame. Your little daughter isn't the only problem, but the entire family who participates in her performances, making her behavior possible in the first place, is involved. The key figure is probably you. After three sons, having a daughter was so important to you that you developed an overly close relationship with the child. This made it possible for even the little child to play the dominant role in the family through you as a mediator. The current situation is annoying not only for you but also harmful for the sons.

Most importantly, the daughter herself needs help. Although she manages to achieve her goals through all available means, she's not really doing well. I would strongly recommend family therapy. All family members can only benefit from it, and your little princess gets the opportunity to come out of her lonely special role and become a normal child among other children.

The Boy Is Different From Other Children

I always say I'm a seasoned grandmother. Since I became a widow twelve years ago, I've been looking after children from my family and my large circle of friends. Word has spread that I'm happy to step in when parents need to run errands or go on trips. I also have four biological grandchildren who love coming to me.

The youngest grandchild, a two-year-old boy, is now somehow concerning me. I find that the boy is different from other children. The parents don't want to hear about it; they just find him difficult. I always thought that all children love cuddling, but not Patrick. He didn't like to be held as a baby, not even by his mother, and seemed happiest when left alone.

It's hard to really interest him in anything. He acts like he doesn't hear and looks the other way. We recently had some kittens, and all the children were delighted, except Patrick. When I tried to take his hand, he ran away screaming. Watching over him is really difficult because he's very wild and doesn't respect prohibitions. Sometimes I think he's somehow delayed because he keeps doing the same foolish things and gets hurt.

Otherwise, he often seems quite smart to me, although he doesn't talk much yet. Somehow, I'm not happy with this child. I have him three afternoons a week and still don't have a warm relationship with him. Whenever he is picked up, I want to talk to my daughter-in-law about him. But she brushes it off and says, "Yes, yes, he does the same at home; he's quite content with you, what do you want?" I'm at a loss and just continue. But my bad feeling remains.

Answer

You have a lot of experience with children and good observational skills. Both equip you to notice something about little Patrick that the parents may not see, or perhaps don't want to see. I assume Patrick is the first child, and the mother has no basis for comparison. The boy is showing what are called autistic traits in his behavior.

Early childhood autism is a very serious condition that must be treated; otherwise, developmental delays will become increasingly significant as he grows older. You describe behavioral abnormalities in Patrick that are typical for autism: The child has difficulty making contact with others, including the mother, and rejects affection. Sensory activity is limited, making the child difficult to engage visually and audibly. New experiences scare him more than they pique his interest.

These children usually resist any change strongly. They cannot recognize or remember real dangers, leading to repeated injuries. They are physically very active. Language development is delayed, but there are outstanding individual abilities that don't correspond to their overall developmental level, making them appear very intelligent.

Perhaps you have also noticed other peculiarities. Early childhood autism also includes the following behaviors: Outbursts of laughter, crying, or anger at minor or invisible triggers for others. Monotonous handling of objects, especially favorite items. Repeating the same games over and over. Isolating oneself, withdrawing to corners.

You should and must speak with the boy's parents. There is a serious suspicion of early childhood autism here. A precise medical diagnosis is necessary for clarification so that, if necessary, appropriate therapeutic measures can be initiated immediately.

The Children Are Being Raised Incorrectly

Recently, I went on a long car trip with my daughter-in-law and my two grandchildren and was thus very intensely involved with them for a whole four days. I love my grandchildren and also like my daughter-in-law; this being the case, it turns my stomach to witness their parenting methods.

Only prohibitions, commands, and threats are issued, and the children are rarely attended to. The children react accordingly: initially shy with the unfamiliar, and then so uncontrolled that it makes my hair stand on end. People on the street are kicked or hit. Most react kindly, as the children are still young. In stores, everything is touched, cabinets and drawers are opened, and so on. Where is this leading?

I would like to share my concerns with my children, but then I'm told: Don't interfere! Yes, it's even possible that they might react incomprehensibly and not know what I'm talking about. I suspect that my daughter-in-law is passing on what she herself experienced in her family. I treated my son differently when he was little. He doesn't have the main influence on the children, and I don't want to hide behind him. What should I do, that's my question?

Answer

As difficult as it will be for you, you can't do much without causing unrest in your son's family. The youngsters must live their lives and make their own experiences. Whether something is still perceived as help or already as annoying interference depends on the feelings that your son and daughter-in-law have towards you.

It is, of course, correct that such a suppressive and restrictive upbringing is not good for the children and leads to behavior that oscillates between extreme reticence and defiance. Since you react so alarmed, I assume that you can assess how much damage is being done to the children. You raised your son differently, more attentively and affirmatively.

If the nature of your relationship with your son allows, I would first try to have a conversation with him and share your concerns. Perhaps once alerted, your son can consciously counterbalance with his different attitude towards children.

As long as a direct conversation with your daughter-in-law is not possible, you can only cautiously do something indirectly, such as drawing attention to books and courses on parenting issues. Perhaps your daughter-in-law can be reached this way. Since she surely has a lot of trouble with the children, she will be interested in learning how she could make her task as a mother easier.

You best guard your own peace of mind by avoiding such long and intense time spent with your daughter-in-law and grandchildren in the future.

I Live Only for My Son

I have been a widow for four years and have lived only for my son since my husband's death. He is now twelve. Lately, I've been worried about him and would like to hear your opinion. He is increasingly falling into bad company. Every afternoon he's with two thirteen-year-old boys. I rarely know exactly where they are because my son doesn't tell me anymore, or simply lies to me. But there have already been serious problems twice.

They broke into a garden shed and smoked there, and they "borrowed" a stranger's bike on the street, which was later broken. My son has changed a lot since he's been with these boys. My advice does nothing. He used to always be at home, helping me, or we would watch TV. Now he is constantly away.

I am getting increasingly sad and am also afraid that I won't be able to assert myself anymore as he gets older, as he already does what he wants. I don't want to make a parenting mistake. Especially when you're alone and carry the responsibility, it is very difficult.

Answer

It is certainly difficult to raise children alone, even if you don't have immediate financial concerns, because you have to deal with all problems alone. But you share this fate with many single mothers and fathers. To relieve your burden, I suggest you connect with an association for single parents. Contacts and conversations with people in the same life situation can help you break out of your isolation.

Like many single parents, you make a very common mistake. You focus too much on your son. The boy is a replacement partner for you, and no child can handle that role. A twelve-year-old is already striving for his own circle of life outside the family. In addition to school, he needs self-determined activities with peers.

You should be concerned about a child who mainly stays at home at this age and seeks the closeness of his parents. Either he has not yet developed enough independence because he is overprotected, or he is – openly stated or silently – needed for tasks in the family, so that he experiences his own wishes only with a guilty conscience and therefore prefers to give them up.

In your case, the latter seems more likely. You need your son at home because then you don't feel so alone. Your son is probably trying to claim a freedom that you don't want to give him at the moment. You are right to fear that this behavior will increase rather than decrease in the future.

Change the situation for yourself and your son. You need adult friends and your own interests that go beyond your child. The boy needs new friends, new activities, and a space to try out new things. Think with him about what could bring him joy. Encourage him. Maybe he wants to play soccer or go fishing and doesn't dare to say it. It's time for you to stop living only for your son, otherwise, in the end, the boy will have to live only for you because you have no other support in life than him.

Stress With Homework

I'm a grandmother who looks after her neighbor's children twice a week. Since my children and grandchildren live further away, this is a nice activity for me because I like children. I enjoy playing and crafting with them. The girl is four and goes to kindergarten; the boy is eight and is in elementary school. Now he is supposed to do his homework with me. He is a good student, but very slow when it comes to homework. He fidgets at the table, explains all sorts of things to me, and takes forever. When the parents come home, they are naturally annoyed if the homework isn't done, because the next leisure appointment like playing tennis or badminton is on the schedule.

Then, loud words sometimes follow, which I hear next door. How should I behave? People always say that you shouldn't talk about how it used to be with my children. I want to help the young parents. I've noticed that the older one likes to play with things that concern the age group of three- to five-year-olds. Otherwise, he is a sharp little guy and can read very well. I enjoy listening to him a lot, and he enjoys it too. He just needs twice the time for homework because he always lets himself be distracted.

Are today's children too over-scheduled? What can I do so that the child completes his homework joyfully, and still has free time, and grows up without stress and tears?

Answer

First of all, I want to say that I find your commitment to the neighbor's children very commendable. If all grandparents without grandchildren would take care of children in their immediate neighborhood, it would be a great win for both sides. I also agree with your view that children at this age should not have stress and should have enough free time to play. There are many poor children who have a timetable like an adult manager. Most of the time, it is the parents' ambition that leads to more extracurricular tasks than are good for the children. Then, the children simply have to function well to fit everything in. Procrastination with homework could also be understood as a silent protest.

But your eight-year-old can have many other reasons for why he takes so much time. If he can read well and is otherwise sharp, as you write, then the homework is not the real problem; rather, it is a fundamental issue that arises.

For you as a surrogate grandmother, it will be difficult to find out what it is. An open conversation with the parents could be useful. It would also be interesting to find out how he behaves at school. He cannot be a good student if he takes as much time there as he does at home. So, he would have a problem that has less to do with performance and more to do with relationships.

Perhaps he is jealous of his little sister. She was born when he was at a very sensitive age himself. Your observation that he does not play with age-appropriate toys suggests that he wants to be small again to get as much attention as his little sister.

You may be focusing intensively on the little one when the older brother is supposed to do homework, and that is what distracts him. He tries to draw attention to himself by telling you things. I am sure that with careful observation, you will find out what it is. It would also be possible to talk openly with the little one. Sometimes even children at this age know very well what they lack.

The Daughter Has Transformed

"Small children, small worries; big children, big worries," so the saying goes, but I never thought that our only daughter would cause us so much trouble. She is twenty-two, and my husband and I always agreed that we have a model child—in every respect. She has never given us cause for concern. Neither in school nor anywhere else. Her nature is friendly, and wherever she goes, she becomes a favorite.

Now, however, she is unrecognizable. She has transformed and no longer shows any consideration; she doesn't care about the feelings of many dear people anymore. The cause of this change is a man she's been seeing for six months. One would think he's inciting her. This man is married, has two small children, and is pulling the wool over our poor daughter's eyes, as she believes everything he says. Rational persuasion is futile.

To fully understand this misfortune, you need to know that our daughter has been engaged for a year to a decent young man who sincerely loves her, and whom we greatly appreciate. Because of the expected marriage, we've also entered into business connections with the young man's family. Both families have also financially contributed to building a house for the young couple.

We all suffer greatly with the young man, who is like a child in our house. His parents naturally find our daughter's behavior disgraceful and urge him to break off the engagement. However, he continues to hold onto his love for our daughter. I can't bear to watch what he has to put up with anymore. My husband has retreated into bitter silence. I stand there, helpless. I cannot stand by idly as our daughter destroys her happiness.

Answer

I assume that, although you don't state it explicitly, your daughter is having a sexual relationship with another man beside her fiancé. The blame for her transformation is not really on the other man who influences her against her fiancé, but rather it's a natural event: Your daughter has fallen in love with another man! It's her feelings that are bringing about this change in behavior, and they are apparently strong feelings, otherwise, she wouldn't have the courage to act openly against the expectations and agreements of two families.

What you consider your daughter's happiness—the decent young man, the new house built by the families—may not necessarily be what your daughter desires. That she has always been an exemplary child and has always met her parents' expectations suggests that she has probably suppressed many of her own desires that would have put her in conflict with her parents. Perhaps she's seeking something in this new relationship that belongs entirely to her and isn't sanctioned by her parents.

As unexpected and bitter as this development must be for you, you should stay out of it or better yet, try to understand what your daughter is going through. She's facing the disapproval of two families, which is undoubtedly difficult for her and likely causing her much guilt. How your daughter ultimately decides should be entirely up to her. It would be good for parents from both families to have a discussion—not to assign blame, but to establish reasonable arrangements in all practical matters, creating a space where the young people can decide for or against each other without parental pressure or material constraints.

The Niece Is Spiraling Out of Control

My brother and I come from a very broken family, so for both of us, it was important to create order and harmony in our own families. I have four children, and my brother has only one daughter. This daughter is the apple of his eye. He has spoiled her since she was young, and I've always feared that this could backfire. My niece is now sixteen and has been terrorizing her parents for the past two years.

My brother has always done everything she wanted. He makes good money and has accommodated all her whims. Essentially, he's adjusted his whole life to suit her moods. My sister-in-law is not in good health and has never had much say in anything. My niece seems to repay her father's love very poorly. It started with her lying to him shamelessly, dragging him into embarrassing situations. When confronted, she'd lash out at him verbally.

Her daily behavior became more and more princess-like, and she would not lift a finger at home. My brother attributed everything to puberty and was understanding about it all. But then, the household became a scene of constant fighting. My niece became more and more defiant, slammed doors, and even threw dishes. I slowly became scared of her and saw my worst fears confirmed.

Recently, when my sister-in-law was away at a health re-treat, a massive argument erupted between my niece and her father over a boy in her class. My niece got so angry that she took a kitchen knife and stabbed her father in the back, narrowly missing his kidney. My brother pulled out the knife, and then comforted his crying daughter. He even concocted a lie to the doctors to protect her from the police. How can we go on like this? My niece is absolutely out of control. I want to help my brother, but how? What do you think?

Answer

At the risk of provoking your anger, the issue here is not your niece; it's your brother. Your niece is sixteen and has a father who suffocates her with his misplaced love. She's resorted to stabbing him in desperation, yet even that hasn't distanced him from her. He continues to indulge, excuse, and deny the hatred expressed through her actions.

What more does she have to do? Your brother has showered his daughter with love, albeit an exaggerated form, likely to cover his own painful childhood experiences. Whether your niece senses that her father's love wasn't genuinely about her, but more about fulfilling his own emotional needs, is debatable. Either way, she's now at an age where good fathering should mean granting independence, something your brother can't seem to do.

You're right: excessive pampering does no good. Your niece is still at an age where development isn't complete. She urgently needs to move out, perhaps into a supervised living community where she can learn boundaries. Your brother, however, will likely resist this, believing he can't live without his daughter.

Unless he lets go, your niece, in her understandable quest for autonomy, may resort to desperate measures. Your brother urgently needs psychotherapy. Talking to him will be difficult. If he doesn't listen, you may have no option but to involve child services.

He's Taking My Grandchildren
Away From Me

I am ashamed of my problem. Even my husband thinks that such ugly feelings don't suit me at all. But I am jealous, so much so that I can hardly think of anything else. Here's the sad story: At 27, after five years of marriage, I got divorced. The entire time was a nightmare, and when it was over, I was left with two young children, no money, and no career. My ex-husband was untraceable abroad and paid nothing. I had a very hard time.

Two years later, I got married for the second time and have been happily married for twenty-two years. We don't have children in this marriage, but my husband has always treated my two daughters from the first marriage like his own children. Both daughters are married and live nearby, and we have—now I must almost say 'had'—a lot of contact. I care deeply for my grandchildren, two boys and a girl. They bring me great joy, especially the youngest one, whom I looked after for months when my daughter was ill.

But here's the twist: A year ago, my ex-husband reappeared. He's widowed and reasonably wealthy. He bought a house here and actively sought a relationship with his daughters. After twenty-five years of silence, this man dares to stake claims on his children, whom he never cared for! At first, I couldn't believe it, but it looks like he has succeeded—primarily through the grandchildren. Particularly one daughter values him, often invites him, and accepts gifts. The grandchildren are quite smitten with him because he's amusing; he plays madly with them, while my husband is more reserved.

Every family celebration has become a torture for me. Will he come or not; then I won't go, as I can't bear the sight of this false harmony between him and the children. He poisons the atmosphere for me. I feel like he's taking my grandchildren away from me, and it gnaws at me. So this is the thanks for thirty years of effort and worry! And everything just falls into his lap. I've almost had a falling-out with my daughters over this. They say I'm selfish and irreconcilable. My husband is just bewildered by me.

Answer

You indeed have a bitter pill to swallow. I completely understand your anger and jealousy. It's essential now to take these ugly feelings seriously and not to be ashamed of them. They are there and justifiable. Talk in detail to your husband about it so that he can understand and empathize with you; otherwise, you will feel abandoned by everyone.

You can't do much more than watch how this story unfolds—a story that is complicated for all involved. On your side, the old feelings of anger and bitterness against the father of your daughters, who deserted his family, resurface. Your daughters are forming new, completely independent relationships with their long-lost father, over which you have no control, but they are also caught in a loyalty conflict with you.

For the grandchildren, it's easiest—they simply gain a new fun grandfather who spoils them. Your ex-husband might be trying to make amends through the grandchildren for what he failed to do for his own children. He is actually taking something away from you that had solely belonged to you—the love of the children and grandchildren. This seems like a great injustice to you. But, unfortunately, you have to live with it.

My Son Is Always Daydreaming

I'm concerned about what will become of my son if he doesn't learn to work without dawdling. He's now eleven and in the fifth grade of middle school. If he continues like this, he won't make it to the next grade. He consistently brings home poor grades, not because he doesn't understand the material, but because he only completes half the tasks in the allotted time. The same goes for homework; everything takes an eternity. Even the slowness with which he draws lines drives me crazy.

But it's not just schoolwork. It's the same with everything else. If I don't push him, he spends an hour in the bathroom and another at the breakfast table. With a roll in his hand, he stares out the window and daydreams. Heaven knows where his thoughts are; certainly not on what he should be doing. His father is similarly inclined and, for that reason, hasn't achieved much. When we separated four years ago, I swore I would make sure my son didn't turn out the same way.

I'm solely responsible for him because his father doesn't care at all. I try both carrots and sticks with the child, but instead of getting better, things are getting worse. What can I do? I want the boy to have a good future.

Answer

The difference in pace was apparently a significant point of contention in your marriage. You could separate from your husband because you were incompatible, but you can't do that with your son. Your slow-paced husband and now your slow-paced son are certainly types opposite to your temperament, and I can understand that their daydreaming gets on your nerves.

It's unfortunate for both of you that your son doesn't take after you. But you can't reprogram him against his inner nature; you must learn to accept him and his ways. Your constant prodding could potentially make things even worse. Perhaps in protest against the imposition of being like his mother and not being allowed to be himself, he may slow down even more.

If you continue to project the disappointment and anger you had in your marriage onto your son, and if you already see in the 11-year-old's daydreaming the precursors of later failures as an adult, you're harming him instead of helping him. He already has a hard enough time keeping up in school; at home, he desperately needs his mother's understanding.

Maybe try to find out what the boy is actually dreaming about. I would guess it's situations where he, or a character with whom he can identify, succeeds and is loved and admired by everyone. If he received a bit more recognition in reality, he might not need to daydream as much. As hard as it may be for you, practice patience. Children want to become themselves, not the children we adults would like them to be.

The Youngest Son Is the Odd One Out

We have been a solid craftsman family for generations, we have a carpentry business, that's for starters. We have three sons. The oldest has just finished his training and will one day take over our business, the middle one is in his final year at a secondary school, and our youngest is in the ninth grade of high school. The high school was already a concession by my husband because the boy's teacher pressed for it. What we get out of it becomes clearer every day. The boy brings ideas and opinions home that repeatedly lead to conflicts with my husband. I regret this very much. Until now, I have always been on my husband's side, because I think that the boy has no right to provoke his father, who is a respectable man even if he only went to a public school. But recently, I've had doubts.

My husband has found a way to torment the boy. He accidentally overheard our son reading me a self-written poem. In fact, it is true that the boy has been writing poems for some time, but no one in the family knows anything about it except me. This time it was about a love for a classmate, which as he wrote, unfortunately, was just a flash in the pan. Since then, my husband teases our son whenever he can. He refers to him as "our poet" and uses the word "flash in the pan" ironically in all possible contexts. I find this terrible and see how our son suffers.

But my husband is really furious about it and thinks that the boy is the odd one out. Even if I find his poetry silly, I don't have to tell him that. When he is older, he will laugh about it himself. I already see how our son is increasingly withdrawing.

He has always been more sensitive than the other two. When I ask my husband to be a little more cautious and less ironic with the boy, I hear: He has to be able to take it. My husband is just stubborn, and I have no hope of changing him. My question to you is, what can I do in this case?

Answer

Poems generally deal with feelings, and your problem reflects how your family handles feelings. You probably operate on necessities and the harsh realities of everyday life, and there is no room for feelings and their expression in artistic forms. Your husband is not just stubborn, but he also wards off all feelings, and you are also inclined to find your son's poetry silly. Only your motherly love keeps you from mocking your son too. Your youngest son is to be pitied. He probably feels very lonely in his family where no one really understands him. He has obviously strayed from the norm, and you may want to try seeing that not as an unfortunate event but as a gain.

It's not uncommon for the inclination of a long-forgotten great-grandmother or great-uncle to resurface after generations. Real talents show themselves early. Your son has a definite urge to express himself linguistically. In a family where everyone does this, he would receive recognition and support; in your family, he becomes an outsider. One day he will hate his father for this.

In the best case, he will strive to show his father by trying to gain public recognition for his poems. In the worst case, he will withdraw so far into himself that he becomes depressed. If you love your son and want him to develop according to his inclinations, support him, even if it means having arguments with your narrow-minded husband. Sometimes it's enough for good development to have at least one person in the family who supports you.

My Daughter Is Preoccupied With an Unrealistic Idea

I am worried about my daughter. Her first child, a boy, died one and a half years ago immediately after birth, and since then she seems different to me. Even in her marriage, there appears to be tension now. Of course, I know that as a mother I have few options to help the two of them. But perhaps there is some good advice for my daughter to start with. She really has an obsession.

When her little boy was born, she was still under anesthesia. Later, the parents were asked if they wanted to see the dead child. Both, my daughter and my son-in-law, were so shocked that they declined. So my daughter never saw her baby. She now claims that we, including her husband and the doctors, should have ensured that she saw the child, as she was not in a state to make such decisions. She says as long as she does not know what he looked like, it will haunt her forever.

I am very sad about this whole thing and don't know how to behave. My daughter is not receptive to rational persuasion. But I know that she is tormented. She looks into every baby stroller on the street, sometimes she has a tearful voice when I call her. On her drawing table, I recently saw a whole series of drawings of infants. My daughter is still young, only twenty-three; she can still have other children. But she won't talk about it.

Answer

I can very well understand your concerns and your feeling of help-lessness because you really can't do much. Your daughter must cope with the loss of her first child all by herself. Grief takes time. The only thing you can do is perhaps to stop trying to reason with her. No amount of reason helps against pain, only loving support does. Your daughter may also be right. If she had seen her dead child, she would know what she now needs to say goodbye to.

Psychologically, it's easier to separate from people or things that have existed in reality, because you have to convince yourself anew every day that they are lost, than from objects that have only ever lived in the imagination. There you can continue to dream and pretend nothing has happened. An unborn child is initially more a being of imagination than reality. A dead child one has not seen has hardly more reality.

At the same time, the accusation from your daughter also contains a charge. The question of why you didn't make sure she saw the child also probably aims particularly at the doctors and her husband: You let my child die. The accusation is certainly non-sensical on the level of reason but understandable on the level of feelings. Your daughter expresses her anger about why this had to happen to her. If she finds guilty parties outside, she doesn't have to be guilty and thus depressed herself.

The search for culprits is a stage in coping with such strokes of fate. Otherwise, your daughter seems to be on her way. She deals with the loss instead of suppressing it. A new child can only really be welcome when the dead child has found its peace in its mother's heart.

Why Is the Child Like This?

I live in a difficult marriage. We've considered separating multiple times but always found a way to start anew. Right now, my main issue is not my husband, but my son. He is nine and, unlike his two younger sisters, is mostly a source of worry for me. I want to share just three incidents from the past week that have truly distressed me.

I overheard a conversation in the garage where my son was trying to convince his sisters that they should definitely go with my husband in case of a separation because they'd be better off with him than with me. The way he talked about me was entirely negative.

I took him to the station for a short trip to visit relatives. When I tried to kiss him goodbye, as is customary for us, he dodged me so dramatically in public that he almost knocked over an elderly man.

Lastly, I'll share one more example – although I could mention countless others. He's issued so-called "pass permits" for entry into his room to everyone in the house. To enter, you must know a passphrase and knock in a particular way. The exception is his father, who can enter without a pass. But I have the most complicated passphrase, despite needing to enter his room for numerous reasons (laundry, cleaning).

We have at least three confrontations per day over this pass. Why is my child like this? He was my desired child and received more attention and care than the girls. Is this how he thanks me?

Answer

You are so entangled with your young son that hardly any interaction between the two of you can be casual or carefree. You scrutinize all his reactions to see if they contain another rejection and thereby an affront to you.

Things are going more smoothly with your daughters precisely because you've been able to give them less attention and care. Too much attention is just as damaging as too little. Unlike your daughters, you've had high expectations for your son from the beginning. Now, you are deeply hurt that he doesn't reciprocate your love. The main issue appears to be that you want to be loved and acknowledged by your son more than you want to hold him in your motherly love, regardless of what he does or how he behaves. Your question should not be, "Why is the child like this?" but rather, "Why am I like this?"

We all want to be loved, but especially young children have a right to our love, otherwise they cannot grow. But as adults, we shouldn't have expectations of them. Our subconscious often plays tricks on us in this regard. We carry over certain relational patterns from our own childhoods into our adult lives, often without realizing it. These subconscious patterns are then projected onto all the people close to us, whether it's a spouse or even our own children.

So it seems to me that you've projected an old, unconscious relational pattern onto your son. You experience your little son as a big, powerful adult (perhaps like your father?), from whom you want love but who rejects you. In your emotional world, you are the small child, and your nine-year-old son is the adult. You are reliving your childhood drama of feeling unloved.

There are countless variations to this theme. Whenever parents can't see that it's actually the child who is entirely dependent on them, that they are the powerful ones in the relationship, they are projecting old, unconscious patterns from their own childhoods. I would advise you to consult a parenting counseling service for your own sake, as well as for the sake of your son, so you can become more aware of the unconscious patterns underlying your behavior. Only when we are aware of why we act can we change our actions.

My Son Wets Himself

Our son, eight, has never been completely dry. It works quite well during the day, but there has never been a dry night. For the past two weeks, his pants have occasionally been wet during the day too. I am at the end of my nerves. We have tried everything. Over the years, we've been to the pediatrician, the urologist, and the child psychologist. Reinforcement plans, scolding, or ignoring have not been successful. We've been trying the "alarm pants" for a week now, after reading the book "Every Child Can Get Dry," and it's making me even more desperate.

It's said that you should give the child a good feeling and boost their self-esteem. These are basic things that should be a part of every upbringing, I think, but all attempts to get him excited about something fail. He doesn't want any of it. I spend all day with my children—the youngest is two—and now find myself second-guessing every word, wondering if it's positive enough. I notice that both my children and I find this annoying because it no longer comes from the heart. I believe I have a perfectly normal child who is not wetting himself out of defiance or emotional distress. Everything is so tangled, and I take the wetting very personally—I feel like a bad mother.

No one can tell me specifically who to turn to for help. I don't want to talk about it with acquaintances, firstly because there are no other children who wet themselves, and secondly because my son already overhears so much, and I don't want to keep burdening him with this. Could it be that this problem will accompany us for the rest of our lives?

Answer

To reassure you in advance: If there is no organic disorder, there are no adults who wet themselves! So at some point, your son will be dry, whether due to or in spite of your efforts. But I still think you urgently need help—not your son to get dry quickly, but you as a mother, before you have a nervous breakdown. Why the many methods you've tried haven't worked, I can't say, but one thing seems clear to me: you've fixated too much on this problem. Taking your son's weakness personally may already unconsciously contribute to the failure of all strategies.

By now, there is a massive disturbance in the mother-son relationship. You constantly convey to him that he's only okay when he's dry. Essentially, he will feel unloved because he sees himself as a failure, and even positive words that don't genuinely come from the heart won't help. As long as the central relationship with the parents is not right, most children are not particularly interested in the world or school content.

You can, of course, search the internet or consult your local health department for other affected parents, but that will probably only provide short-term relief. You can speak your mind, but long-term, you'll only get new suggestions on how to fix the problem. My suggestion goes in a completely different direction.

Get out of it! Untangle this complicated conflict knot by cutting it. Not more of the same, but something completely different for once. Wet pants are part of your eight-year-old son, just like blonde or brown hair are part of other children. Relinquish responsibility for the problem, which is much more than just ignoring it. The boy can take responsibility for it himself at the age of eight.

Provide enough pants and laundry, possibly diapers, and organization for where the wet stuff goes, and leave the rest to him.

Don't ask, don't check, it's his problem. Everyone else in the family should also stick to this. It would be helpful for both you and him if you could separate for a while. Apply for a health retreat for yourself, and if you can't organize that, then take better care of yourself than of the children in the future. Arrange for a babysitter and do your own things without the children. It rarely benefits children when they are the sole focus of their mothers' lives.

My Children Lie

There are always problems with the children, but at the moment I am very concerned. About both, my older son who is seventeen and my little daughter who is just four years old; both children are lying. From the older one, I hardly get any information that doesn't make me suspicious. Time and again I find out later that he has told me another lie. Often, these are entirely unnecessary lies, or he should have thought that I would soon find out the truth.

For instance, when I asked him the name of his current girlfriend, he gave me a false name. There is no girl with that name in his circle of friends. I had seen him with the girl, and we have nothing against him having girlfriends, as he is a good student. I don't understand why he does something like this. My love for truth is proverbial in the family, and I have tried to raise my children the same way.

I'm writing to you today because I'm quite shocked about an incident with my four-year-old daughter who is also starting to lie. She insists she went for a walk around the duck pond with her grandmother, who lives nearby. My mother, however, knew nothing about this when I asked her. When I confronted my daughter, she couldn't admit her lie but instead started to wail loudly. I am now unsure whether I should punish her for this lie. What will become of her if she starts at four years old! Lying is second only to stealing for me. It is utterly terrible for me that my children lie.

Answer

There is a big difference between a seventeen-year-old and a four-year-old lying. Children before the age of six can only partially distinguish between fiction and truth. It is a part of the development of young children that they live temporarily in a world of fantasy. In playful lying, reality is altered by the child's imaginative constructs. The false statement is true and unreal to the child at the same time.

If you insist on the presentation of the truth, you are asking something from your little daughter that she cannot deliver. She's not lying; she's testing reality. I understand that you are also sensitive to your daughter's lies because you are having similar difficulties with your older son at the moment. However, your son's lies seem more like evasions, with which he wants to defend himself against your control and interference.

You are fighting with your son about truth and untruth, but secretly it's probably about an entirely different topic, namely, separation from you. Your son is trying to grow up and lead his own life. Leave him alone, don't pressure him with questions. Perhaps then he will voluntarily tell you something true about his life.

I Can't Stand My Son

I've experienced something that I can't really comprehend. It's about my children. I have three adult sons who were the most important thing in my life for a long time. I've tried to be a good mother, knowing that there is no ideal mother, and you always do something wrong. I find my relationship with them, as well as with my daughters-in-law and grandchildren, very harmonious, sometimes even blissful.

Now I am affected by a feeling that suddenly overwhelmed me last weekend when I was with my second son, and it seems very foreign to me. I was at his home. It was before dinner. My daughter-in-law was with the kids in the kitchen. We were both standing by the window and talking about the garden. He spoke in that very specific manner he often has, about weeds that should be eradicated root and stem.

Suddenly, I realized I actually can't stand my second son. He was immediately repulsive to me. Even articulating this feeling now makes me horrified about myself. Yet I still hear his tone in my ears and, as soon as I think about it, the discomfort resurfaces.

For nearly thirty years, I've tried to talk to him about his extreme attitudes and achieved nothing. I've become tired and never allowed myself to also be unhappy with him. I wonder, and that's why I'm writing to you, what did I do wrong, what can I do?

Answer

It took me a long time to figure out what exactly you want to know and why you have written. I now think you want permission to be an imperfect mother because you have not fairly distributed your love among all three sons. One has received less than the other two. It's been difficult to love him, and you've become so tired of it.

And if you look closely today, you have to realize that you actually reject this second son. You would have never suspected such a feeling in yourself, and it scares you because it questions the image you have of yourself as a mother. If parents were always open and honest with themselves, it would be spoken much more frequently how different the feelings are toward the children. There's always a favorite, secretly or openly: Mommy's darling or Daddy's darling, and there is almost always also a child that attracts a lot of criticism or even rejection.

When older people talk about their childhood, they usually see very clearly how love, indifference, and rejection were distributed in their family. Parental assurances like "But we loved you all equally" are of no use. Distance sharpens the view. You too can only recognize your true feelings now that the sons have long been adults.

It hurts to be an unloved child, but it also hurts not to be able to love a child as you would like to. Make peace with the reality of your different feelings for your sons. Worse than too little love is false love.

The Children Snack Too Much

I would like advice on how to stop my children's enormous candy consumption. At the moment, I'm fighting a losing battle. My older daughter is eleven, the younger one eight. The grandparents, the numerous relatives, they all continually give the kids treats.

At all children's birthdays, there are sweets, not to mention the cake. Every store, every trip to the city means for them: ice cream, candies, chocolate bars. It has become completely normal for them that there are always sweets somewhere.

The worst is my husband, who himself can't watch TV without stuffing chocolate, candies, and cookies into himself. For the children, if they beg long enough, he always has something sweet or gives them money so they can get something.

Of course, regular meals suffer as a result. For dinner, the children regularly have little appetite. Despite my great efforts to bring balanced whole foods to the table for my family. It's pretty frustrating when the dear family doesn't appreciate it. I read everywhere how harmful so much sugar is. But no one in the family wants to listen to me. Both grandmothers are big cake bakers, and nothing works without sugar. It also makes no impression that both children already have multiple filled teeth. I feel like a spoil-sport, but after all, the children's health is at stake.

Answer

You are really fighting a losing battle. At least with your husband, you would have to agree on the dietary style in the family to really be able to make a quick change. You are absolutely right: sugar is not a food but a luxury item, and too much harms health, especially teeth. The fact is, however, that not only your children but also many adults are made to believe by advertising and general consumption habits that an oversupply of sweets is normal.

Strict prohibitions can only be enforced on very small children, and they then also feel like outsiders. The only thing you can do is patiently steer a counter-course and not be discouraged by failures. Just as your children take their father as a (bad) role model in terms of sweets, you could also become a good example over time.

Such a counter-program could look like this: You offer enough sweets in the form of whole foods at meals. You show the children that not every tension, every disappointment, every boredom has to be soothed with sweets, but you can also talk about it and look for real solutions. And instead of sweets and money, you give your children something that takes much more effort but is much more valuable than material pampering: attention, time to listen, understanding.

If you represent this attitude with emphasis (but without aggression) and are yourself the best example of how well you can live without the comforter sugar, you will have long-term success and perhaps even convert your husband.

How Can I Protect My Daughter?

I have a thirteen-year-old daughter, who is my one and only, as further children have been denied to me. My husband has often been abroad for his job, so my daughter has always been the center and purpose of my life. Now, I see with growing concern how she is being drawn into my unhappiness, suffering under the circumstances just as I do.

The core of our problems lies in my husband's behavior, her father. He started an affair two years ago with a younger, also married woman in southern Germany. She has two small children and probably was just playing with my husband. For us, however, it was a disaster because she turned his head so much that he became ill. When I found out, I was able to quickly put an end to the affair, and my husband promised to break off all contact with the woman.

I forgave him for this disappointment and trusted him again. Now, I have found two (!) phone numbers of this woman in his notebook. I was beside myself. My daughter had to witness my shock. I tore out the page with the numbers. My husband noticed it immediately, from which I can conclude that he wanted to call her again. He could hardly come up with any justification.

I then called the woman's husband and told him to keep an eye on his wife. That ended the story. But I am outraged and deeply hurt by this betrayal. My husband's behavior pains me, especially because of my daughter. She is noticing everything. Won't she lose respect for her father? How can I protect her?

Answer

I'm sorry, but I don't think I can give you the answer you'd like to hear. You're seeking validation that your husband is behaving horribly, and your concern for your daughter is fundamentally an indictment against the man who has disappointed you. While it's certain that you're emotionally suffering right now, and your daughter is suffering along with you, from an outsider's perspective, I must say that you are the one directing this family drama.

In relationships, it's never the case that one person is solely at fault and the other is entirely innocent. You can't even see your own contribution: there is something you cannot give your husband that he seeks from another woman. You evidently exert so much pressure on him that I am not surprised he no longer wants to explain himself, let alone that he is still around. He was forced by you to promise to break off contact; such promises are not worth much.

It's not him, but you who are committing a breach of trust by snooping in his notebook and then making such aggressive moves as tearing out a page. With your call to the husband of his lover, you are trying to put in place the same control systems there as you have at home, as if they were not adults but children to be watched over.

Finally, it is you who involve your daughter in the family drama by making the thirteen-year-old your confidante and partner replacement. That is too much for any child! If you really want to protect your daughter, keep your outrage and hurt feelings to yourself, discuss them with an adult friend, or seek help from a counseling service. Children often lose respect for their fathers when the mother belittles or disparages him.

The Ingratitude of Children

It is bitter to think that with good intentions and love, you have done everything for your children, only to reap accusations in return. Quarrels and disputes have broken out in our family, poisoning the lives of my husband and me. I want to ask you, what did we do wrong to deserve such ingratitude from our children? We have three adult children—a son living with his family in Switzerland and two daughters here; the older one is also married, and the younger one isn't yet but has a boyfriend who already thinks he has the right to make demands.

A death in our circle of friends a year ago made us realize how discord can break out in the family if there is no will. Since we are not getting any younger, we subsequently drew up a will with a notary, in which we thought we had fairly distributed our assets among our three children. I gave this division a lot of thought.

For example, I had various older pieces of jewelry appraised to ensure that no one would be disadvantaged. Since we told our children about our decisions, all we hear are accusations. The daughters claim that the brother got the lion's share. When we argue that they have all received equal shares in value, they become unreasonable and bring up ancient, sometimes ridiculous incidents where he was allegedly favored.

I have always tried to show my children that all three are equally loved by us. But even the son, who is the eldest, is not satisfied. He thinks that the better educational opportunities we partly financed for his younger sister should be factored in. I am flabbergasted. We meant so well, and our children are talking and acting as if we were terrible parents. What have we done wrong?

Answer

Executors of wills can tell you all about the bitter family scenes that wills can trigger. In the inheritance that falls to the heirs, the love and appreciation that the deceased had for them materialize—or the love and appreciation they wished they had received. The fight over money, houses, land, jewelry, and the like is essentially always about love and the question of self-worth. With this question, old conflicts naturally re-emerge.

What seems to you like laughable and long-forgotten childhood stories are individual memories your children have retained as representative of many similar incidents where they felt the same way. So, your children are actually fighting about material assets on the surface; in reality, they are fighting for the recognition of their feelings. I can imagine that it must be difficult for you to acknowledge that your children do not feel equally treated—neither now nor in the past—even though you have always tried.

Perhaps it is also an illusion to believe that you can love all your children equally. Children, through their developing personalities, also contribute to their relationship with their parents. As no child is like the other, different emotional relationships arise between parents and children. You must have sensed something of this, or else you would not be striving for fairness so much.

Perhaps the only mistake you made was not keeping quiet about your will. If you alone, based on your assessment and monetary value, decide your legacy, then those should be your final words, beyond any further discussion. The other option is to openly discuss the will with your children from the beginning. This would mean really talking to each other. You will need strength for this, as children almost always come with accusations when they really open their mouths. No mother in the world can be so good as to have done everything right.

My Son Is Too Generous

I am concerned about my young son's behavior and would like some advice. He's nearly nine and in the third grade. He is very popular among his peers, which isn't surprising as he freely shares everything he has, whether it's his breakfast, money, or toys. He excels in school and lets everyone copy his work. His best friend borrowed his new bike (a much-desired birthday gift) and has forgotten to return it for days. My son doesn't seem to mind and forgoes biking to school. When I tell him to insist on getting his bike back, he defends his friend.

Within our family, the pattern is similar. If I'm not careful, he always ends up getting the short end of the stick. During holidays like Christmas and Easter, his older sisters regularly consume all his sweets. For a few kind, albeit empty, words, he willingly takes on his sisters' chores like emptying the dishwasher or taking empty bottles to the recycling bin. Both sisters have come to expect that they can delegate their unwanted tasks to him. They look out for their own interests, but my son allows himself to be exploited by anyone who tries to take advantage of him.

Answer

It's possible that your son has inherited this trait from his father, either genetically or by emulating his behavior. For children, adults serve as significant role models. Your daughters look to you for how to behave as adult women, while your son views his father as his masculine role model. When you first met your husband, it was his helpful and selfless demeanor that attracted you, and you've undoubtedly benefited from this quality yourself. Over time, these once endearing traits have become a concern you feel you must address.

For both your husband and your son, this manner of conduct is their unique way of fostering relationships with others. In principle, no one has the right to demand they change—certainly not a mother towards her child. However, there are exceptions. If your husband feels burdened by his office role and asks for your counsel, or if your son seems unhappy, then intervention may be warranted. But as long as your son is content, thriving among his friends and family, and performing well academically, there's no urgent need for maternal interference.

Should I Notify
Child Protective Services?

My nephew and godson is now thirteen years old, and I am deeply concerned about him. He's the son of my sister. His father works in sales and is rarely at home. Since the birth of his younger siblings (twins, three years ago), he's often left to his own devices. I've noticed he's slowly becoming neglected. Last week, I saw him at the train station during school hours, smoking cigarettes and drinking alcohol with four older boys.

His academic performance has significantly deteriorated since joining this group. His new "friends" are known troublemakers; most are unemployed and don't have apprenticeships. No one really knows how they make a living or where they get the money for their binge-drinking. I suspect drugs might also be involved.

I've tried talking to my nephew multiple times, but he's become quite dismissive, even toward me. We used to have a good relationship. Three years ago, we took him with us on our family vacation to Italy.

My sister doesn't take my concerns about her son going down a dangerous path seriously; she dismisses and downplays the situation. She believes it's normal for a boy his age to rarely be at home and even to not come home some nights, attributing it to puberty.

Moreover, I feel my sister has been overwhelmed since the twins were born. She rejects offers for help and avoids conversations. How can I help my nephew and my sister? Should I inform Child Protective Services? I fear for my nephew, but I think my sister would never forgive me.

Answer

It's hard for me to judge whether they will intervene, but if you're unsure, definitely contact them, describe the situation, and they will assess it for themselves and decide whether they want to take action or not. I can understand your concerns for your nephew. You would never allow your own children to behave in such a manner. But he is not your child, and just because things are different in his family doesn't mean he's necessarily neglecting himself. "Neglect" is a strong term, suggesting the child is entirely unattached.

I think the real issue is your relationship with your sister. Both of you likely hold extreme positions on not just this matter but life in general. Where your sister minimizes problems and lets things slide, you magnify them and want to intervene in a controlling way. The middle ground between these two stances is probably a more realistic attitude, especially concerning adolescents.

As an aunt, your influence is inherently limited. Discussions with your sister are unproductive as they ultimately turn into battles over the "correct" perspective. Your best course of action is to actively engage with your nephew. Talking won't help; action will. So make offers and hope he accepts them.

The invitation to vacation in Italy was a great start. As his godmother, you could also spend time with him alone. But please don't use the opportunity to lecture him. Show him what else life has to offer outside his family and social circle—things that are also enjoyable.

The Child Is Destroying Our Relationship

I am simply unhappy, even though we finally have what I've always wished for: a child. Our son is one and a half years old. We were a happy couple for two years. My husband, as they say, fulfilled my every wish. We both work in artistic professions and have always been able to give each other a lot of inspiration. We traveled a lot and embarked on many an adventure; there was always something to laugh about, and I was absolutely sure of my husband's love. We wanted a child, actually, I wanted it more than my husband did because I've always imagined a happy family.

But everything has turned out quite differently. Even if my husband denies it, since our son has been here, our relationship has been on a decline. He no longer understands me as he did before. It started with the difficult birth. I lack recognition for what I have accomplished. I was sick for a long time and did not want sex, which he held against me. Then I breastfed for six months, and he didn't understand that he now has to take on more household chores. When we were alone, we shared everything; there were no problems, but now it feels like I bear all the responsibility alone. I always have to remind and ask him. Then there is an argument. We never had such issues before.

Don't get me wrong; we both love our son, but if I had known beforehand that a child would cost me my relationship, I would not have wanted one. I feel like the child has destroyed our beautiful relationship. My husband says he would actually be quite happy if I were not so dissatisfied. But I don't believe him. Everything has changed for him too. We argue all the time, we are no longer affectionate with each other, instead of creative conversations, we talk about the organization of everyday life. We both work and share the care of our son. When I tell him what I miss, he does not understand. What should I do?

Answer

You were a love couple, now you are a parent couple. Nothing lasts forever in this world, as much as we might wish. Even without a child, your beautiful relationship would have changed over the years. The birth of a child, however, brings about an immediate, drastic change. It seems that you've dreamed of a family as it appears in advertising, focusing only on the idealized facade. Family, however, means work and a lot of organization, something you weren't prepared for. The difficult birth alone shattered all illusions you had about wanting a child. This disappointment you have to process yourself; no man can alleviate your pain with special understanding.

Pregnancy, childbirth, breastfeeding, and even temporary sexual disinterest are female experiences that men can only partially understand. But when sexuality takes a back seat after the birth of a child, the man is quickly inclined to see in his wife only the mother and therefore, maybe as he knows it from his mother, shove the responsibility for the shared life onto her. He often feels easily excluded from the tender mother-child unit.

The birth of the first child is always a very critical time for both partners. A few conversations at a counseling center or with a psychologist could probably help you gain an understanding of each other's needs. Since you are the one who is suffering more, you will probably have to be the driving force. If you handle this turning point well, your son will not destroy your relationship but deepen it.

Our Only Son Lives in Chaos

We married late, and I was very grateful to give birth to a healthy child at the age of thirty-eight. Our only son was the apple of our eye. He is now almost eighteen and finally found a suitable apprenticeship five kilometers away from us after a long search. He found himself a room in a shared apartment with other young people. We helped him set up his room nicely, including some quite expensive leather armchairs.

At first, he came home every weekend, but then his visits became increasingly rare. In the last six months, he has only shown up once for two hours. Last weekend my husband and I visited him to see how he was doing. Our son was very embarrassed and said he had not expected us at all. We could quickly see that for ourselves.

I must say, we were shocked! His room was unrecognizable. A chaos of used dishes, leftover food, full ashtrays, empty bottles, CDs, and discarded clothes—all of this more or less on the floor or on randomly scattered mattresses. His bed was dismantled. The leather armchairs were in the hallway and seemed to serve only as a storage area. Instead of his landscape photos, which had always been his hobby, he now had rather obscene posters on the walls. I was appalled! Do teenagers have to be like this?

My husband was just disgusted. We endured half an hour on a mattress and drank tea from sticky cups, then we left. We were totally shattered, also by the behavior of our son, who acted as if all this was quite normal. We don't understand it at all. He has always been neat and even as a child placed great importance on having a beautifully furnished room, and now he lives in such chaos!

Answer

The almost-adult son has moved out and is starting his own life. If it's to be his own life, it must—at least initially—be different from life with his parents. Your son is now adopting the deliberately casual to chaotic lifestyles of a certain youth subculture, contrasting it with the bourgeois, sheltered world of his childhood.

Take his chaos as well as his rare visits home as necessary attempts by your son to separate from his parents and go his own way. This detachment phase is usually a hard time for parents and pushes them to the limits of their understanding. Your son conformed to your norms for a relatively long time; now his protest phase is quite drastic. Many parents experience the chaos you described already within their own four walls.

The more tolerant you are now, the easier it will be for your son to reconnect later. Make no more surprise visits in the future. Spare both yourself and him such uncomfortable situations. Respect his wishes for distance. True adulthood can only be achieved away from parents.

No Reward, No Effort

I know that views on child-rearing have changed a lot over the past twenty years, but not everything that was commonplace in the past should be considered bad today! For us children, it was a given that we had duties around the house and had to help our parents otherwise. These services were expected of us, and no big deal was made about it. Our parents did the same, helping neighbors and friends where necessary.

I now worryingly see that my only two grandchildren, a fourteen-year-old girl and a twelve-year-old boy, are not taught this attitude. The stark opposite is true. They don't lift a finger on their own accord, are served hand and foot by their parents, and live completely selfishly, focused solely on their own desires.

What my daughter-in-law does, in my eyes, is bribery. She promises the children something special, or most often just money, as an incentive for some form of help. Even in academic achievements, negotiations take place on how much a grade of "one" or "two" in this or that subject brings! I can hardly bear to hear it. Everything operates on the wrong principle: "No reward, no effort."

A reward for good performance should be something additional, not a prerequisite for making an effort in the first place. I believe that my grandchildren are not learning very important things like solidarity, compassion, and also taking responsibility for their actions. Instead, they learn to consider profit in all their actions.

Am I old-fashioned? I find this parenting style simply impossible. And is it worth talking to the daughter-in-law? She is mainly the one advocating this parenting style; my son is unfortunately rarely at home.

Answer

You'd better stay out of it; you'll likely only sow discord. Parenting topics are very heated issues between adult children and parents and quickly reopen old wounds inflicted by upbringing. What you observe so intensely and worryingly in your grandchildren today probably didn't just arise last year. Your daughter-in-law and your son have likely always interacted with their children this way; it just wasn't as visible as it is today when it comes to money and bigger desires.

You are right: Helpfulness and solidarity with close people are valuable attitudes and are sadly becoming more and more obsolete. It is hard for parents and children to live and convey such values in this consumer society. Your daughter-in-law passes on what she experiences herself. Education works through examples, not talk. Show your grandchildren, whenever you are with them, that you don't partake in this performance-reward thinking in the family, and that there are reasons other than profit to make an effort.

My Daughter Is Stealing Money

I'm appalled. While cleaning her closet, I found so much brand-new toys hidden under the clothes of my eight-year-old daughter that I had to confront her. At first, she claimed to have traded them for books with a friend but eventually admitted that she had bought the items with my money. I was shocked; I would have never expected this from my daughter.

The worst reaction came from my husband. He raged, accusing our daughter of betraying our trust, and said that if she starts like this, she will end up in prison. He imposed four weeks of grounding and suspended her allowance indefinitely. Moreover, he is no longer speaking to her. I find this to be very harsh, and after discussing the matter with other mothers, I am starting to doubt whether we are handling this correctly.

On the other hand, I do think she needs to be punished. When I sum up all the retail prices, she has taken between twenty and thirty Marks from my wallet in the last eight weeks. Naturally, I also wonder what I have done wrong. I am a stay-at-home mom and available for the children all day. Within our means, we also fulfill their wishes. Why would our daughter do this? Should I really be worried about her development?

Answer

You probably haven't done anything wrong—at least not until this draconian punishment. Most children try to take money from their parents' wallets at some point. It's not a big deal, as long as the parents don't make it one. However, such an incident is a reason to clearly define boundaries and make binding agreements so the child knows what is allowed and what isn't.

To children, the mother appears to be an inexhaustible source of satisfaction. They constantly demand love, comfort, attention, food, warmth—so why not money as well? With the same ease as they usually take what they need, they take from their mother's wallet. The concept of ownership is gradually acquired by children over the course of their development. Talking about theft, as adults understand it, is hardly applicable to children under ten.

Your husband's overreactions likely have more to do with his own fears and childhood experiences regarding such matters than with the reality of your young daughter. Ask your husband how it was when he himself had stolen something as a child. If he remembers, he might be more willing to empathize with the child's feelings. It would be good if all three of you could sit down to discuss everything calmly now.

Not only are you as parents disappointed by your daughter, but your daughter is also disappointed by her parents. It would be best if you revoked all the punishments. Your daughter will understand that you initially went overboard out of anger. Show understanding that it was not entirely clear to her that her mother's wallet, like any other money lying around the house, is off-limits for her.

Check if the child has an adequate allowance. Raising it after such an incident is pedagogically more effective than taking it away. Avoid leaving money lying around in the future, so as not to tempt the child. Review your expenses more often so you notice if something is missing. If your daughter secretly obtains money again, you should first consider whether she lacks something for which money serves as a substitute satisfaction.

Homesickness Comes in the Evening

I always thought I had very low-maintenance children. But now, our six-year-old daughter is getting on our nerves, especially mine, since I deal with it the most. We moved here exactly four months ago from a small village 30 kilometers away. Here, we not only finally have enough space in the apartment for the children but they also have a large garden to play in. The external circumstances are much better. Nevertheless, my daughter cries almost every second evening before falling asleep, saying she wants to go back. She helped raise rabbits at a neighbor's house there, and she also wants to return to her trees and a pond where she fed ducks.

I can't convince her that she can have all that here too. My husband even offered to build a rabbit hutch in the garden, but she refuses. The homesickness always comes in the evening. During the day, she's quite cheerful and has adapted well. She's still being held back from school, so she attends kindergarten and has even found a friend. She's quite independent and explores the area on her own.

After four months, however, her evening reactions just don't seem normal to me. I also get the impression that it's getting worse rather than better. Her four-year-old brother had no issues adapting. I really don't know how to handle my daughter anymore.

Answer

Your daughter's daytime cheerfulness is not at odds with her evening sadness; they both go together. It's the same for us adults: During the day, we're distracted, the accomplishment of new tasks gives us a good feeling about ourselves, but in the evening or during leisure times, when we can no longer keep our fears and pressing feelings at bay through distractions, they overtake us. In the evening, your young daughter is likely becoming fully aware of all the pain she feels from leaving her familiar surroundings.

However, I do find it alarming that this reaction still occurs after four months and, according to your impression, is even intensifying. Moreover, your daughter is homesick only for animals and nature, which is a bit unusual for a six-year-old. There might be other yearnings behind her behavior. Perhaps her evening crying has solidified into a ritual that always unfolds in the same way because that's when you are emotionally available to her. Even if you can no longer comfort her and instead scold her, she still gets your attention.

What is your daughter trying to tell you with her crying? Maybe she is unconsciously trying to say that she feels lonely and not loved enough. The strong relationships she developed with animals and nature in her old home could indicate that her relationships with people—primarily with her parents—are not holding up.

Even in the new environment, she is often on her own. Perhaps she is less emotionally independent than you think. Being held back from school attendance points in the same direction. Her younger brother seems to feel emotionally safer. In any case, your daughter's crying expresses a lack. I would strongly recommend that you seek child counseling.

Our Daughter Accuses Us

I am writing to you today because we are struggling with a problem concerning our daughter. Our oldest daughter, who is almost forty, has been in psychotherapy for a year, and since then, we've had no joy. There isn't an encounter or a phone call where she doesn't level the most severe accusations at us, sometimes with tears or wild outbursts of anger.

We have done everything within our power. I can't help that I got divorced, that my first husband mistreated this daughter. Now our daughter says I should have protected her. But I was scared of my husband myself. I later remarried, and I am happy with my second husband. Initially, he also made a lot of effort with my daughter, but when we had three more children together, she became less important to him.

She had many difficulties in school and had to go to a special school, which was a shock for our family. She then trained as a seamstress. She is certainly not stupid, but she just couldn't make it in school. She also blames us for this. Before therapy, everything was so beautiful between us. She often visited, always brought gifts, and was there when I was sick. My question is, should we go to her therapist to set the record straight and tell them what discord they have brought into our family?

Answer

I can understand how hurt and outraged you are. Within a year, what you perceived as a good relationship with your adult daughter has turned into a constant source of insults due to her therapy. Talking to the therapist probably won't change much, as what you're experiencing now is part of the therapeutic process and unavoidable.

However, you could gain a better understanding of your daughter's current emotional state through such a conversation. Most difficulties in life that we have as adults—both with ourselves and with others—originate in childhood. Parents and other significant figures do many harmful things to children, usually without realizing it. In this sense, all parents become innocently guilty concerning their children.

In therapy, many of these old childhood wounds are reopened. The old feelings of children, especially anger and pain, are revived. What was good in childhood and what the parents did right is seen as normal and not given further attention, but the mistakes and oversights of the parents can only be forgiven after experiencing the anger and sorrow over them. Your daughter is evidently still in the phase of aggression and pain.

At the moment, she is also not able to consider your shared history from your perspective. There are usually two stories: one from the parents and one from the children. These two stories often don't match at all because parents and children experience the same events very differently. Try, as difficult as it may be, to be patient. After therapy, a new and much more genuine relationship between parents and adult children is often possible.

Children to Show Off

I am hurt by the behavior of my siblings and would like to ask you for advice. I am the second of three children; both my older brother and my younger sister have no children of their own. We have a fourteen-year-old daughter and a twelve-year-old son. Our daughter has been riding horses for six years and has won many prizes in tournaments. Our son is talented in athletics and had several significant successes at championships last year. I am happy for the children and, of course, proud of them.

At a family gathering, my husband showed videos of the children that he took at various championships. While watching, my siblings and my sister-in-law made only sarcastic comments; only my brother-in-law and grandma had something appreciative to say. Among other things, my sister said to me, "You finally have something to brag about," and my brother spoke disparagingly of "showpiece children."

I was hurt and showed it. The farewell was very frosty. Now I blame myself. Did we impose too much on them because they have no children, even though they would have liked to? We just wanted to share our joy about our children with them. There's nothing wrong with being proud of one's children. It has nothing to do with bragging. What do you think?

Answer

Your siblings are probably the wrong people to share the joy of your children's success with. There appears to still be too much sibling rivalry from childhood between you, your brother, and your sister to genuinely share in each other's happiness without envy. Maybe you also unconsciously wanted to get back at the two of them by showing off your children, and the siblings retaliated.

I would let the matter rest and be more reserved about this issue with your siblings in the future. Show the videos to grandma or other understanding people and enjoy your children's successes with them. It's only natural to be proud of them. A house of one's own, a new car, or even a successful craft project—any achievement we have invested energy into makes us proud, and we want to show it off. Why not children? Especially them!

Children represent a life achievement for parents. For decades, a large part of their energy, feelings, fears, time, and income is devoted to their children. When the children manage well in life, perhaps even have special talents, the joy is only justified. Conversely, the hurt over troubled children goes very deep. Parents like these naturally react very sensitively to success reports about other children.

Therefore, consider beforehand who your conversation partners are. Also, pay attention to how your children feel as "showpiece children." Some children think it's great; others are more embarrassed. The reactions depend on how the relationship is with the parents otherwise. In any case, you should take your children's feelings more seriously than the reactions of your siblings.

The Guest Child Is a Concern

We have taken in a friend of our daughter for four months. Both are ten years old, go to the same class, and have known each other since they started school. Therefore, I had no reservations when Julia's parents asked us. Both are artists and have an engagement in Japan. If they had taken their daughter with them, Julia would have missed too much at school. We have known the little girl for four years now, she is well-behaved, very sociable, and talented. We have never noticed anything problematic about the child. The girls were looking forward to living together.

Julia has been living with us for over a month, and I find the girl's behavior increasingly strange. I am a trained educator, so I can assess whether a child is behaving normally. At first, I thought it was due to the separation from her parents and the new situation, but then it should weaken over time and not intensify, and it does. So, the little girl brought three stuffed animals with her, besides a teddy bear, a donkey, and a crocodile. She carries them around everywhere. Wherever she stays for a longer period, these three are arranged in a specific order: while eating, doing schoolwork, watching TV, sleeping, of course, but also in the kitchen when she came just to lick the remains of the cake dough from the bowl. If one prevents her from doing so, she starts to cry.

When doing schoolwork, she looks more into the air than into her notebook and has also declined in her school performance. My daughter says that Julia sometimes cries in her sleep at night but knows nothing about it in the morning. She is very jumpy and starts at loud noises and sometimes can't calm down at all. On a class trip to the zoo, she absolutely did not want to go and made such a fuss that a teacher had to stay with her on the bus.

What really made me suspicious was when I discovered that she has hidden small packages of food everywhere under her clothes in the closet. Half a slice of bread with cheese wrapped in a sheet of paper, half an apple, a cooked potato from lunch. I haven't said anything and left everything as it is. But before it all spoils, I have to do something, but I don't know what. I am worried about Julia and am hoping for your help. I also have a responsibility for her, even if she is only our guest child.

Answer

Your concern is justified. The little one has some serious problem. Fundamentally, I see two possibilities. Either something happened to Julia before her parents left, which has disturbed her and she can no longer suppress now that her parents are not around, or something has happened to her shortly after moving in with you that she cannot talk about. Children express themselves through behavior, and Julia's behavior and her reactions are indeed alarming. There is a suspicion that the girl has experienced something that has traumatized her. One does not immediately have to think of abuse, but one should not exclude it either. Accidents, surgeries, experiences of violence can also be traumatizing.

A trauma arises whenever a person feels helplessly exposed to terrible experiences and no one helps them process what has happened. Whatever happened to Julia, if she has help talking about it, she will get over it well. You can offer this by trying to talk to her about the food packages.

You shouldn't forbid her from doing it, but rather consider with her what she could do instead because she packs these packages out of inner necessity. These are attempts to solve a need she cannot cope with otherwise. You should observe her closely and ask many questions. Probably there is an animal in the zoo that scares her particularly. The reasons Julia gives for this are clues to what might be going on. Children often tell what has happened, but it is so encrypted that one only gradually gets behind it. It's best to take notes.

To relieve yourself, you should seek professional help. Child protection centers are good points of contact who can help you make good use of the time until Julia's parents return. They are trained to find out through play scenes what is troubling children and what they need to become cheerful and carefree again.

I Only Meant Well

I have only one son. He got married in the summer to a much younger woman. He is thirty-six, she is twenty-three, and comes from, as they say, a simple background, very different from our family of teachers and doctors. I was invited to their place for Christmas, which I was looking forward to, but I left very disappointed. First of all, the apartment they have been living in for six months was only half furnished. Very uncomfortable, I must say. Their clothes, for example, were hanging on an open rack like you see in stores. The apartment had no cabinets. Even in the kitchen, dishes were simply on shelves. No plants, no rugs. My son is used to something entirely different at home; I don't understand how he can feel comfortable there.

The only Christmas decoration was a white (!) plastic Christmas tree. I nearly walked out the door when I saw it. My son thinks it's "unique." On Christmas Eve, we had sausages and potato salad, and she didn't even make the salad herself but bought it. After we exchanged gifts, which were wrapped very thoughtlessly, we watched TV for the rest of the evening. No songs, no music, no festively set table, no group games. I was quite frustrated.

On Christmas morning, I woke up early and, since I didn't know what else to do and they were still asleep, I set the table as beautifully as I could. I found candles and napkins, and even went outside to cut a few evergreen branches for decoration. It ended up looking quite nice, and I thought they would be pleased.

But the opposite was the case. I only meant well, but it was the start of a fight and a bad atmosphere that lasted until my departure. My daughter-in-law forbade my interference, saying they have their own style, and that I had kept my son in "plush" long enough. To my great disappointment, my son had no kind words for me, but rather sided with his wife. Now, I am back home, in my "plush" as my daughter-in-law calls it, and I wonder what I did wrong, and how I should behave in the future.

Answer

I wonder why your son invited you. It's possible that this invitation was a point of contention between the young couple. She might have preferred to celebrate alone with her husband rather than have his mother join them. In any case, you were not wholeheartedly welcome by both, and this was demonstrated to you with minimal effort in organizing the festivities. But there are other motives. Perhaps your son simply wanted to show you how he now lives, to signal that he no longer feels like a son but as an adult, married man. His behavior indicates this too; he sided with his wife during the dispute. I understand that this hurts you, but your son owes his wife solidarity; otherwise, he jeopardizes his marriage.

Everything happens in the young couple's apartment; that is essentially their domain, and you have no say there. You're just a guest. The young people still have to find their style and establish their own Christmas traditions. Your daughter-in-law was right to reject your table-setting as interference. If you are honest with yourself, you will also realize that you wanted to show your daughter-in-law "the right way" to do things through your decorations. Your ideas of Christmas are not the only correct ones, and the young woman might have very different ones. Moreover, this daughter-in-law, coming from simple circumstances, is not to your taste, and she rightly sensed your criticism in your actions.

I believe you still have to truly accept the fact that your son now belongs to another woman and has a different, independent life. Once you have managed that, everything else will follow naturally.

Problems With Others

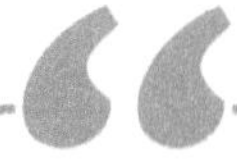

Conflicts with others are often reflections of our own inner struggles. Those who understand themselves find it easier to get along with others.

—**Brigitte Halenta**

Anger at the Tenants

I am extremely annoyed with my neighbor, who scolded my three boys (seven, nine, and eleven) for running over her freshly seeded lawn in their excitement for soccer, so much so that they came home crying. This neighborhood is complicated for me anyway. We live pretty close to each other with four families. It's a large courtyard, and my parents gave up farming a long time ago. My parents still live in the old house, I live with my family in a converted barn, and two more adjoining houses are rented out. One is occupied by the neighbor I'm annoyed with, along with her husband and three children, and then there's an older, single couple. Both houses have their gardens in the back but overlook the former courtyard.

Now, the older couple behaves like the grandparents of the young family. In the summer, life takes place collectively on the courtyard. The old man, who dictates everything, has built a large table outside and created a barbecue area, where they all sit and grill in the evenings. Whenever I manage to join them, which takes a lot of effort on my part, I am always greeted kindly, but I somehow don't feel truly welcome, as they never invite me over themselves. My parents are not an issue in this respect, as my father is in need of care following a stroke, and my mother would never leave him alone.

The two families have now beautifully redesigned the courtyard. Grass was laid and more was seeded after we removed our stored firewood. Technically, it's our property and was not rented out with the houses, but my parents don't care.

My husband always says that I shouldn't get angry at the tenants' unauthorized actions but should say something. After all, I am the heir, but as long as my parents are alive, I don't have the right to do so, I believe. Besides, they would all look rather stupid if I suddenly wanted to decide something. But now with my boys, and how she scolded them, it really makes me think. What do you advise me?

Answer

You should listen to your husband and develop a realistic view of the situation. The fact is that both families are overstepping their boundaries. Apparently, the old man has taken over your sick father's role as the authority figure. As long as no one sets limits, he will continue doing what he wants. The redesign of the old courtyard is only as pleasing as it aligns with your interests. Theoretically, you could also park vehicles there, create a soccer field for your boys, or do whatever you want. But these two families seem to have lost their sense of the actual ownership situation. Your annoyance with the scolding neighbor is therefore very understandable.

What makes it difficult for you to act as the future owner? This could be related to your special relationship with your parents today, or even with very old childhood patterns. Obviously, you couldn't leave to start your own life elsewhere, and now that you've stayed, you can't grasp what will eventually be yours. There are surely powerful unconscious motives responsible for your behavior. Use your anger with the neighbor as an opportunity to change. You need to break away from your internal position as a daughter in relation to your parents. You're no longer a child, but an adult. However, you still feel small next to them.

Ironically, you can only assume your role as the heir when you can identify with your parents as the owners of the courtyard. But you are currently still rejecting this internally. You don't want to be like your parents, from your child's point of view. Only when you can change your perspective and look at the old parents and the courtyard with adult eyes will you become capable of acting. If this change in perspective doesn't work for you, you should seek psychotherapeutic support.

My Neighbor Is Intrusive

Even while the movers were carrying my furniture into the new apartment, my immediate neighbor already came over to introduce himself, brought a bottle of Prosecco to toast to good neighborliness, and immediately announced that I could turn to him trustfully for any arising problems. He said the building had a particularly good community where everyone could rely on each other. I've been living here for half a year now, and I don't find that people here interact differently than what I'm used to in other apartment buildings. But my neighbor gets on my nerves with his pushiness. He must be around 50 like me and is also single but, unlike me, he is an early retiree.

At first, I thought it was all just an act, but now I know he has tried to establish some form of trust with everyone in the building. Others had already warned me about him. It has been easier for the other tenants to fend him off than for me. Ever since I had him over for tea once, I can't shake him off. I think he actually waits for me in the stairwell. He finds everything I do or wear fantastic. Meanwhile, he talks non-stop. I hardly get a word in. Now he wants me to give him my keys when I go on vacation, so he can take care of my mail and plants. I can't manage to tell him that I don't want this.

For such cases, I always ask my friend, but he thinks it would be more practical if he did it, as we live door-to-door. The guy is just slimy, and I can't counteract it. I wonder what he actually wants, and I've even started fantasizing wildly. For example, that he only wants to spy on my apartment in my absence to then empty it out in a disguised burglary. What do you think is going on with this man and how can I keep him at a distance?

Answer

Neighbors are a matter of luck, and yours is quite a special case. To me, it doesn't sound like the man is dangerous but rather like he has nothing to do and feels very lonely. The fact that he is insensitive in his contact-seeking and doesn't respect the boundaries of other people probably belongs to his character. The reasons he became this way are speculative, but such self-centered people need very strong signals to realize what others want from them. And that leads us to your problem.

It seems like you belong to the people who express their wishes only very cautiously and politely. Rude words are probably foreign to you. To complicate matters, you're easily convinced by kindness. The neighbor plays the role of the charming person very well, so you dare not push him away strongly and firmly. But that's exactly what you have to do. Politeness won't get you anywhere in this case. You probably adhere to life beliefs that you don't want to hurt anyone; you should set these aside if you want to keep the neighbor at a distance once and for all.

In your value scale, the way you tell him that you don't want this much contact and certainly not for him to look after your apartment in your absence must already fall under 'causing offense'. He may withdraw offendedly, or he might lash out—many reactions are conceivable with such people. However, that shouldn't matter to you. You should only focus on one goal: to guide the unpleasant neighborhood into more bearable channels for you.

My Efforts Are Not Appreciated

I am a general practitioner in the countryside and have a problem that you may be able to help me solve. I am chronically overworked; there is simply no time for my private life or the urgently needed exercise program. I also eat poorly because I'm always stressed and don't feel like cooking for myself in the evening. I keep taking on more and more work, and often know just two minutes after agreeing that I can't possibly manage it all. This applies not only to my medical practice but even more so to my various social and political commitments. There, I volunteer for three different institutions on my own.

When things got too much for me again, I tried to analyze my situation and noticed the following: This total stress, coupled with a feeling of complete overwhelm, only occurs with women. Where I deal with men, even after long conversations, I feel more satisfied that what could have been achieved has been achieved. Unfortunately, outside the practice, I deal almost exclusively with women. I don't know if it's me who simply can't deal with women, although I am a woman myself, or if women are simply more difficult due to their greater emotional focus. As I write, I realize that I actually only get upset about women, especially when they portray themselves as victims and have great expectations of me.

In general, my commitment is great; I do what I can, but I always feel that my efforts are not appreciated enough—by women, with men it's different, as I said. Do you have any advice on what I could change?

Answer

You've already identified the most important point yourself, namely that your relationship with men is different than with women. This is not due to the fundamentally different nature of women, but to the different way you experience and react to women. With men, you can set good boundaries and realistically assess what is achievable. With women, the boundaries of your person as well as those set by reality seem to blur. You let women seduce you into making the impossible possible, and that is associated with a type of stress that makes you sick. Of course, you can't achieve that, so you fail and blame yourself.

You don't write anything about your family of origin, so I can only deduce from today's conflict what happened to you as a child. There must have been an important reference person whom you could not satisfy despite your great efforts. The core of the feeling of being overwhelmed when solving actually unsolvable tasks will already stem from this time. You have repressed all unbearable feelings from back then; they reappear today in the form of other suffering women. You have a very strong unconscious motivation to eliminate suffering, because that would secretly also comfort the suffering child you once were. Because you unconsciously identify with suffering women due to your repressed own experiences, the boundaries between you and others blur, leading you to lose touch with reality.

Our greatest reality is time, but you lose sight of that when dealing with women, leading to situations that are then objectively unmanageable. When dealing with women, you belong to the so-called helpless helpers who are always trying to save others, although they should actually be saving their own inner child. Your goal should be to deal with women as adult-like, i.e., with defined and reality-appropriate boundaries, as you do with men. Then you will no longer feel overwhelmed, and your efforts will be appreciated not only by men but also by women.

I Don't Want to Give Up Hope

I need some advice on how to behave. For two years, I've been pursuing my neighbor, who lives alone, without much success, but I don't want to give up hope. I've told her that as well. We live in a row house, side by side. In one half, my wife and I, and in the other, our lovely neighbor. We are all of mature age. My wife has been suffering from dementia for twelve years after a heart attack. Her short-term memory is destroyed, so she needs help practically all day. She goes to a facility three days a week where she feels comfortable. During the day, I have a caregiver for a few hours, so I can move freely; otherwise, I take my wife everywhere with me, although she doesn't benefit much from it and gets tired quickly. You can imagine that I welcome any conversation, any diversion.

I liked my neighbor from the moment she moved in shortly after us. At first, she didn't pay any attention to me and kept the inevitable contacts, due to our close gardens and terraces, as short as possible. Gradually, however, we have gotten a little closer. I've helped her a few times with heavy work in the garden; as a thank you, she has sometimes invited me for a glass of wine on the terrace in the evening when my wife was already asleep. I always enjoy our conversations very much. She's a very interesting and intelligent woman. At some point, I hugged her as a greeting and gave her a little kiss on the cheek. That's as far as it went, but she always pulls away.

I've tried to explain my situation to her, simply that I like to hug her because my wife no longer tolerates any touch. There's nothing wrong with that, as I would never cheat on my wife, even if she would never find out. I've explained this to her as well. But my neighbor keeps saying: Neighborly friendship, yes, but nothing more. But I don't want to give up hope. I'm practically alone, and so is she. What else could I do to win her affection? Do you have any idea?

Answer

You have a tough fate, and your selfless care for your wife is highly commendable. However, you have to come to terms with reality. Your needs are understandable, but you must sort them out and see how you can implement them. Indeed, the best thing that could happen to you would be if your neighbor were fond of you. But it's clear that she can't envision a closer relationship with you. To linger in front of a closed door and not want to give up hope that it will still open is a waste of time. You should accept the neighborly-friendly relationship as it is and give up your wishes regarding your neighbor.

This will be easier for you the more honest you are with yourself. You long for closeness to a woman, for touch and exchange. You should review your perhaps outdated idea of eternal fidelity to your wife in light of the situation. You're not taking anything away from your wife by having a relationship with another woman.

In your free time, you should be around people as much as possible to satisfy your need for contact. Instead of courting your rejecting neighbor, you should specifically look for a friend. In that regard, I agree with you: you shouldn't give up hope. It must be possible to find people even at your mature age, with whom you can find a balance besides caring for your wife.

Cohabitation in Old Age

You often hear in the media about living communities for older people, but usually, there are a lot of problems involved because older people have certain ideas about life and are not as open to new things. Three years ago, I founded a shared living arrangement that has been very successful, meaning we all get along splendidly and feel that we have all gained something. However, we are facing opposition from the outside. The neighbors, who find our lifestyle immoral, are the least of our problems; worse are our adult children, who are all unhappy with us.

As I said, I am the initiator. I have some wealth and a debt-free large house. After my wife died four years ago, I was faced with the question of what to do with the house, which is too big for me alone. Selling it was hard for me because I am very attached to the garden. First, an old friend, also widowed, moved in with me. Even then, my sons grumbled that I was taking too little money from him. My friend only has a small pension, and his company is worth much more to me than a few bucks. Over time, two women joined us, so now we are four. I have two sons, and the two women together have three more children, who like mine are married and have their own lives.

While my sons and daughters-in-law make snide remarks at every contact that I am being taken advantage of by the others and am squandering the wealth, the children of the women say the opposite. They take every opportunity to proclaim—right to my face—that their mothers are being financially exploited by me. However, the four of us have a communal agreement about finances, and everyone is satisfied. But visits from children or even just phone contacts constantly disturb our peace and well-being. One cohabitant, in particular, suffers greatly from the accusations of her son. I fear that one day he will wear her down, and she will move out.

We all agree that the children have no right to interfere in our affairs, but we would still like some advice on how best to handle such a situation.

Answer

Your problem is not on a rational level; it's clear to you and all other thinking people that older individuals have as much right as younger ones to determine their lives. Rather, your issue lies on an emotional level. Your reactions are based on the various relationship patterns between parents and children. If you were overly involved in your children's lives when they were younger, perhaps even crossing boundaries, they now claim the same right with you. Depending on how strong emotional dependencies still are today, the resulting conflicts are greater. The cohabitant who suffers the most undoubtedly has the closest bond with her son.

You should all sit down together and clarify in an open discussion what your living community is worth to you. Perhaps you should invite a neutral friend who understands and can moderate the conversation. If you are united not only financially but also emotionally, you are strong as a group. You should develop a unified strategy and wording for visits from children. You should all four refuse to discuss your lifestyle, and you certainly should not have to justify yourselves. That is unnecessary.

Society is changing, older people are establishing new ways of life, and the younger generation has to accept that. Everyone has the right to dispose of their hard-earned money even in old age.

The idea that one must do everything to increase the wealth to be inherited by the children is outdated. The five children related to you are only pursuing selfish interests.

I Could Strangle Her

I am busy with an upcoming staff meeting that I have to conduct. An independent opinion on how best to handle the situation could help me make a decision one way or another. Some details about me: I am the head of an office in a mid-size municipality, fifty-five years old, married, and have two adult children. The issue is about a subordinate employee. The woman has been in service for over thirty years and is going into early retirement next year. I've only been in this position as her immediate supervisor for three years. I immediately noticed she doesn't like me, and the feeling has become mutual. We only talk business when absolutely necessary.

The situation is as follows: The employee collects donations and sometimes also revenue from events. According to our by-laws, these funds belong in the municipal budget. However, for the third time this year, she has been distributing these amounts at her own discretion to charitable organizations of her choice. Three years ago, I built her a bridge by making it clear in a one-on-one conversation that she should stop. Last year, when she again did not comply, I was so irritated by her disloyalty that I issued her a formal warning. Which, as you can see, did no good. I could therefore terminate her employment without notice, putting her early retirement at risk.

A friend and colleague advised me to keep a low profile, so I have now scheduled a staff meeting that six people in total, including myself, will attend. How the conversation goes will depend on how I lead it. The thought that it may result in another formal warning that she will again ignore infuriates me. Just seeing her sour smile could make me strangle her. She reminds me of my adoptive mother who always looked at me askance. In your opinion, how should I best behave?

Answer

Your colleague is right; keep a low profile. Your emotional reaction is a bit too extreme for the situation at hand. Whenever there's a mismatch between the trigger and the reaction, we should ask ourselves what the issue has to do with us. Formative experiences in childhood and adolescence can easily be activated by similarly structured events today, leading to the same emotional storm as back then. This can lead to inappropriate actions. You've already found the key to your anger over this employee's misconduct; she reminds you of your adoptive mother.

Your one sentence already hints that your relationship history with your adoptive mother was difficult and probably full of injuries for you as a child. You offered her your childlike love, and she didn't reciprocate properly. She was "disloyal," just like the employee today. The overwhelming anger you feel likely comes mostly from these old sources. However, you are no longer as helpless and powerless as you were as a child; now you have power. By firing the employee and messing up her retirement, you are unconsciously taking revenge on your adoptive mother.

If you become aware of these connections, it will probably be easier for you to maintain your composure during the staff meeting and, along with others, find a realistic solution that you can support. The employee likely has no idea how serious her situation is. Given her many years of service, she probably feels secure and certainly feels entitled based on older rights than you have. Your colleagues may feel the same way. In your case, I would go along with the majority opinion. The remaining anger and irritation that you then still feel, you can no longer project onto the employee but will have to take responsibility for yourself.

Am I Too trusting?

I just had to experience a great disappointment, and one could really lose faith in the honesty of one's fellow human beings. I had lent my apartment to the children of a friend for fourteen days while I was away. It was my friend's daughter and her husband. They got married in December, live in cramped conditions with their in-laws, and wanted to spend some time here for their belated honeymoon.

I don't know the young people myself but trusted my friend. She had my keys and was to instruct the young couple. When I returned from my trip, I found my apartment in a state that appalled me. Not only had the young people not bothered to clean before leaving, but there was even used dishes still in the kitchen; I also had to find out that they had broken a lot of things.

Here is my preliminary list of damages: The knob on the electric boiler is overtightened and no longer works; there are large, indeterminable stains on the cover of my TV chair that I can't get out; the teapot of my best china has a crack, and a plate is missing; the door of the wardrobe is only hanging on one hinge; the TV programs were so messed up that I had to call a technician. Every day I find something new. I am deeply disappointed that the young people have abused my generosity.

When I asked my friend to pass on my complaints to her children, everything was denied roundly, and I suddenly appeared as someone petty and fussy. I was very depressed about it. My son thinks I'm simply too trusting, and that's why such things happen to me. Do you agree?

Answer

You are a bit naive, so in that sense, your son is right. Leaving strangers in your apartment will leave traces; you should prepare for that. You should have locked away your good china and left notes with operating instructions on electrical appliances. The habitual way you handle these things, which seems so obvious to you, is not for strangers. You should exercise a bit of imagination to put yourself in others' shoes.

However, your main mistake seems to be that you didn't personally get to know the young people. You didn't check if you wanted these people in your apartment at all. By simply relying on your friend, you already programmed your disappointment. If such disappointments accumulate in your experience with others, I would ask myself what I am actually doing to create these situations repeatedly?

In the case of the inconsiderate holiday guests in your apartment, you certainly had a strong hand in directing the scene. Maybe you unconsciously need the confirmation again and again that you yourself are generous and magnanimous, and that others are bad. Maybe in this case, you can manage to be a bit bad yourself. That's the best way to prevent disappointments. Tell your friend how disappointed you are and ask for the address of the young people. Write a brief letter to the young couple, include the bill for the incurred costs, and ask for reimbursement. That's your good right.

I See No Solution

We are a community of twenty-five homeowners who have mostly grown old together over the past thirty years. There have been many disputes in the past. All problems could be solved – sometimes unfortunately through legal means – but the solutions were not always accepted. Tensions linger because almost everyone in this house has their own interpretation of the law. Now there is an owner who is increasingly advocating that decisions should only be made according to the letter of the Condominium Ownership Act, so that everything is only "fair". This is very commendable, and no one is against it, but – and here comes the problem: The woman exercises her fanaticism for justice with such vehemence and downright obsession that an owners' meeting had to be repeatedly abandoned because all the co-owners simply walked away.

Because if a certain word acts as a trigger for this woman, she starts like clockwork, and there's no stopping her: Her voice gets louder and shrill; she insults and offends her former adversaries – even if it has nothing to do with the matter, but refers to previous events; lets no one calm her down, pacify her, stop her. She speaks without commas or periods, like a tank she rolls over everyone. No one can listen to her anymore; it is unbearable. And she even follows the people who leave the meeting and continues to scold them on the street. And the best part: She feels completely in the right.

I now think that it is unacceptable for one person to tyrannize twenty-four others in this way, but I see no solution. The most sensible thing would be to exclude her from meetings, but this is probably not legally permissible. Otherwise, this resident has maneuvered herself into an "out" for years due to her own behavior. Do you have any advice?

Answer

On one side, there is this tyrannical owner; on the other side, there are twenty-four others who allow themselves to be tyrannized. This unbearable co-owner is actually sick. She uses the meetings to act out her neurotic patterns at the right trigger. If twenty-four other people have put up with this for years, or escape by fleeing rather than taking action, it can only be understood that there is so much aggression in this woman's behavior that everyone, more or less consciously, is afraid of her.

You are right with your idea that there is a lot to regulate in an owners' meeting, and this woman is a disruption that prevents any reasonable work. You should clarify the legal background, but I cannot imagine that a resolution by the twenty-four others to exclude this person would not be legally valid. Besides, you can meet behind this woman's back wherever you want.

Against this unbearable co-owner as a common external enemy, the smoldering disputes can certainly be set aside for a while. Unity is strength. It should be possible to come to common resolutions in small groups before an official exclusion. All goodwill proposals are useless in such a case. Talking is pointless because the woman, due to her neurosis, cannot come to any insight. Only drastic measures will help.

For this, all the others have to give up their underlying fear of the co-owner's aggressiveness and suspend their ideas of polite coexistence in this case. It is likely that this woman will gain access despite being excluded. Then there must be residents willing to remove her from the room using physical force if necessary. If she then causes a disturbance, you will have to call the police.

How Do I Tell My Neighbors?

I'm grappling with a problem that grows daily and increasingly angers me. However, I don't know how to solve it. It's about my neighbors, with whom I share the same floor. It's a young family that has recently moved in. They are decent people, just to be clear. The kids, eleven and nine, are well-behaved, the man works as a bricklayer, and the woman is a hairdresser.

The issue is that all family members leave their shoes outside the door. Apparently, no one is allowed to enter the apartment with shoes on. Recently, I counted nine pairs of shoes outside the door. I'm not bothered by the sight or even the fact that with so many shoes, space is limited, and they're almost at my door. What bothers me is the foul stench emanating from these shoes.

The worst are the man's work boots and the children's sneakers. By now, the whole stairwell smells, and the stench even rises to the next floor. The tenants above have already complained to me about this nuisance, but they also dare not say anything to the family. I feel the same way. On the one hand, I find it embarrassing for them; on the other, I wonder why they don't notice it themselves. The smell is so intrusive that even airing out the stairwell does nothing. If my own front door is open for longer because of the mail carrier or a delivery, I have to open all the windows afterwards. I'm getting really disgusted.

At least three times a day, I wonder how, when, and what words to use to approach the family. Or would it be better to write them a few lines? In any case, I can probably forget about a good neighborly relationship, which I would actually wish for, after that. So far, we have hardly exchanged a few words. Can you advise me on what to do?

Answer

The problem with the neighbors is much easier to solve than you think. But first, you probably have to solve the problem you have with your own aggression. Each time that intrusive smell enters your nose, your anger and indignation grow. Apparently, your level of aggression is already so high that the simple request for the neighbors not to place their shoes outside the door feels like a bomb that, once detonated, will make peaceful coexistence impossible. To keep your anger from growing further, you should act quickly. The following considerations may help you:

You perceive the stench as a personal attack committed by these people. In reality, the family probably has no idea that their shoes emit such unpleasant odors. The feet that have been in them give off the same smell in their socks and in the apartment, and generally, people don't smell their own stench or find it particularly bothersome. Therefore, the family needs external clarification about this. This doesn't have to be embarrassing, as it is now well known that the emergence of such odors has nothing to do with personal hygiene but with specific, less breathable footwear, like that favored by children and adolescents.

My suggestion would be to leave your anger at home and knock on the family's door with a flower in hand, preferably at a time when all the adults are home. Apologize for having a request at the beginning of a neighborly relationship and express the hope that they won't take your request amiss. The friendlier you are, the easier it will be for the other party to accommodate your wishes. It is quite conceivable that such a visit to the new neighbors could be the beginning of a friendship, and not, as you think, the beginning of neighborly hostilities.

No Day Without a Skirmish

I'm actually a peaceful person who loves comfort, but the circumstances around me have developed to the point where I'm essentially living on a battlefield. Originally, we were two young, friendly married couples who bought an old house together and renovated it. Strangely, there was never any argument during the construction phase. The arguments only started after we had moved in and threw a big housewarming party with all our friends. While previously important decisions like what tiles should be laid in the entrance area were made in agreement despite differing opinions, tensions now arose over minor issues, such as stacking old paper in the basement.

About a year after moving in, my wife took on a lover, whose existence the other two knew about before I did. Our communal living situation had already fallen apart by that point, though I didn't want to admit it. My wife moved out, and I kept the apartment not only because it's nice but also because it's conveniently located for my job. From then on, the atmosphere with the other couple turned frosty. I didn't let it bother me, but whenever I brought a girlfriend home, sarcastic comments would follow. I acted cool, but internally I was boiling.

Then, much to my satisfaction, my friend started having an affair with a colleague from his office, and since then, he and his wife have been fighting loudly and consistently late into the night. I would actually not care about this if I didn't constantly get caught in the crossfire. If I arrange with him to hire a window cleaner for a basic cleaning of the skylights, she can-

cels it. A long-established bulk trash date is sabotaged by him because I started cleaning out the shed with her. And so on. No day goes by without a skirmish. This is slowly getting on my nerves. Do you have any advice for me on what can be done?

Answer

You have remarkably good nerves if you haven't lost your temper yet. But it seems you're more than just a peaceful person; you're someone who avoids conflict at all costs. However, avoiding conflict isn't a virtue and usually leads to a really big blowout or worse. In the development of your housing community, you only see yourself as the victim. Your wife, the other couple, they're the ones causing the changes. But you're equally responsible for everything that happens. If you let things happen without intervening, your contribution is your passivity or adaptability.

This living situation seems to me to be suffering from some naivety that emerged from initial enthusiasm—everything will sort itself out. As long as everyone had a common goal, namely, the renovation of the house, you got along well. But without that unifying idea, the problems in the relationships between the couples came to the forefront. A set of house rules and binding agreements for managing daily life should have been made by this point.

An additional complicating factor for you is that the emotional wound from your wife is linked to the other couple. Without a clearing conversation, the discord in the relationship with the other two was already pre-programmed. If you don't want to continue living on a battlefield, catch up on these steps as soon as possible. Only this way will you not get dragged into the marital war between the two.

Maybe you're lucky, and the two separate and move out; otherwise, your last option is to find yourself a new peaceful apartment.

I'm Disappointed in My Friend

I've known my friend for a good twenty years, and we've been close friends for ten. We're both divorced and have confided a lot in each other. Unfortunately, her behavior has been giving me more and more to think about. She flirts with men in a way I never thought she would. For example, she invites them over, has them do small repairs, teaches her how to use the computer, and keeps more than a few on a long leash.

She shares very little and tends to deflect the topic when I ask. Ten months ago, she met a man who has really captured her interest. At first, she didn't tell me anything about it; after three months, she started sharing a bit more but always reservedly. For the last two months, she hasn't talked about it at all, but I feel that she has changed, and I believe the relationship has solidified.

I never pry. If she wants advice, I'm always there for her. If she doesn't want to say something specific, she laughs in a strange way, and it bothers me a lot. I've always been very open and thought it would be nice to share in this respect as well. I'm happy for her when she does something with him, but I've emotionally let her go a bit. Isn't it completely normal to go out with a man—can't you tell your best friend about it? I'm very disappointed and would prefer to distance myself.

She's already noticed that I'm not reaching out to her as often. I wonder if I'm overreacting? Is it worth jeopardizing the friendship over this? Can't I make my openness and trust the standard? Is she acting this way to maintain a "clean slate" publicly? Please reply, I'm very curious to hear what you think.

Answer

I think you're asking yourself the right questions. You are indeed overreacting, but there are two important reasons for that. First, you're likely envious that your friend can do something that you can't, which is to interact with men in an easy and hassle-free manner. Secondly, you're rightfully afraid of losing your friend to a man.

After your divorce, the relationship with this best friend was undoubtedly very important and has become increasingly closer over time. But that doesn't entitle you to be possessive. I believe your friend senses what's going on inside you and that's exactly why she's not telling you anything. As long as both of you aren't truly open with each other, the friendship will suffer more from all this fog between you than from the men who come between you.

Instead of retreating, offended, you should really make your openness the standard and tell your friend how you feel. Everything you've told me, you should tell her. Then maybe she can also be open about her friendships with men. Friendships between women can easily be thrown off balance by a man, but that's precisely when trust and openness are important to maintain the friendship.

Deep down, you find your friend's behavior towards men reprehensible, which makes it hard for you to approach her openly. Your friend isn't degrading herself by flirting, accepting help, or even falling in love. I think she's just afraid of you and your strict norms when she doesn't tell you anything. It would be better for you to learn something from your vivacious friend than to end the friendship. Who knows, maybe in the end there will be a joyful quartet.

My Acquaintance Annoys Me

I would like to know how to deal with the following problem. Among my acquaintances is a woman who lives alone and is increasingly getting on my nerves. Her constant phone calls are filled with dissatisfied rants, and I find myself becoming more and more impatient. Sometimes it's about her rude son, whom I think really doesn't treat his mother well, or about her landlord. I feel an unspoken pressure to take care of her.

This lady has a summer home by the North Sea, where she keeps inviting me. It's actually an appealing offer, but I can't imagine wanting to spend that much time with her. I don't want to accept her invitation, but I also don't want to offend her, as she is very lonely.

In essence, she's a smart and stimulating person, and I'm sure she likes me very much and cares about my well-being. However, it's also uncomfortable for me to have to tell her everything. She won't let go until I've shared all the details. She doesn't hold back her opinions on my matters, and sometimes her judgment is quite harsh. Yet that's only one side of it.

Lately, there are more and more accusations like, "You were supposed to call me," or, "I expected you to get in touch," or, "Why didn't you tell me that?" The whole relationship is becoming too much for me. How do I get out of this without offending her?

Answer

Like many other people who find it hard to say no because they take other people's expectations more seriously than their own desires, you've gotten yourself into a situation where your room for decision is slowly shrinking. Your behavior so far has probably been so accommodating, despite your reservations, that your acquaintance feels entitled to make demands and express wishes.

If you decide to pull back now, it's likely unavoidable that your acquaintance will feel snubbed. However, if you want to feel good yourself, you have no choice but to have an open conversation with her and tell her how you feel about this relationship and how much or how little contact you wish to have with her. Honesty, even if it initially hurts, is always better for human relationships in the long run than misunderstood consideration. Your sympathy for this acquaintance, because she is so alone that you feel you have to take care of her and can't impose anything on her, leads to such misunderstood consideration.

If you just want to help, without any expectations of your own, that's a different matter, but then this woman wouldn't annoy you in the first place. You really don't have to be grateful for the fact that she likes you and cares about you. It's an offer that you can accept or reject. What you want to share and what you prefer to keep to yourself is entirely your decision. Be brave and clarify the situation.

I'd Prefer to Quit

I've experienced a situation that feels like something out of a movie. Even after three days, it still seems so surreal to me, as if it didn't really happen and I only dreamt it. I work in the social sector and have a somewhat older colleague who took me under her wing when I started four years ago. I always believed that I could trust her completely and that she would definitely stand by me if there were any problems. Sometimes it was difficult to work with her, but I always forgave her because she has her own burdens with her family – she has two children.

Three days ago, I unexpectedly entered our meeting room and heard her talking about me with another employee in the tea kitchen next door. I was stunned! She said things about me and my work that I still can't believe. Among other things, she called me a "slut," "unreliable," "selfish," and only focused on taking the easy way out.

I should add that I am still unmarried and my family lives far away. My job means everything to me, and I invest a lot of energy and often more time than I need to. The accusations are absolutely unfair, but what hurts me most is that she would say such things behind my back. I left feeling numb.

What now? I can't even find a standpoint on this. How should I face her after this disappointment? How can people be so two-faced: friendly to one's face and mean behind one's back! I'd prefer to quit. Should I?

Answer

I can well understand that the situation feels unreal to you. On the one hand, you have a strong tendency to deny this unpleasant experience—as if you could wake up, and it was all just a dream. On the other hand, you're tempted to escape by resigning, thus avoiding confrontation with the undeniable reality. Torn between the two, you just feel confused.

However, neither denial nor avoidance is an appropriate response to this real emotional hurt. Even if you overheard the conversation unintentionally and nobody knows you listened, you should now take action and put your cards on the table. Rather than quitting, confront the situation head-on, or else your workplace will become unbearable in the long run. You need to clear the air between yourself and this motherly colleague who turns out to be not so motherly!

Apparently, over the past few years, you've lived more according to wishful thinking than reality with this colleague. It's unlikely that her hostility hasn't already shown itself in many small gestures. But you didn't want to see it, and where you did notice it, you excused it away. You've idealized this colleague, meaning you've seen her as better than she really is. Now, like it or not, you have to face reality.

Make a fresh start! Tell your colleague what you've heard and how it hurts you. Distance yourself from her and, above all, pay closer attention in the future, even if it hurts, so you understand what's really going on between you and others.

Our Neighbors Have Changed

I need to share my sorrow with you and hear what you think about this story. We have lovely neighbors with whom we've lived side by side for nearly thirteen years. We've celebrated many wonderful events together. It touched me deeply to witness the setbacks our friends have had to endure in recent years. They've had a lot of bad luck and illness in their family, and, to make matters worse, the husband was forced into early retirement against his will due to poor business conditions.

As a result, their financial situation deteriorated to such an extent that they had to sell their house. They now live not far from us in a four-family home, so we can continue to nurture our friendship. Unfortunately, both have changed so much since the move that it breaks my heart to see it. My friend now sits lethargically in her chair and leaves the house only for shopping and doctor's visits, even though she is usually a lively and adventurous woman.

The worst part is the atmosphere created by her husband. When we visit, we have to arrive at a specific time because that's when the landlord has gone out. Our old neighbors have had several disputes with this man. We have to be very quiet in the apartment. Firstly, because our friend wants to verify whether the landlord has really left, or if he's just pretending, and secondly, so the landlord, if he's still around, cannot hear what we're saying. We found the whole situation to be absolutely bizarre, but we couldn't counter it. If the lower apartment was completely silent, it was just proof that the landlord was deliberately not making noise to eavesdrop on our conversations. Only later, when the radio downstairs started playing, could we talk normally.

I feel sorry for both of them, but I don't know how to help. We've already suggested that they move again, especially since they've had so many difficulties with this landlord. But they don't want to hear anything about it.

Answer

I think you may have to come to terms with the fact that you've lost these neighbors as friends. The behavioral changes you describe are so profound that it's unlikely they'll ever be their old selves again. You're probably so deeply affected by the situation because you sense that a good period of togetherness has come to an end.

I believe your friends haven't coped with the blows of fate they've endured in recent years. The husband primarily sees himself as a victim to whom things are being done. The events during your visit point to a pronounced case of paranoia, a mental illness that often develops in middle age, usually under the pressure of external events causing great emotional hurt. Once the initial signs of illness appear, many avoidable problems with the environment also develop.

It's also possible that your friend's changed behavior contributed to his forced early retirement, just as the disputes with the landlord may also be provoked by him. Sadly, people with such paranoia aren't receptive to reality; they always see others as the cause of everything that happens to them. As long as they're not doing too badly and aren't a danger to themselves or others, no one can help them.

What's truly unfortunate is the wife, who in this case has clearly resigned herself and can only express her despair through illnesses. Stand by your friend as best you can. Perhaps, through careful conversations, you can help her realize that her husband is mentally ill and she needs to consider how to arrange her own life under these circumstances.

I Should Lie for My Friend

I find myself in a tough dilemma regarding how to act. It's about my longtime friend, who I care for despite the relationship always having been difficult. Since she got married, and her strong-willed husband always has to be taken into account, it's become even more complicated. We have such a situation right now. I had to organize a children's birthday party and wanted to take nine kids to a bowling alley. When no one was available to take the second batch of kids, my ever-helpful friend stepped in, even though she was supposed to take her baby to the doctor. She drove ahead with four kids, while I followed with the rest. Along the way, I was pushed aside, resulting in two cars separating us. At a busy intersection, my friend had an accident.

Fortunately, none of the children were injured, but the other car suffered significant damage. The police documented the accident; I didn't have to make a statement because I was taking care of the children. My friend claims she signaled, while the other party claims the opposite. I immediately told her I saw nothing. My friend insisted that I could say I saw her signal, but I refused.

As long as it wasn't clear if her insurance would pay, peace prevailed, but now they've denied the claim, stating she's at fault for not signaling. Now all hell is breaking loose. I'm being pressured to claim something I didn't see. My friend, after some back-and-forth, understands my refusal, and our friendship won't break over this, but her husband won't accept my refusal.

He says it would be ungrateful and disloyal not to help my friend, who after all did me a favor. Without her helpfulness, this would never have happened, and now they're stuck with the costs. If I don't support them, he will ensure his wife no longer associates with such a conscienceless person as me. Do I really have to lie to keep my friend?

Answer

Your friend's husband is very adept at twisting the truth. Apparently, he is the one who has no conscience and manipulates reality for his benefit. He is exerting moral pressure on you, but he is dealing with a false morality. Stick to your refusal. Truth and law are on your side. Making a false statement could lead to unpleasant consequences you can't yet foresee. Emotionally, lying against your inner voice will also not make you happy.

The whole situation appears like a classic conflict: Either you act against your convictions and keep your friend, or you stay true to yourself and lose her. The reality will be that your difficult friendship will be tested either way.

If you lie for your friend, you'll unconsciously blame her; if you refuse, her husband threatens war. Your friend has the most difficult problem—she has to find her own position between her relationship with her husband and you. This is certainly not easy for her, and it means you'll also need to show a lot of patience to give the friendship a chance to survive.

In such crisis situations, usually, old conflicts resurface. The difficult relationship you've always had with your friend will not get any easier. You should prepare for that. Don't let her raging husband intimidate you. Make sure any conversation with him takes place only in the presence of witnesses.

Friends in Need

I'm just recovering from an extreme crisis and wondering how to deal with my so-called friends who abandoned me when I was down. Just now, my up-to-this-point best friend called and asked if I wanted to go to the movies; she'd even pay for me. However, when I was severely depressed and didn't know how to feed my children, she was nowhere to be found. She knew exactly what was going on. I had left my two children, aged four and seven, in her care when I had to go to the hospital unexpectedly for acute appendicitis.

When I came back a week later, my husband had used my absence to flee, probably to Holland. He took anything of value and emptied all the accounts. The human situation combined with the financial ruin, until social services finally stepped in, was a nightmare. My friend did not comfort me; instead, she told me it was my fault for not giving my husband enough free- dom and restricting him. Then she went on vacation.

It was more or less the same with all the people I had con- sidered my friends. My sister, my stepfather, former colleagues, mutual friends of me and my husband, they all let me down. The one who helped was an almost unknown student from my building. She took care of my children, cleaned my neglected apartment, accompanied me to social services, and made sure the kids had something to eat in the worst initial days.

A woman from the neighborhood, who I only knew by sight, brought food that she usually collects for a social station; my sports trainer, who I'd always thought was arrogant, had long conversations with me and lifted my spirits. I called him at two in the morning once, and it was okay. Now, as normalcy slowly returns, I don't know how to act toward all those who have disappointed me. What do you advise?

Answer

There are always many understandable reasons why people react the way they do. However, when you urgently need help and can no longer empathize with others, actions speak louder than words. Your old friends have proven themselves useless in times of need. This is another blow on top of everything you've been through. It's an old experience that hard times reveal who true friends are. You have found new friends who have helped, and you must be thankful for that. If you show your gratitude, perhaps lifelong reliable friendships, proven in times of need, will develop.

Regarding the old friends, whom you now don't know how to deal with, you'll have to decide on a person-by-person basis what still connects you and what you can get from them. With some, it will make sense to openly discuss how disappointed you are, with others not, because they don't want to understand. Either way, you'll have to test your childlike trust in family bonds and be very careful with your heart when dealing with old friends.

If you can go to the movies with your friend and enjoy it, but don't expect anything more from her than a nice movie night, you have regained a large part of normalcy and also learned something essential for yourself and your life: that you can never get more from someone than what they are willing to give. You should learn to realistically adapt to this fact.

The Hostile Neighbor

The trouble with the neighbor never ends, and I am seriously considering suing him. But first, I would like to know what an impartial expert thinks about it. We have been neighbors for about twenty years. We built our single-family homes around the same time and, in consultation, planted a thirty-meter long hedge as the boundary between our properties.

In the beginning, everything went well. With his consent, I placed my garage close to the boundary. His and my children were still small and played alternately in both yards. He is technically quite inept, and whenever there was something to repair in the house, I was always happy to help. Only later did I realize that he was also taking advantage of me in this regard. The tone, however, remained neighborly friendly—until his wife died six years ago.

After that, everything changed. He kept bringing new young women into the house; even his adult children turned against him. He showed consideration for no one. Music often blared from his house late into the night, his garden became overgrown, and weeds crept under the hedge into my garden. Friendly conversation made no difference. When the fruit was ripe, he took fruit from my trees without asking. He didn't even spare my flowers. Once, he practically cleared an entire rose bed. Recently, he installed a motion sensor on his terrace that frequently goes off in the evening, casting its light directly into my living room. I've asked him to lower the lamp, but he plays dumb and doesn't know what I'm talking about.

Now, my wife and I were away for three days. When we returned, we couldn't believe our eyes. Without prior agreement, the neighbor had commissioned a company to trim the two-meter high Thuja hedge between our properties down to a height of just sixty centimeters. Only shrubs remained of the beautiful evergreen hedge. Until it grows back, we must endure this ugly sight. On our side, the flower bed along the hedge was trampled down, many plants destroyed. My wife was beside herself. Since talking to the man is no longer an option, I want to go to a lawyer now. What do you think about that?

Answer

Somehow, you still have reservations about taking this step; otherwise, you wouldn't be writing to me. Indeed, such an action needs to be carefully considered as it really constitutes an official declaration of war. Such neighborhood disputes are among the absolutely most unpleasant tasks that neither lawyers nor judges appreciate. Quite apart from the costs, it would certainly be better to resolve this without litigation. Your neighbor is behaving in a boundary-crossing manner in the truest sense of the word, but I'm not sure if he even realizes what he is doing. What rightly comes across to you as hostility may not necessarily be meant that way from his side.

Some evidence suggests that your neighbor has undergone a personality change after the death of his wife and is now simply living in his own isolated world, taking what he needs. He may even have delusions, as the hedge trimming is also entirely nonsensical from a gardening perspective. The long years of familiarity with each other may have reduced his perception of boundaries and respect for others' property.

But even if that were the case, you need to do something to protect yourself. Clearly, you have accumulated a lot of resentment over the years, but that should not lead you to overreact now. If you don't want to consult a lawyer right away, perhaps you could first write a clear letter with a friend, which you would send to him by registered mail. In it, you should forbid him from entering your property under threat of legal action. If that doesn't help, you could make an official visit to him with a witness. During that visit, you could assess whether the neighbor is still in his right mind, because only if that is the case can legal measures be effective.

I Don't Want to Be Xenophobic

Half a year ago, two foreign families moved into our immediate neighborhood. I have to be honest and say that I was initially not very comfortable with this—like many other residents, by the way. Particularly, the very dark skin color seemed extremely foreign and out of place to me. However, we have since gotten used to them, and I have put my prejudices aside. We've gotten to know one family quite well; they have four children aged between six and twelve. They have also leased a piece of our garden, so we often see each other.

Now, however, I'm in doubt about how to behave. The two middle boys from the family, aged eight and ten, broke into our garage and took various tools. I saw the boys running away with them but did not intervene. Even then, I was unsure about how to react. Running after them seemed too silly to me.

When I ran into them a few hours later on the street, I would have liked to confront them, but there were other people present, and I didn't want to appear xenophobic. The fact that they are foreigners makes the situation complicated. My husband was very upset and wanted to go to the parents immediately, which I just managed to prevent. There are also language barriers. The atmosphere in the settlement is already a bit tense; I don't want to cause a stir, but what to do?

Answer

The least conspicuous course of action would be to accept the loss of the tools and act as if nothing happened. However, this benefits no one in the long run. Your mistrust towards foreigners would grow, and the two boys might feel encouraged to try it again. Instead, you should consider this incident as a typical childish prank that has nothing to do with the skin color of the young perpetrators.

The best thing to do would be to take the two boys aside. Take them into the garage and make it clear to them that you know what happened and expect the tools to be returned. Be friendly but firm and consider the matter closed afterward. Only speak to the parents if you can't handle the children. If language understanding is sufficient for neighborly interactions, it should be sufficient for resolving this issue.

The fact that this incident causes you so much trouble has more to do with yourself than with the foreigners. You still have very mixed feelings and are afraid that your rejection might show. This excessive caution makes you unable to act as freely as usual. Extremes are always suspicious: the total demonization of foreigners as well as forced and exaggerated friendliness.

The truth is that both foreigners and locals have difficulty with each other and that both sides need patience, tolerance, and openness if they want to get used to each other. This won't happen without conflicts. Overcoming shared conflicts, however, builds trust and strengthens relationships. If you can honestly admit to yourself what you dislike and like about the foreigners, then you have a realistic basis for maintaining neighborly relations. Then you don't have to react overly cautiously and can adequately resolve the issue with the stolen tools.

Conflict in the House

I live in the attic apartment of a three-unit rental building. The woman who lives below me has undertaken the responsibility to maintain cleanliness. She is supposed to clean the staircase, clear snow, mow the lawn, and sweep the street; in return, she pays less rent. My question is, where does the staircase start and where does it end? The woman who is supposed to clean always starts cleaning in front of her door. The two flights of stairs leading to the attic are not cleaned; she believes that this upper area is my domain and she doesn't need to clean it. I have already involved the landlord, who also confirmed to me that she should clean from top to bottom; he said he would talk to her.

When nothing happened, I spoke to the property management again and asked them to please clarify the matter. But still, nothing happens, even though the property manager was there to read the water meters and heating. Two weeks ago, a letter was left on the staircase, in which she called me a deceitful, disagreeable, and unfriendly person. I should not say that she doesn't clean; it's been cleaner now than it ever was in all the years before. She has been living in this building for exactly one year now! I did not respond to this letter and avoid any contact with her.

My question to you is, should I speak to the landlord again and show him the letter? The landlord only talks, but doesn't take any action. He stays out of the matter. As long as his rent is in the account, he's happy. How can one label other people as

Answer

You ask questions that I cannot answer. Where your staircase starts and ends, in your case, where cleaning needs to be done, is a matter of agreement or a written contract. If the property management confirms that the two flights of stairs to your apartment, which you probably use alone, are included, then the objective facts are clarified. How this obligation is met in a community is more of a human problem, and it seems to me that you have unnecessarily stirred up a war. Your first point of contact should be the neighbor who has committed to cleaning. Probably a friendly approach from your side right from the start would have resolved the matter.

But you go straight to the authorities, namely the landlord and the property management. There could be many reasons why she didn't clean your stairs; you don't have to assume malice right away, you should have asked her. The neighbor may feel like you've maligned her, even if from your point of view, you're just telling the truth.

I get the impression that you can't stand this neighbor anyway. Perhaps it also bothers you that she receives a reduction in rent, and in your opinion, she should do proper work in return. In any case, the neighbor felt attacked, otherwise, she wouldn't have written such a letter. But neither writing such a letter nor ignoring it leads to better relationships in the house. You'll say, she should just clean my stairs, nothing else. But when living under the same roof, all parties are responsible for a good atmosphere in the house.

I understand the landlord not wanting to get involved. A dictatorial word from his side, even if you desire it, won't solve the problem. Take matters into your own hands. You may need to step out of your comfort zone. Buy a bouquet of flowers and pay the neighbor a visit to offer peace. Suggest that there are probably only misunderstandings on both sides. In a friendly conversation, where the focus should not be on who is right, you'll surely find a solution that both can live with.

Must I Put Up With This?

I work in a male-dominated profession and am used to being the only woman in most groups. I don't have any problems with that in my daily work, but things usually get difficult only during parties. I had another such situation recently, and I must say, it was extremely uncomfortable. Here's what happened: I drove to a client's place in another city with two colleagues. We had intense negotiations throughout the day and finally reached a mutually satisfying conclusion. Naturally, this had to be celebrated in the evening. So, we went out for dinner with two senior gentlemen from the client's side.

I was thus with four men—two colleagues and two clients. One client was already drunk after the meal, but he insisted on going to another venue. Since he was a client, we gave in. On the way there, he began groping me. I found it disgusting; he was already someone I found unsympathetic. I wouldn't want to deal with him privately.

My two colleagues just looked away. At the venue, he wanted to dance with me. He was so persistent that I had no choice but to reluctantly comply. On the dance floor, he became really intrusive. Words no longer affected him. When the dance ended, I made sure we went back to the hotel. The drunken client wouldn't shake off and wanted to come to my room. I finally escaped and locked myself in my hotel room.

The next morning, my colleagues found everything to be "within the realms of normality." They nearly said that I was overreacting. I'm very angry and also quite helpless and don't know what steps I can take. I don't have to put up with this, do I? What do you think?

Answer

You don't have to put up with this, but sustained protest against it won't be without consequences. You probably know the structures in your company well enough to estimate your chances. You'll have to do an internal cost-benefit analysis because it won't be easy. As long as women who refuse to comply are labeled as "difficult" in male-dominated hierarchies, subtle career impediments are common. The secret solidarity among men is evident from the behavior of your colleagues. They should have been the ones to intervene, but the client was more important to them than their co-worker, and who knows if they weren't secretly amused.

You'll have to decide whether you want to keep this issue low-key or if you're finally concerned about the principle. In the first case, you should talk to your colleagues and clearly express how you experienced their behavior and develop a model for how you'll act in such situations in the future. That could mean, for example, letting your colleagues know that you will leave if there are any advances.

In the second case, I would aim for a conversation with the works council, if there is one, or go straight to the top boss. Preparing for such a conversation with a letter might be useful.

Taking successful action, however, requires that you be very sure in your assessment of the situation. The fact that you tolerated the drunk client for so long suggests that you might be hesitant to set strict boundaries, or that your self-confidence, where it isn't about job performance, is not strong enough. A few consultations at a counseling center could help prepare you for confrontations at work.

They Are Playing a False Game With Me

Ever since I can remember, I've been singing. Even as a child, I wanted to become a singer. Unfortunately, life took a different turn. I learned a decent profession, as my parents wanted, got married, and had children. However, I still managed to get the singing training I always wanted. Now, at thirty-six, I've finally found a band that suits my musical style. They were looking for a temporary replacement for their lead singer who was on maternity leave, and that's how I joined them. Within two weeks, I had mastered their entire repertoire, and secretly, from all sides, including band members, I heard that I was better than the previous singer.

For six months, I sang at all gigs and felt totally accepted and belonging, until my predecessor showed up again, and since then, everything has gone awry. I feel cheated. The most outrageous things are happening. They have gigs with the other singer, about which I know nothing, or the rehearsal is suddenly rescheduled, and she's already on stage when I arrive and won't come down.

Recently, we had a performance at a company party where the boss explicitly wanted me to perform. Two band members confidentially told me they'd much rather work with me, but when it comes to taking an official stand, they cite their six years of collaboration with the previous singer.

I'm devastated and don't know what to do anymore. The bandleader is a soft-spoken type and can't assert himself; everything that happens is decided by the group, but they are playing a false game with me. Do you have any advice for me?

Answer

The first step toward solving any issue is to clearly acknowledge the reality of the situation. In your case, it's evident that clear agreements were not made before you even took on the role, leading you to forget that you were just a stand-in. You've pushed aside the entire issue of what happens when the original singer returns. Perhaps the band didn't expect the replacement to be better than the original, assuming things would revert to the old status quo. Their current behavior appears to be more out of helplessness; I don't think they are deliberately playing a false game with you.

It rather seems they don't want to lose you. Instead of dwelling on setbacks, I'd suggest appreciating the tokens of favor, because, realistically speaking, you have no entitlement to the role. Since this band doesn't seem to operate on a strictly commercial basis where your superior performance would tip the scales, personal relationships take precedence, and six years outweigh six months. Don't rush things and be patient, as difficult as it may be; the group is apparently not yet ready to make decisions. Your place is in the background, painful as that might be.

However, you could try having an open conversation with your rival. Perhaps the two women can achieve what the men find so difficult: a compromise that everyone can live with.

Thank You & A Look Ahead

Dear Valued Reader,

As we arrive at the final page of this book, I want to take a moment to extend my heartfelt gratitude to you. Thank you for embarking on this journey with us. Books have the magical power to transport us to different worlds, offer solace and hope, or spark imagination, and it's a privilege to have been a part of that experience for you.

I sincerely hope that you found what you were seeking within these pages—whether it was answers to lingering questions, an escape from the everyday, or simply a few hours of entertaining engagement with words. Your time and attention are precious gifts, and it's an honor that you chose to spend them on this book.

But wait, the literary adventure doesn't end here! I'm incredibly excited to announce that there are many more captivating stories and enlightening books from the talented Brigitte Halenta on the horizon. As you read this, translations are already underway to bring her remarkable novels to the English-speaking market. Brigitte Halenta's works are treasures waiting to be discovered, filled with complex characters, intricate plots, and emotional land-scapes that are sure to resonate with you.

In true American fashion, let's get a bit sentimental: Books are the bridges that connect us, regardless of where we are in the world or which language we speak. And in this rapidly changing landscape, that's something truly special to celebrate. So, stay tuned! An enthralling literary journey awaits you, and it's just a page turn away.

Thank you once again for your companionship through this book. It's readers like you who make all the late nights, revisions, and creative struggles worth it for authors and everyone involved in the process of bringing a book to life.

If you've enjoyed this book, we'd be incredibly grateful if you could take a moment to leave a review or rating. Your feedback not only helps us improve but also helps others discover this work. Every review contributes to keeping this story alive and enables us to continue sharing new ones with you.

Here's to many more literary adventures together, in worlds both familiar and yet-to-be-discovered.

Warmest Regards,

David Halenta

P.S. Life is short; read fast. The best is yet to come.

Eager to keep the literary suspense going? Dog-ear this moment and hop over to **brigittehalenta.de** to sign up for our newsletter.

In every story, just like in life,
there are lessons to learn,
emotions to feel, and
choices to make. The art of living
lies in turning your own life story
into your masterpiece.
—Brigitte Halenta

Book Preview

Old Is Great — usually

You can find countless books that tell you all the things you should do to age healthily—this book, however, will tell you what you shouldn't do, and more importantly, what you shouldn't think. Because our thoughts program us to age. It's not what we do that determines our health and longevity, but how we perceive it.

An English translation of this riveting book is on the horizon! Stay in the loop and be among the first to get your hands on it by subscribing to our newsletter at www.brigittehalenta.de.